MONEY & DIVORCE

THE ESSENTIAL ROADMAP TO MASTERING FINANCIAL DECISIONS

LILI VASILEFF

Cover design by Cory Ottenwess/ABA Design.

Library of Congress Cataloging-in-Publication Data
Names: Vasileff, Lili, author.
Title: Money and divorce : the essential roadmap to mastering financial decisions / Lili Vasileff.
Description: 1/e | Chicago : American Bar Association, [2017] | Includes index.
Identifiers: LCCN 2017040391 (print) | LCCN 2017040667 (ebook) | ISBN 9781634259934 (ebook) | ISBN 9781634259927 (pbk.)
Subjects: LCSH: Divorce. | Divorced people—Finance, Personal.
Classification: LCC HQ814 (ebook) | LCC HQ814 .V37 2017 (print) | DDC 306.89—dc23
LC record available at https://lccn.loc.gov/2017040391

Printed in the United States of America.

21 20 19 18 17   5 4 3 2 1

ISBN: 978-1-63425-992-7

e-ISBN: 978-1-63425-993-4

Discounts are available for books ordered in bulk. Special consideration is given to state bars, CLE programs, and other bar-related organizations. Inquire at Book Publishing, ABA Publishing, American Bar Association, 321 N. Clark Street, Chicago, Illinois 60654-7598.

www.shopABA.org

Contents

Preface

Over 25 years ago, I had a successful career and budding family. But suddenly I found myself going through a divorce with two small children, one of whom has special needs. My once perfect world was crumbling out of my control. I had no idea what to expect from my soon-to-be ex-spouse or the legal process. I was overwhelmed by uncertainty and frightened to make financial decisions that would be long lasting and final. I could not even envision my own goals for the future.

Somewhere in the middle of my divorce, I realized that I was the only one who could empower myself to negotiate my outcome. Rather than let this transition destroy my family, I learned how to rebuild it and thrive post-divorce. I found a community. I then began to teach and guide others through divorce. I witnessed their sense of fulfillment grow as they took charge of their own financial decisions.

Financial planning for the future is an essential part of every divorce settlement. Separating couples often face a significant financial transformation. The bottom line is that two households must now survive on the dollars that formerly supported one. Transition is a critical time when you need the most help to understand the pros and cons of your financial options, how to set priorities, and when to reach a settlement with confidence.

Over the years, I have worked with thousands of couples and individuals to offer divorce financial planning before, during, and after divorce, as well as mediation, collaborative divorce, financial forensics, expert testimony in court, prenuptial and postnuptial agreements, and wealth management. Because every divorce is unique, expert guidance can often be the ace needed to effectively manage the settlement process and guarantee not just financial survival, but also success. It is my hope that this book will help many more accomplish their goals with dignity, confidence, and a sense of security. I am eternally grateful for the opportunity to clarify the confusing world of divorce.

I thank my two fabulous children and my beloved mother for helping to rebuild our life and family. Without their strength and everlasting love, I never would have followed my passion, instincts, and vision to assist clients through the difficulties of divorce and improve upon their experiences.

About the Author

Lili Vasileff is a pioneer and a nationally recognized expert in the field of divorce financial planning. She is author of the *Ultimate Divorce Organizer* (featured recently on HBO's *Divorce*) and has received numerous prestigious awards for her pro bono services to individuals and nonprofits. Her passion is evident in her ongoing efforts to improve upon the divorce experience and combat perceived injustices in the legal system that fail families in the long term. Motivated by her own divorce—and by being a single parent of two young children, one of whom has special needs—Lili is determined to make a difference for the better.

Specializing in divorce, litigation support, and tailored wealth management services, Lili offers customized financial guidance. She has strived for more than two decades to give clients a sense of confidence during difficult times.

Lili works successfully with attorneys to provide litigation support, serves as an expert witness, and consults behind the scenes for case evaluations. She's developed a reputation as the "go-to" neutral expert by mediating uniquely challenging financial issues in cases that aim to settle.

As President of Divorce and Money Matters, Lili is a fee-only Certified Financial Planner Professional™; a Master Analyst in Financial Forensics (MAFF™), specializing in Matrimonial Litigation; a Certified Divorce Financial Analyst™; and a Registered Investment Advisor. She is regularly quoted and interviewed across print, radio, TV, and online, and she is a featured contributor to the *Wall Street Journal*, *Financial Times*, CNN Money, CNBC, Bloomberg News, Reuters, *AARP Magazine*, *TIME*, the *Journal of Financial Planning*, the *New York Law Review*, the *New York Times*, and more. She is regularly invited to author articles for several national law journals, including the *New York Law Review* and the *Domestic Law Journal*. In keeping with her original mission to make a difference for the better, she's also written for *Working Mother Magazine* and *USAA* online, which provides assistance to military families.

Lili received the prestigious national 2013 Pioneering Award for her outstanding public advocacy and leadership in the field of divorce financial planning. She is currently the President Emeritus of the Board of Directors of the national Association of Divorce Financial Planners (ADFP). During her 15-year tenure as President of the ADFP, Lili has successfully helped grow a small regional group of professionals into a national organization of over 6,000 accredited practitioners in the United States, Canada, and several foreign countries. Through many of her efforts, divorce financial planning is recognized as a professional financial planning specialty niche by major national financial planning organizations and the Certified Financial Planner Board of Standards.

Email: Lili@Divorcematters.com www.divorcematters.com **203-622-4911**

1 How This Book Can Help You: Your Financial Guide to Divorce

A Step-by-Step Roadmap

Most people head straight into divorce without preparing themselves for the journey that lies ahead. Whether or not the divorce is of your choosing, you need the necessary guidance and useful information.

The primary purpose of this book is to help you make informed and intelligent choices concerning financial issues in divorce. In plain English I explain the fundamentals—illustrating how to set goals, deal with finances, navigate the legal process, and protect against unforeseen events.

This book is, in essence, a step-by-step roadmap of everything you need to know about the financial aspects of divorce. You are initiating self-empowerment to take control over your divorce.

How to Make Your Best Financial Decisions During Divorce

In this book, I focus on the three primary financial components of divorce: maintenance, child support, and property. I explain all financial topics and legal terms. I outline approaches for making critical financial choices, tips for managing your costs, strategies for successfully negotiating property division and support, and tactical advice (as well as cautionary notes) for ensuring a sustainable and reasonable divorce settlement.

Think of this book as an indispensable financial resource and guidebook for anybody thinking about divorce, going through divorce, or experiencing post-judgment financial challenges. You will gain the knowledge and tools you need to advocate for yourself as well as measure your capacity to obligate yourself financially.

This book does not provide any legal advice or legal opinion. You must work with your own attorney to get legal advice. I am not an attorney. I am a divorce financial expert, and this book is designed to provide you with accurate financial information, as I believe that thorough financial preparation will make a huge difference in your divorce experience and outcomes. From a basic introduction to a sophisticated analysis of finances, this book is a must-read for anyone interested in getting the best results for their divorce.

This book describes:

- The divorce process
- Property law
- Financial issues
- Financial definitions
- Financial strategies
- The pros and cons of short- and long-term financial decisions
- Taxes and tax implications of decisions
- What-if's
- How-to's
- Debt and creditworthiness
- College planning for divorcing families
- Special needs planning for divorcing families
- Negotiating, how to settle, or when to go to trial
- Your financial situation after divorce

Yes, You Are Unique

It is commonly said that 50 percent of all marriages in the United States end in divorce. Recent divorce statistics show that 41 percent of first marriages end in divorce, with that percentage creeping much higher for second marriages to 60 percent and for third marriages to 73 percent.[1]

No matter how prevalent divorce seems to be, your situation is unique. Everyone's divorce story relates to money, and you must therefore get at the heart of your values to enable good decision-making. Only you know your personal priorities, concerns, and challenges. Do not let a third party dictate what they are to you, or worse yet, make permanent decisions for you without your informed consent. Divorce is not just about the money—it's about your life.

Most people head straight into divorce without being prepared for the journey that lies ahead. Divorce client's concerns vary with age, and many people go back and forth trying to decide how and when to pull the trigger to divorce. Spouses may be at odds when it comes to slowing down or speeding up their divorce; however, you will find that divorce is both a marathon and a sprint. In addition, there are many different ways to divorce. Few are wrong. But no matter if your divorce is planned, unplanned, expected, or unexpected, you must be fully prepared.

This is not just any book on divorce. This book outlines each phase of divorce so you can better understand how to start planning for your outcome. This book

1 The U.S. Census Bureau and the CDC: Centers for Disease Control and Prevention National Vital Statistics System for 2000–2014.

will help you take back control of your life. You will learn the language of finances and the art of negotiation, and you will discover what you need to know about money and divorce: How to determine what you need, what you want, what you are entitled to, and how to reinvent yourself after divorce.

In addition, this book contains valuable, essential information about the divorce process and related financial issues. It describes in detail how to protect yourself financially before, during, and after divorce. Whatever you are feeling, this book provides guidance not only to educate you, but also to help you thrive during the process and afterwards.

What You Do Not Know Can Hurt You

You need to know how to navigate your divorce to achieve a successful outcome for you and your family. Divorce is one of life's biggest trigger events and touches many aspects of people's lives, including legally, financially, emotionally, and psychologically. It is multidimensional and marks the transition from being in an economic partnership to a single independent life.

No one can diminish the impact of divorce on families. However, the concept of minimizing risk, cost, and pain has brought about the novel idea of holistic divorce. Legal options for divorcing are evolving accordingly as more couples yearn for a better approach to ending their marriages.

If You Are Feeling Overwhelmed

Divorce is not the best time to learn about how to deal with money and financial decisions. More than ever, couples and families have greater resources for engaging a team of professionals (such as your attorney and divorce financial planner) in their divorce process. It is therefore important to be aware of the various stages of the divorce process, the role of each professional, and how best to evaluate who you need on your team.

You are pivotal in driving your divorce, and you are your own best advocate for your needs. The reality is that you will be called upon to make some of your biggest decisions when you are least ready to cope with them. You must take your time and assume responsibility for understanding all of your financial information and decisions. As hard as this sounds, divorce is a business transaction that will affect the rest of your life.

Preparation

The key to surviving and thriving after divorce is to understand as best as possible how to prepare for it. During a divorce, you will discover that there are certain components over which you will have little or no control. It is to your advantage to recognize early on which parts of your divorce fall into this category so you do not waste your time and energy working against, rather than with, the system.

This book will help you get ready to deal with your divorce. It provides comprehensive factual information about divorce each step along the way. You will find checklists, personal and financial information forms, charts, and references to resources. This book is broken into chapters and organized by topics relating to your personal life. It will help you get organized and focus on the key essentials of divorce while dismissing many distractions. Each chapter can be read separately, but it is best if you read all of them to understand the legal framing of all issues impacting divorce finances.

Mistakes to Avoid

In this book you will find information about some of the biggest and most common financial blunders in divorce. For many of these, it is crucial that you have advice from a divorce financial planner so that you do not get sucker punched or commit to an unsustainable agreement.

Learn the ropes, think for yourself, get a divorce financial expert involved early on, and use the actionable ideas in this book to tailor everything for your particular situation.

Beware of Tall Tales

All too often, well-meaning but misinformed colleagues, friends, and family members will want to share their stories and advice about divorce with you. Even though everyone claims to have your best interests at heart, often their information is rife with myths and false facts. At a minimum, it is one-sided or biased, and at worst, it can be dangerous for you to rely upon. If you are feeling confused and overwhelmed, you may discover that searching various websites for answers to your divorce questions may be unsatisfying as well.

If Only I Had Known That . . .

Instead of regretting decisions and saying "I wish I had known," this book will provide you with straightforward, easy-to-understand, reliable answers to many of your questions:

- How do you prepare for divorce?
- How do you start the divorce process?
- How much will it cost?
- How long will it take?
- Who do you need to hire?
- How do you protect your children?
- What is your financial situation?
- What do you own and what do you owe?
- What are the financial decisions you need to make?

- How will you divide property, what amount of child support will you need, and what amount of spousal support will you need?
- How do you negotiate a final settlement?
- How will you survive financially?
- Do you have any special circumstances?

What's Covered in This Book

Chapter 2: The First Steps: What You Should Consider When Contemplating Divorce

- ❑ This chapter details how to detect signs that you are heading toward divorce and what should be your top considerations. It provides an overview of the different phases of divorce, various legal options, what you need to know about contested and uncontested divorce, fault, how to pace yourself, and how to manage the costs.

Chapter 3: You Have Decided to Divorce, Now What? An Outline of the Divorce Process

- ❑ This chapter provides an overview of the legal sequence of events, important dates to know, how to keep your divorce private, how to protect yourself from financial chaos, steps you can take to prepare for divorce, inherent pitfalls of divorce, and common financial mistakes to avoid.

Chapter 4: Preparing for Your Financial Divorce

- ❑ This chapter is an overview of the primary financial issues in divorce, including defining property ownership, defining equitable distribution versus community property, dividing marital and nonmarital money, addressing a family-owned business, and commonly asked questions.

Chapter 5: The Financial Phases of Divorce

- ❑ This chapter describes the financial sequence of events in a divorce, including what information you need to gather, how to prepare a Net Worth Statement, how to fit all the pieces of the financial puzzle together, and how a divorce financial planner can help.

Chapter 6: What If I Don't Know . . . ? How Do I . . . ? The Unknowns That Keep You Awake at Night

- ❑ This chapter answers key questions, including what to do if you don't have enough or accurate financial information, when you should be suspicious of the other party, and how you can find hidden assets. It also walks you through what to do if your spouse declares bankruptcy during or after divorce, prenuptial and postnuptial agreements, and your and your spouse's obligations after divorce.

Chapter 7: Splitting Up Your Property: The Balancing Act

- ❑ This chapter describes how to value and divide property and defines financial terms you need to know, such as cost basis, liquidity, real after-tax value, and type of asset. It also helps you determine what an asset will cost to keep, what assets you will be forced to trade or sell, and how to ensure that all transfers to you are accurate and timely.

Chapter 8: Financial Investments: What Are They?

- ❑ This chapter is an overview of the different kinds of financial investments and practical tips for dividing investments, including cash, publicly traded securities, real property, life insurance, annuities, nonpublicly traded securities, precious objects, personal belongings, and a family-owned or closely held business.

Chapter 9: Retirement Assets: What Makes Them Special?

- ❑ This chapter lays out the various types of retirement plans and accounts, pre-tax and after-tax contributions to tax-deferred accounts, and dividing retirement assets. It also explains the Qualified Domestic Relations Order (QDRO) and when it is required, as well as practical tips for your QDRO and risks with future assets.

Chapter 10: What Is a Contingent Interest in the Marital Estate?

- ❑ This chapter describes contingent interests, how to identify deferred compensation benefits, how to divide benefits, and strategies to protect your fair share, as well as taxes, trusts, and income interest in divorce.

Chapter 11: Real Property and Your House: Sell It, Keep It, or Transfer It?

- ❑ This chapter provides an overview of the financial options for real property, including factors in making a decision, making sense of your decision, dealing with mortgages, ownership after divorce, spousal support paid as a mortgage payment, tax benefits of owning, taxes on the sale of your house, reduced exclusion for a second home, and commonly asked questions.

Chapter 12: Child Support

- ❑ This chapter focuses on child-related expenses, child support guidelines, deviation from guidelines, modifying support, custody types, tax implications, and the tie breaker for tax filing status.

Chapter 13: Spousal Support, Also Known as Alimony

- ❑ This chapter provides an overview of different types of spousal support, statutory factors of entitlement, calculation of spousal support, duration factors, taxes, the Internal Revenue Service (IRS) alimony recapture rule, and the IRS child contingency rule. It offers in-depth explanations of forms of payment, waivers, and modifying or terminating support, as well as what happens if your spouse dies during or after divorce, and late-life divorce and its unique considerations.

Chapter 14: Debt, Credit, and Credit Worthiness: How to Protect Your Credit

- ❑ This chapter describes the nature of credit, including different types, how it is reported and used as a credit score, responsibility for debts in marriage, protecting your credit, what you need to know about your equal opportunity rights under the law, and practical tips about divorce and credit.

Chapter 15: Divorce and Children with Special Needs

- ❑ This chapter defines special needs and the "best interests" of the child, as well as parenting plans and special needs lists, child support and added expenses, public benefits planning before and after age 18, special education, transition planning, spousal support implications, and estate planning.

Chapter 16: College: The Effects of Divorce on College Financing and Financial Aid

- ❑ This chapter is an overview of the financial aid process for divorced parents, how to maximize your financial aid, how income and assets of parents and children are counted differently, key things you need to know, and practical tips for Free Application for Federal Student Aid (FAFSA) applications.

Chapter 17: Taxes and Divorce

- ❑ This chapter looks at the tax impact of divorce, tax facts in divorce, how the timing of your divorce impacts taxes, who gets tax credits and can claim deductions, whether your ex-spouse can place you at risk with the IRS, and what happens to your taxes after divorce.

Chapter 18: Getting to "Yes": Negotiating a Settlement

- ❑ This chapter outlines the top reasons to settle, strategies to reach a settlement, how to determine if your spouse is sabotaging any agreement, why to avoid trial, why you must obey orders, and practical tips to thrive post-divorce in your new life.

Chapter 19: The Light at the End of the Tunnel: Your Financial Situation after Divorce

- ❑ This chapter describes how to rebuild your financial life, including how to set goals, create a budget, build an emergency fund, update key financial areas of your life, keep up with changes in taxes, take care of your debts, and plan for retirement.

Pearls of Wisdom

Fashioning a realistic, creative, money-saving agreement goes a long way toward achieving a more holistic divorce and lasting peace. Families and couples deserve thoughtful and comprehensive guidance for important financial decision-making. Whether your spouse cooperates or not and whether your divorce is amicable or acrimonious, this book lays out how to craft a strong final settlement. When you face tough economic and personal times, this is precisely the right book to read to protect your privacy, family, property, money, and rights.

2 The First Steps: What You Should Consider When Contemplating Divorce

Marriage is a complicated partnership. It is a legal contract, a joint economic venture, a social pact, and an emotional commitment. When it starts to come undone, no matter how well prepared you are for its ending, there will be many choices you have to make that may be unfamiliar to you.

What is a divorce? It is a legal order called a Court Judgment that ends a marriage. It's more permanent than a separation, and it involves a "legitimate" reason. Because laws govern your marriage contract, property ownership, and parental rights, you have to also reckon with the legal system to untie your marriage knot. While you may think your divorce will be "simple," there are many bureaucratic hoops to jump through from beginning to end.

Grounds for divorce vary widely among jurisdictions and states, and even from county to county. Divorce laws are not static and evolve with the social norms over time. Divorce is fairly common today and is generally regarded as a morally acceptable choice.

At its core, divorce is about people and money. Divorce means change, and breaking up is hard to do. Sometimes both spouses want to divorce, and sometimes one wants to while the other doesn't. Divorce is very personal, and many factors influence how you experience the process. Your divorce is intensely subjective; it's about you, your past, your present, and your future.

If you are at the crossroads of contemplating divorce, you will benefit from knowing more about divorce laws, statutory factors, and common reasons that people give for divorcing. Often people considering divorce have some idea of what to expect, but divorce can be unpredictable, especially if you have unrealistic expectations or are too frightened to understand the reality of divorce.

You need to be prepared and informed—legally, financially, emotionally, and practically—because you will be forced to make critical decisions with long-lasting consequences when you are feeling the most vulnerable. It is therefore wise to know what divorce can and cannot do for you so that you have a better chance of having your expectations met realistically and being satisfied by your outcome.

With the right planning, you can take charge of your divorce and represent yourself in the process better. In fact, you have an obligation to yourself to participate fully in your divorce and to hold yourself accountable for your decisions.

Signs You May Be Heading Toward Divorce

The idea that you should prepare for your divorce *before* the battle is ever fought mirrors good financial planning techniques—that is, plan in advance for all contingencies or life transitions that might lie ahead. How do you know if your marriage is troubled and possibly heading toward divorce?

Arguing about money is a top predictor of divorce and the primary reason for 90 percent of divorces. Finances is one of the great stressors in marriage and is usually more intensely argued about than any other type of marital discord. It usually isn't about the amount of money—it's about differences in spending habits and lack of communication. It's about a lack of compatibility in the financial arena.

When you are at an impasse, personality plays a major role in your financial problems. There is no right way for married couples to manage money, but there are plenty of wrong ways. Instead of solving your financial problems together and avoiding further conflict, you or your spouse may shoulder all of the financial problems alone and keep them secret from each other. This lack of communication escalates quickly into conflict, and divorce seems the only logical conclusion.

Few people ever plan for a divorce in the same way they passionately planned for their wedding. Here are some tell-tale, classic signs that should alert you that money problems are imminent and divorce may be on the horizon.

Classic Tell-Tale Signs of Change in Your Spouse's Behavior About Money Signaling a Possible Divorce

1. Frequent arguments about money.
2. Money is missing and your spouse offers no explanation.
3. Your spouse has stopped direct deposits of paychecks into your joint bank account.
4. Your spouse starts talking "budget" and demands an accounting of all of your spending.
5. Your spouse takes out large cash withdrawals from personal or business accounts.
6. Your spouse pays for his or her credit card bills; you do not see them.
7. Your spouse redirects mail, and his or her credit card and bank statements now go to their office.
8. Your spouse goes on more business trips and has greater travel and entertainment expenses than usual.
9. Your spouse blindsides you with unusual, lavish gifts and trips.
10. Your spouse reduces contributions to savings or retirement—excess cash is now spent or socked away somewhere else.
11. Your spouse increases debts because it is a "smart" financial decision during times of low-interest rates.

12. Your spouse begins spending a great deal more on personal items, grooming, or care as a way to increase the standard of living.

Financial difficulties plague a lot of marriages. Stress is an obvious result that may manifest itself by your spouse complaining *a lot* about money, how bad business is, the risk of a disappearing bonus, or sudden risk of job loss. Your task is to evaluate your current state of finances realistically.

Are you having real money problems? Money problems could be real, but it could be possible that your spouse is manipulating you into believing something that is not totally accurate. People do premeditate divorce and will intentionally aim to lower your financial expectations at the outset of the divorce process so that they have an advantage over you when negotiating support and property division. Attorneys even have a name for it: RAIDS (recently acquired income deficiency syndrome).

⚠ **Caution:** Pay close attention to changes in financial behaviors, attitudes, communication, and changes in spending.

ⓘ **Tip:** You should realize that divorce cannot guarantee a resolution for your financial woes.

Manipulation Tactics to Lower Your Financial Expectations

1. Your spouse complains all the time about money woes.
2. Your spouse says he or she is at risk of being replaced with a less expensive employee.
3. Your spouse's bonus is reduced or nonexistent.
4. Your spouse says that company layoffs are imminent or overdue.
5. Your spouse has a reduced sales territory or cutback in job responsibilities despite solid job performance and company profitability.
6. Your spouse says his or her employer is discriminating on the basis of age.
7. Your spouse says that the "family" spending is rampant and unsustainable with probable loss of income/job.
8. Your spouse says that "you" must go on a strict budget and that every penny needs to be accounted for.
9. Your spouse blames the economy for the need to cut back.

If you recognize any of these tell-tale signs of behavior that is different than usual or surprising gloomy comments about money, you have an opportunity to address them head on with your spouse. In doing so, you may be able to sidestep the risk of divorce, or, if not, at least better prepare yourself for divorce.

Everything depends on how one enters into a divorce: You can either be prepared or not prepared. Divorce can result in either a win–lose, win–win, or lose–lose situation.

What Are the Key Issues in Divorce?

- Children
- You and your emotions
- You and your money

Before You File for Divorce: What Are Your Top Considerations?

- Protecting your children's well-being and interests
- Getting professional support
- Being effective
- Protecting your privacy
- Controlling costs
- Minimizing negativity
- Preparing for the rest of your life
- Creating a sustainable outcome
- Avoiding unnecessary subsequent legal action (post-divorce)

Recognize That Divorce Is Home Grown

Each state legislates its own laws for divorce, separation, and annulment. A divorce is a formal court procedure, and the time required to obtain a divorce, the waiting period between filing an initial petition and receiving a final divorce decree, separation prerequisites, residency requirements, legal costs, and court costs may vary greatly by jurisdiction depending on which type of divorce is filed.

> ⓘ **Tip:** It can be helpful to ask different divorce attorneys to assess your case. You may want to ask about types of settlements that local judges approve or what the "norms" are for your jurisdiction.

All states offer some version of "no-fault" divorce, which defines any divorce where one spouse does not have to prove that the other did something wrong. However, individual states put their own spin on the no-fault rules, and interpretations of divorce law can even vary from judge to judge.

What Is Fault?

Divorce courts are concerned more with money than with morals. The main role of the court is to resolve property disputes and ensure the welfare of the children. However, the concept of fault may play a part in a court's rendering of a financial award. In states that accept versions of marital misconduct as grounds for divorce (fault), the most commonly cited are the following:

- Adultery
- Fraudulent contract
- Constructive abandonment (refusing to recognize the marriage or to act married)
- Intolerable cruelty

- Willful desertion
- Physical incapacity or legal confinement in a hospital because of mental illness for a specified period
- Addiction and habitual use of drugs or intoxicants
- Commission of an infamous crime or a sentence of imprisonment for life

What Kind of Divorce Is It? Contested or Uncontested?

There are two kinds of divorce: contested and uncontested. A *contested* divorce is one in which you and your spouse cannot agree, either about getting divorced or about the terms of one or more issues in the divorce. If you cannot reach a settlement, you ultimately may have a trial and a judge will make a binding decision for you.

In an *uncontested* divorce, you and your spouse have negotiated all the issues, agreed on everything, and reached a final agreement. Therefore, you do not need the court to make any determinations for you regarding custody, property division, or support. An uncontested divorce moves more quickly through the legal system, is less complicated and less costly, and is more likely to be the product of spouses "doing their own divorce."

When you first meet with an attorney, she or he will ask you if your divorce will be contested or uncontested. This question refers to how far apart you and your spouse seem to be, and the answer may not be simple. Many times, it is not easy to initially determine how your divorce will proceed, and what may seem to be uncontested actually ends up being contested as things heat up.

> ⓘ **Tip:** About 90 percent of divorces reach a settlement and do not go to a court trial.

What Are the Different Phases of Divorce?

- The Legal Phase
  - The legal phase of divorce includes:
    - Petition (filing for divorce)
    - Answer
    - Discovery
    - Evaluation
    - Negotiation
    - Finalization (trial or settlement)
    - Transition
- The Financial Phase
  - The financial phases of divorce are:
    - Fact finding and gathering information
    - Preparation
    - Investigation

        - Analysis
        - Planning
        - Projections
        - Transfers and monitoring
- The Emotional Phase
    - The decision to divorce can be filled with contradictory emotions. Divorce triggers a seemingly endless array of emotions from which you must recover, or else your behavior will impact the process.
- The Practical Phase
    - Know what you are getting yourself into ahead of time.
    - Decide where you will live during the divorce.
    - Decide how and when you will tell your children.
    - Put into place realistic financial arrangements, such as who will pay the bills and living expenses. Dividing one household into two means compromises; divorce puts a strain on anyone's budget.
    - Try to avoid involving friends, family, and colleagues in your conflict/affairs.
    - Do not criticize the other parent.
    - Do not alienate the children from the other parent.
    - Try to communicate effectively with your "ex-spouse."
    - Only notify those persons who need to know about your change in address or communications—usually the sooner, the better, such as landlords, banks, government agencies, credit card companies, utilities, schools, doctors, childcare providers, organizations, places of worship, etc.
    - Avoid taking on new debt.
    - Develop strategies for personal growth and make an action plan to decide how you will deal with this event.

Tip: Divorce is an opportunity for change.

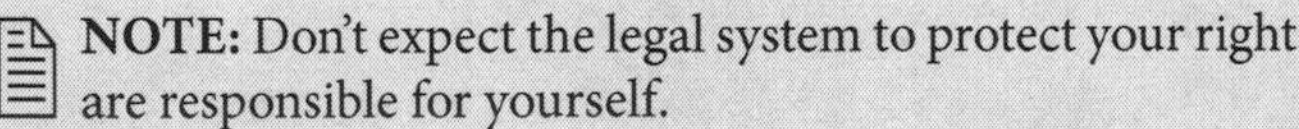

NOTE: Don't expect the legal system to protect your rights and needs—you are responsible for yourself.

How Can You Best Focus Your Energies Before You File for Divorce?

- Make your financial concerns, challenges, and priorities the essential core of your divorce.
- Treat your divorce as business, not personal.
    - The two most important subjects that will affect your result *significantly* are legal and financial. In each case, how you address these two issues will have a far-reaching impact on every aspect of the aftermath of your divorce.

Caution: Emotions run high during a divorce. Greed, revenge, guilt, victimization, and many other reactions all taint divorce and are counterproductive to the proceedings. Your feelings can sidetrack you easily and end up making your divorce more costly, time-consuming, and adversarial. Thinking strategically leads to much better decisions.

- Know your personal responsibilities and obligations.
  - Avoid common client mistakes, such as
    - Using your attorney as your therapist,
    - Expecting justice after proving your spouse's guilt,
    - Having unclear objectives and lack of priorities,
    - Believing everything your spouse tells you,
    - Blaming your attorney for your distracting behaviors,
    - Not checking the details or paperwork,
    - Not communicating with your attorney,
    - Not being flexible, and
    - Not asking enough questions because you feel intimidated.
  - Do research about your state's divorce laws and be realistic about what are considered reasonable outcomes. You often will not get everything you want, nor will you lose everything. Recognize your status quo. Courts are reluctant to change the status quo.
- Know your legal options.
  - Determine which option is the right legal process for you:
    - "Do it yourself" or "*pro se*,"
    - Mediation,
    - Collaborative divorce, or
    - Litigation.
  - Determine how to find the right legal representation, as well as what to ask, what to tell, what to expect, and what it will cost.
- Build your professional team.
  - Find the right experts as needed, such as
    - A divorce financial expert,
    - A mental health professional,
    - A child specialist,
    - A business valuation appraiser, and/or
    - A trust and estate attorney.
  - Know what each of these experts do and define the scope of their tasks and costs of their engagement.
  - Find out if they have experience in the legal process that you choose.
  - Ask how can they help you, such as
    - What value they will add to the final resolution,
    - If they are available to be involved in the process or will be limited to work product (all writings, notes, reports, conversations and confidential materials that reflect impressions, conclusions, opinions, research, or theories) and
    - If they are available and have experience with testifying in court, if needed.
  - Assess their professional standards and work product and how their work product can be used effectively by your attorney.
  - Determine if there are any conflicts of interest.

Taking Your First Steps: Your Legal Options

There are various legal options for divorce. Sometimes you will begin one process and switch to an alternative by choice or out of necessity.

In considering which approach is the best for your divorce, it is vital to research each option carefully and make sure you understand the benefits and risks of your particular decision. The following are the different legal processes you can choose from, although not all may be available in your state:

- "Do it yourself" or "*pro se*"
- Mediation
- Collaborative divorce
- Litigation

Pro Se

"*Pro se*" means that you represent yourself in court without the assistance of an attorney. A "do it yourself" divorce is best for those who agree on everything and who have no children, a short-term marriage, and/or uncomplicated finances. A *pro se* divorce is the least expensive option and is usually the quickest. Nevertheless, not having legal representation may pose perils, even in a seemingly uncomplicated divorce.

Problems with a *pro se* divorce include the following:

1. One spouse may exert undue influence, coerce, or threaten the other under duress to sign an agreement in the absence of legal counsel.
2. Many people do not understand the tax consequences of transferring property and get stuck with huge tax bills later.
3. Some assets may be "missed" (i.e., overlooked) or believed to be separate when they are actually marital property and one party fails to get their fair share.
4. All retirement accounts are valuable assets, and they can be mistakenly undervalued, their tax impact may be underestimated, or they can be overlooked or incorrectly transferred. As a consequence, full benefits are not allocated.
5. Many people do not understand the long-term (or even short-term) impact of the legal decisions they make in a divorce, and there can be serious legal and financial ramifications.

⚠ **Caution:** Not knowing what you do not know can be dangerous, jeopardizing your long-term financial security.

Mediation

Mediation is a form of alternative dispute resolution. Divorce mediation is a voluntary process in which spouses try to negotiate an acceptable divorce agreement with the help of a neutral third party: the mediator.

The mediator helps the spouses to communicate and negotiate a mutually agreeable resolution but does not make any decisions for them. The mediator is trained to use various techniques to open or improve dialogue and empathy between the spouses, aiming to help the parties explore options, make good decisions, and reach an agreement.

The professional practice of family mediation draws practitioners from various backgrounds such as law, finance, mental health, social work, and education. Mediation remains strictly confidential and private, and the mediation process takes less time than moving through standard legal channels in a litigated divorce.

A mediator also may encourage or insist that each spouse has legal review counsel to help them make thoroughly informed decisions, without the threat of coercion or undue influence, before a final agreement is reached. While a mediator may charge a fee comparable to an attorney, generally speaking, the mediation process is less expensive overall and can be a lower-cost option.

The challenges of mediation include:

1. The inability to be open to compromise
2. A lack of motivation to settle
3. Failure to navigate an impasse or conflict
4. Inadequate or dishonest disclosure of all finances, including assets, debts, income, and expenses

⚠ **Caution:** Mediation is not for all cases, especially if domestic violence or addictions are present.

ⓘ **Tip:** Mediation is usually the least-expensive approach to divorce. The benefits are that it is a nonadversarial approach and maintains both parties' privacy, with only one court appearance at the end of the process.

Collaborative Divorce

Collaborative divorce is also a form of voluntary alternative dispute resolution as it relates to family law matters. It is a process in which the parties and their individual attorneys (who are trained in collaborative divorce) commit themselves to resolving all issues by negotiated agreement without resorting to, or threatening to have recourse to, expensive court proceedings.

It encourages the resolution of disputes and early settlement of potential litigation through good faith efforts. The parties and their attorneys sign a contract binding each other to this process and disqualifying their individual attorneys' right to represent either one in any future family-related litigation.

The collaborative process allows the spouses and their attorneys to add to their "team" at any time, such as other specially trained professionals in finance and mental health, to educate, support, and guide the process toward a balanced and lasting agreement. This process protects confidentiality and avoids publicity, and it may reduce financial, time, and emotional costs of a litigated divorce.

The drawbacks of collaborative divorce include the following:

1. If the process falls apart, you have to start all over again with new legal representation and a new professional team.
2. Failure to disclose all finances honestly, including assets, debts, income, and expenses.
3. Few states have collaborative divorce statutes in effect.
4. The collaborative process potentially weakens the attorney-client privilege because information is shared freely between parties and professionals. Should individuals decide to pursue litigated divorce, they may find that they have waived their attorney-client privilege.

> ⓘ **Tip:** Benefits are a nonadversarial approach and privacy for both parties, with only one court appearance at the end.

Litigation

This is the most familiar and traditional process in which each spouse hires an attorney who advocates his or her client's position and separate interests. Your attorney negotiates property, support, and custody issues for you. Litigation is the most widely chosen option since in the vast majority of divorces, one spouse wants the divorce and the other doesn't. Your attorney files for divorce, and the clock starts ticking.

Litigation is a word that paints a picture of going to court and fighting for what you're entitled to. Though litigation is by nature adversarial, attorneys often negotiate cooperatively and strategically to reach reasonable resolutions. The majority of litigated cases end up being settled out of court. Fewer than 5 percent of all litigated cases are tried before a judge who will make the final decision.

The steps in the litigation process are sequential. It can take a lot longer to divorce due to the comprehensive discovery process; the exchange of financial information; mandatory disclosure requirements; depositions; case management conferences; motions (if applicable); pretrial conferences; and, if necessary, a trial. Further, time and costs are expended by correspondence between attorneys, between the attorneys and the two parties, between other professionals who become involved, and by the timetable set by the court's calendar. Litigation for a contested divorce is the most expensive option.

The downside of litigation includes the following:

1. There is potential for an adversarial approach that is costly and damaging to your family.
2. If you cannot settle, the judge or trial court (someone else) decides your future, including child custody and finances.
3. If your children are caught in the middle, the court will probably appoint an attorney for the children, and this may involve invasive psychological evaluations of the family.
4. Your personal and financial information may be open to the public.

> ⓘ **Tip:** Litigation can be *cooperative* among opposing attorneys and respectful of each party's desire to not be acrimonious and to foster civility and respect.

How Can You Manage the Cost of Divorce?

Each divorce is different, so it is impossible to predict how much it will cost or how long it will take. However, you can follow several steps to manage and control the cost of divorce:

- Budget for divorce
  - Oddly enough, people budget for everything but divorce: weddings, baby showers, graduations, etc. People rarely sit down to plan for divorce and allocate resources for how they will pay their divorce.
  - Find out how much you will need to pay for legal and other professional retainers and hourly fees.
  - Make a plan for where will you get the funds (the idea is to think about it and then act).
  - Anticipate how long it will take you to get the funds.
  - Find out how you can keep control of your divorce.
  - Be prepared to track all and any expenses related to divorce; some expert fees may be tax deductible.
- Know the different kinds of costs
  - Costs should not be the sole motivating factor for how the two parties choose a legal process—choosing the least-expensive option may be foolish and short-sighted, with negative long-term consequences.
  - Ask your attorney up front about the usual costs involved and what to expect.
    - Each legal professional and allied divorce professional will charge their hourly rates and retainers—there is no consistency except what the market will bear based on expertise, experience, and geographic location.

  - Find out if you can minimize costs by doing anything yourself, such as making copies, organizing information, avoiding delays, etc.
  - Do not be bullied or persuaded by your spouse to be cheap about divorce—this is a common intimidation tactic by the spouse who is more knowledgeable about finances and controls funds. You need to make smart, informed choices when hiring your attorney and team.
  - Ask which professional divorce-related expenses may be tax deductible for you in the year you are divorced. Only legal fees incurred relating to spousal support issues are tax deductible if you itemize and are divorced.
- Know what can impact costs
  - Do not leave decisions up to others to make for you. They cannot fully understand your financial concerns, priorities, or challenges because they are not you!
  - Client behavior—the good, the bad, and the ugly—can have a significant impact on overall costs.
  - The nature of the case itself can be costly, including financial complexities, the scope of the discovery, the valuations of assets, appraisals of properties and debts, child-related and parenting issues, etc.
  - Sometimes it is necessary to bring in other professional experts to value a business, licenses, earning capacity, assets, and lifestyle standard.
  - Clients may try one attorney or one legal process, only to fire them or drop out and begin fresh all over again with new and different legal representation.
  - Legal professionals may fire their clients. Clients bear the cost of hiring once again and getting their new attorney up to speed plus updating their stale financial information.
  - It takes time to schedule court calendars, court motions, attorney travel, and determine availability for all parties to meet, negotiate, and appear in court for trial.

> ⓘ **Tip:** The true cost of divorce is seldom discussed honestly or is even knowable at the outset, including the emotional impact on the family.

How Can You Pace Yourself When You Decide to File for Divorce?

- Know when time is on your side
  - Time is on your side to:
    - Do your best to research your divorce laws
    - Know in which jurisdiction where it may be in your favor to file divorce
    - Find your legal representation and build your professional team
    - Ask your questions and follow up
    - Organize your financial information
    - Gather resources to pay for divorce
    - Ensure you are prepared to initiate or respond to a divorce filing
    - Apply long-term thinking to your divorce decisions

- Know when time is against you
  - Time is against you when:
    - You are at risk, and there is abuse
    - There is dissipation or waste of marital property
    - You are denied or lose access to financial accounts, property, and/or credit cards
    - You do not wish to be "conflicted out" from engaging your preferred attorney or team member because of your spouse's tactics
      - A "conflict" refers to situations where it is inappropriate for an attorney to advise you because of previous or ongoing work (including initial consultations) with your spouse. Sometimes a spouse will have an initial consultation with many different attorneys as a tactic to preclude the opposing spouse from hiring specific attorneys.

ⓘ **Tip:** Pace yourself—divorce is a marathon, not a sprint.

How Long Will Your Divorce Take?

In divorce, everything takes longer and costs more than you expect. Be aware of the general timelines for different legal processes in your state and how they work.

- Residency: In all states, one spouse needs to have been a resident for a certain period of time for the court to have jurisdiction to divorce you. This can range from six weeks up to one year.
- Waiting or "cooling off" period: A mandatory waiting period, also commonly referred to as a "cooling off" period, is the amount of time the state requires a person filing for divorce to wait until the court grants the divorce. Some states have no waiting period, while others have waiting periods up to two years.
- "Separation requirement:" A separation period is the amount of time that both spouses must be separated before getting a divorce. In some states, the separation period must be met before a divorce can be filed, while in others, it just has to be satisfied before the divorce can be finalized.

It is hard to say or know how long your divorce will take. The entire process can take as little as a few months to as long as several years. The average length of an uncontested divorce is 3 months, while the average contested divorce takes 18 months. The actual length of time for your divorce depends on local rules, the number of issues, and the extent of your negotiations.

Generally speaking, you can manage and control the process to cooperate and agree to reasonable compromises to expedite settlement. However, once you embark on an uncontested divorce, the types of proceedings from state to state are similar but not identical, and they may even depend on the jurisdiction where your case is filed.

 **NOTE:** No one can accurately predict how long your divorce will take.

What You Need to Know If You Stop Your Divorce

The only person who can stop a divorce is the person who initiated it. He or she must rescind the initial filing.

You can contest the grounds your spouse alleges to in their petition, and you can argue custody and property settlement, but no state will force your spouse to stay married to you if they don't want to.

Also, the ability to stop a divorce after the papers have already been filed depends on the timing of the request. The general rule is that if a judgment has not already been issued, the parties may stop the divorce upon mutual agreement. However, if you miss the statutory deadline in which to halt the divorce action, either spouse will have to file additional motions with the court to overturn the divorce proceeding. Once the withdrawal is finalized, the divorce proceedings are terminated, and you remain legally married.

Be aware that this can get complicated, especially if you and your spouse were separated before or during the divorce process and acquired property. You are at risk of "new" property being reclassified as either separate or marital, depending on laws of your state.

One last point: You and your spouse may encounter some obstacles if you wish to stop the divorce, and it can be considered divorce fraud. Depending on circumstances, a party that does this may face legal consequences, such as contempt of court or even criminal charges. The following are examples of divorce fraud:

- Your spouse was only "pretending" to stop the divorce in order to delay the process in his or her favor.
- Your spouse grossly misrepresents issues and circumstances.
- Your spouse initiated the divorce but then reconciles with you, or still lives separately with intimacy privileges, and leaves the divorce action dangling. This tactic enables your spouse to go to court for a final judgment without even telling you.
- One spouse is encouraged to change his or her mind out of coercion, fear, stress, or duress.
- One spouse rescinds the divorce action, but there are serious issues with safety or health (such as abuse, neglect, violence, or mistreatment, especially of children).

What Will Happen Financially During a Divorce?

During a divorce, you will experience a significant transition in your financial position. Without assistance, the changes that occur can be a tipping point and can affect the well-being and security of you and your family. Remember that the legal process has a beginning and an end, but the financial reality of your outcome is something you will have to live with for the rest of your life.

For each spouse, there is bound to be:

- Distractions and time away from one's career
- Economic upheaval that comes from having two household budgets instead of one, having to account for everything during the divorce process, etc.
- Imbalance of power, such as knowledge about finances, experience, and control over money

In many ways, divorce is a business transaction, but the financial issues you face can be life-changing. As daunting as this sounds, you have a finite period to understand your financial situation completely. You need to focus on planning for the future, and realistically, you will be better off if you discard prior expectations and any sense of entitlement about keeping *more than* your fair share.

NOTE: You are beginning a new life, with all of the excitement and responsibility that goes along with it.

The best way to make decisions about financial issues is to get them *right* before your final agreement is ever signed. It is imperative to disclose all financial information accurately, analyze your options thoroughly, and understand both the short- and long-term implications of your decisions.

Build your professional team at the outset. One of the most important team players besides your family divorce attorney is a divorce financial planner, who can listen to your needs, help set priorities, perform an expert financial analysis, improve the negotiation process, and guide you to reach a settlement with confidence.

Here are some of the other benefits of including a divorce financial planner in the planning process:

- More control of the divorce process
- A clear understanding of the *current* financial picture
- A better comprehension of the *future* financial picture
- A greater focus on reaching a fair and workable settlement
- Being able to negotiate more effectively
- Being able to ensure a faster resolution of all financial matters, equitably, for both spouses
- Minimizing legal fees
- Reducing taxes
- Maximizing marital assets

ⓘ **Tip:** Divorce is a multi-step process. Finances are an issue in almost every stage of divorce and are sometimes very complex, with a variety of long-lasting consequences for both parties.

Remember, information is power. The following chapters give you very detailed information about everything you need to know to confidently complete the divorce process. I walk you through the process and explain how to prepare your financial case; divide up property; protect your assets; understand tax consequences, child support, and spousal support; and identify unique circumstances (children with special needs, etc.). I also address the "what if's," explain what to expect at the very end, and describe how to avoid post-divorce problems.

It is a reality of modern life that many marriages end in divorce and that many children are affected by divorce. Preparing for divorce is your best strategy for comprehensively and successfully addressing your needs and financial security. Heed the old proverb by Miguel de Cervantes: "Forewarned, forearmed; to be prepared is half the victory."

3 You Have Decided to Divorce, Now What? An Outline of the Divorce Process

The Legal Sequence of the Events Leading Up to Divorce

Ultimately, all divorces end up in court because a judge must approve the divorce to make it final. However, before this ending, the legal sequence of events depends on how you choose to divorce. There are many ways to divorce. Most divorces are never tried by a judge or jury. About 90 percent of all divorces are settled out of court.

Do It Yourself

If you and your spouse have decided on a "do it yourself" divorce, you will represent yourself before the court. First, contact the local courthouse for your state's Rules of Civil Procedure (or Practice Rules), Family Court Codes, and any procedures that must be followed. You will draft your papers and file them with the court to request an uncontested divorce. Most states or bar associations provide handbooks to help you complete the forms, understand and comply with timeline requirements of the court, and guide you through the process. You can also go to your local court clerk's office for assistance.

Mediation and Collaborative

If you choose mediation or collaborative divorce, you (and not the court) are in control of both the process and timelines. You have the option to avoid deadlines imposed by the court until you reach a settlement and are ready to present your agreement to the court. At that time, you can start the process with the court by filing an official action.

Litigation

If you choose to litigate your divorce, you and your spouse each hire a separate divorce attorney, one of whom will initiate an action (divorce proceeding) with the court. In a divorce action, one spouse (the plaintiff or petitioner) is suing the other (the defendant or respondent) for a divorce. The petitioner/plaintiff requests the divorce, and the defendant/respondent may or may not want the divorce. Both spouses are called "parties" to the action. An action in matrimonial matters can be an annulment, a separation, or a dissolution of marriage (also known as divorce).

If you choose to litigate, there are very definite timelines relating to a litigated action, and the court mandates the sequence of events:

1. One spouse, known as the plaintiff, hires a divorce attorney who initiates an action for divorce by filing with the court a petition for divorce (also called Summons and Complaint). The petition is served on the other party, also called the defendant.
2. In many courts, there is a waiting period before the court can order the final judgment of divorce. The date of filing the divorce action is when the waiting period starts.
3. The court assigns a case number to the parties for the newly filed action, which is called a docket number.
4. In many cases, once the petition is served, certain orders are automatically entered by the court that apply to both parties. These "automatic orders" are designed to protect the financial status quo while the case is being litigated.
5. A divorce attorney may also file for *ex parte* orders along with the initial petition.
   a. An *ex parte* motion requests immediate relief that can be granted without a hearing. These orders vary from state to state and will apply to the parties until the divorce is finalized.
      i. Orders for personal protection
      ii. Orders for interim financial support
      iii. Orders to maintain status quo on marital property
      iv. Orders for child custody

NOTE: Parties can agree jointly to temporary orders, but they won't be enforced if they are not filed with the court and the order is not signed by the judge.

6. The other party, the defendant, is served with the summons and complaint.
   a. Once served with papers, the defendant files a response, also known as an answer, in order to participate in the litigation. Usually, the defendant also files a counterclaim or cross-complaint to continue the divorce action even if the plaintiff withdraws the petition. If the defendant does not file a responsive pleading, the plaintiff can unilaterally end the action.

7. Many courts require parties to attempt to mediate their disputes before their matter is subjected to the court. Mediation is a method of nonbinding dispute resolution involving a neutral third party who tries to help the disputing parties reach a mutually agreeable solution. Currently 10 states have mandatory mediation for divorcing couples, 5 states allow a judge to order mediation, and 21 states are considering a mediation program.
8. Many states have adopted a policy that requires parents to attend co-parenting classes, although they need not attend together.
9. A financial statement for each party must be filed with the court within a designated time frame (depending on your state, it may be called a Net Worth Statement, a Case Information Statement, a Financial Affidavit, or an Affidavit of Financial Condition).
10. Many states require a court session called an advance case review, case management conference, preliminary conference, or early case resolution meeting, where the parties meet with the judge assigned to their case or with a referee to discuss the issues.
11. The parties exchange documents and information revealing the financial position of each. This is known as the "production of documents" or "discovery." Each state sets a deadline by which the discovery process must be completed. In cases where complex financial issues are litigated, the court may allow the deadline to be extended.
12. Settlement or pretrial conferences are scheduled by the court. In such meetings, the judge or a court referee will meet with the divorce attorneys and parties to discuss the issues and make settlement recommendations.
13. The parties negotiate a permanent agreement for child custody, child support, spousal maintenance, and property division. An agreement is written up and submitted to the court for approval. In most states, the parties and their attorneys appear to declare in person before the judge their intentions regarding the agreement.
14. If the parties cannot agree on all or a portion of the issues, a trial will be held, and a judge/jury will enter permanent orders and a judgment of dissolution of marriage.

Is It Better to Be the Plaintiff or Defendant?

The plaintiff is the person who initiates the action for divorce and files the papers with the court. The defendant is the person being sued for divorce. Being the defendant doesn't mean you have done anything wrong and it doesn't mean your spouse gets to make all the decisions in your divorce. If you are the defendant, you will be served with the complaint. There is no advantage in attempting to avoid service. The divorce action will continue; it may only slightly delay the process.

Years ago, it mattered more which party was the plaintiff and which was the defendant. This distinction applies to trial procedure but seems to be gone from a practical viewpoint. Judges do not care particularly who filed first or which party is the plaintiff.

However, you may have a compelling reason to start the divorce action first. These reasons could include:

- Your need for immediate judicial intervention in the case,
- Your desire to have the action in one jurisdiction as opposed to another if deemed advantageous,
- Your spouse is stalling on starting the divorce action, or
- Other reasons articulated by your attorney; e.g., if your attorney is certain you will go to trial, she or he may want you to be the first to testify.

What If I Want to Premeditate My Divorce and Get My Ducks in a Row?

When you decide to divorce, there are several steps you can take to prepare yourself financially as well as to establish a better fact pattern for your case. A good rule of thumb is to take about six months before taking action to sort through how you will file for divorce.

ⓘ **Tip:** Pre-divorce financial planning is fundamental to achieving the best results.

Can I Keep My Divorce Private?

In litigation, once an action is filed, your intention to divorce is no longer a secret. Court cases are public information and are listed on the court's website by the court docket number, by divorce attorney/firm name or juris number, and by the name of the parties. All of this information is available to the public. The court's website is updated as new information is entered into the case management system.

It is possible that a court will grant a request to seal, or make private, all or part of a divorce file to avoid becoming a matter of public record. The sealed records will remain private and confidential. Commonly cited reasons for requesting the court to seal records include the following:

- The need to protect victims of domestic violence
- The need to protect children from public identification
- The need to protect sensitive data such as Social Security numbers and account numbers
- The need to protect celebrity information from public identification
- The need to protect proprietary business information

If you choose an alternative legal process to litigation, such as mediation or collaborative divorce, your privacy is protected better to an extent. The information sought and exchanged by the parties is not typically filed with the court or discussed with the court. There are no court motions. You can negotiate privately and file only your final agreement with the court. Keep in mind, however, that minimum financial disclosures must accompany the final agreement in most courts. Finally, the final agreement is part of the public record in most states.

⚠ **Caution:** Some states have laws in place to protect the confidentiality of statements made during mediation. No such laws have yet been enacted to protect the confidential nature of collaborative divorce.

Why Dates Are So Important: The Date You Announce Your Decision to Divorce, the Date of Physical Separation, and the Date of Filing

You are probably most concerned with the date when your divorce becomes final; however, other dates may be much more significant, including:

1. The date of marriage,
2. The date of separation from your spouse,
3. The date of filing the petition,
4. The date the judge signs the judgment, and
5. The date the court clerk enters the judgment into court record.

Various states use different dates to mark the end of marriage. That date will be a critical factor, and it sometimes has a *dramatic effect*, in deciding issues related to property division, child support, spousal maintenance, and adultery. Why? The critical date in your state will establish a point in time to value marital assets and marital debts, pension benefits, and business income and ownership. Other important dates start the clock running for a mandatory waiting period before a divorce can become final and determine the maximum amount of time for the parties to resolve the case.

⚠ **Caution:** It is imperative you are mindful of key dates in your state and how they will affect income and property divisions.

In many family law cases, the date of separation plays a focal role and is a hotly contested issue. It can be the difference between whether an asset is community, marital, or separate property, as well as whether a marriage is of lengthy duration such that spousal support may continue for a longer term or indefinitely.

NOTE: The precise definition of the "date of separation" varies from state to state.

In some states, the date of separation is considered the date that spouses no longer physically live together as a married couple, either by relocating from the marital residence or by staying separately in the same marital residence. However, this can be confusing and is arguable. Physical separation from your spouse does not necessarily indicate the end of hope for reconciliation. If you move out, you may have every belief that the move is temporary and conditional for saving your marriage. On the other hand, you may continue to reside with your spouse when you intend to end your relationship in consideration of financial constraints, fear of being regarded as having abandoned the children, desire to retain possession of the joint residence, and for many other reasons.

ⓘ **Tip:** Some states require physical separation; others do not. Divorce is never automatic, and you can live separately for years, but you can't legally move on with your lives until you bring the court in on the process by filing a petition for divorce.

⚠ **Caution:** Be aware that even if you decide to informally separate by moving into separate residences, without filing for legal separation or divorce, this can have a bigger impact than you imagine. Courts may likely consider it as the date of legal separation. You should be aware that an informal separation can be a slippery slope.

In states that use the date of separation as the termination of the marriage, a judge may have to decide the "date of separation" if you and your spouse do not agree. The judge will decide whether the marital relationship was impaired to the extent that there is no hope to resolve the issues that caused the breakdown, and he or she will consider evidence of when you as a couple intended to split, such as the date you hire a divorce attorney, the date you communicate to your spouse an intent to divorce, or the date you file for divorce. The judge may order the parties to agree to a date decided by the court.

In states where the date of separation is less weighty, you and your spouse can agree on a cutoff date. This date must reflect when you intended to make a complete, final break from your marriage and is based on your simultaneous conduct (such as hiring a divorce attorney). Other states use the date of filing for divorce as the unequivocal date for the ending of the marriage and as the start of the divorce process.

⚠ **Caution:** For obvious reasons, you should pay attention to the date your marriage ends because this is when you become legally and financially in limbo until you are divorced.

Important Dates and Abbreviations

Date of Marriage (DOM): The day you were legally married.

Date of Separation (DOS): Refers to the date you and your spouse separated from each other with the intention to end the relationship.

- It may start the court clock for certain mandatory waiting periods for obtaining a divorce.
- It establishes a cutoff date for the acquisition of marital assets and marital debts.

  Some states, especially community property states, use the date of separation (living apart physically) for determining property interest; property acquired by you after the DOS is considered to be your separate property. Commonly, the DOS is a source of disagreement between spouses.

Date of Filing (DOF): Refers to the date that one or both spouses file a petition for divorce. The date of filing a petition for divorce shows the intention of one or both spouses to divorce and officially initiates the divorce process for purposes of the court proceedings.

Date of Divorce (DOD) or Date of Judgment: When the court enters the legal orders on the record, signs a judgment, and enters the judgment on the record or when the court notifies you and your spouse of the entry of judgment. In some states, the divorce takes effect once the parties receive notice of the entry of judgment. Other states have a waiting period of six months until the divorce becomes final.

Bifurcation of Divorce: In states that allow bifurcation of divorce, the court divides the divorce proceedings into two stages. The court first hears the divorce case and rules on the dissolution of marriage; it resolves other pertinent issues like property division and child custody on another date. Once the court orders the dissolution of marriage, the spouses are legally divorced and free to remarry.

How Do You Protect Yourself Financially Before and After Separation or Filing: Your Best Defense Is a Good Offense!

It is normal to feel anxious during the transition period of your divorce. You often hear that the greatest threat in adversarial divorce (litigation) is when parties are determined to scorch the earth so that their spouse will get nothing. This annihilating posture is usually harsh bluster, but—occasionally and mostly in the short term—it may be necessary for you to take action to protect your finances.

> ⓘ **Tip:** Remember the greatest ally you have in divorce is yourself—because only you know your spouse best—when it comes to you, your children, and your money.

How to Protect Yourself from Financial Chaos

If you believe your spouse is purposefully creating financial turmoil, you can request the court to enter orders on a temporary basis to maintain the status quo. These temporary orders may provide for support, custody, or some other relief. Laws and rules vary from state to state regarding *pendente lite* motions or *ex parte* interim orders.

You need protection if you suspect any of the following financial abuse:

- Excessive spending
- Transferring of assets
- Hiding assets
- Disposing of property
- Incurring debts
- Failure to make timely debt payments—risk of default
- Entering into long-term lease or rental contracts, investments, or private deals that tie up money
- Gifting or lending to family, friends, or relatives
- Forfeiting or deferring income substantially or taking alternative compensation (not cash)
- Delaying or failing to file income taxes
- Prepayment of debts and taxes that favor one spouse only
- Closing all joint accounts and credit cards
- Canceling utilities, services, insurances, etc.

Interim Steps You Must Take to Prepare Yourself: Be Proactive

Ignorance about your money issues is not acceptable. The following are several tasks you can do to protect your financial interests before filing for divorce or immediately upon learning that your spouse will or has filed for divorce.

- Open a bank account in your name
- Open a major credit card in your name if you do not have one
- Create a new email account for yourself dedicated to working with your divorce team for divorce correspondence and communications
- Get a current copy of your and your spouse's credit reports from all three reporting agencies and immediately correct any errors
- Pay off and block further usage of any unsecured joint debts (credit cards, HELOCs, etc.) unless you are given notice and you give permission of future usage
- Make sure all insurances are paid and up to date on auto, health, property, life, long-term care, etc., and arrange for the companies to notify you first of late payments
- Don't create any new substantial debt in your name alone or incur debt in your spouse's name alone
- Start a cash emergency fund
- Do not co-mingle any separate property of yours with your spouse's in a joint account or use it for family expenditures
- Monitor all joint accounts as closely as possible, including online passwords, all transactions, and all transfers in and out of accounts

- Maximize cash flow from your paycheck by changing withholding exemptions (this may have future tax implications)
- Hold on to refund checks belonging to both of you until instructed by your attorney how they should be transacted
- Take possession of certain assets during your separation, especially assets you want to use, such as autos and furniture, and any assets your spouse could liquidate privately, such as collectibles, cash, jewelry, and bearer bonds

⚠ **Caution:** Most states set limits on how assets and debts and income can be handled by the two parties once a divorce is filed. The limits may apply even prior to the commencement of the case if the actions are taken in anticipation of a divorce. It is essential that you follow the advice of your attorney, so that you do not violate the statutory limitations. Although it is smart to protect your assets, it is never acceptable to hide assets—or any financial information—from your spouse during a divorce case.

Your Future and the Bigger Picture

In addition to immediate financial concerns, you also need to focus on the bigger picture that lies ahead. What will your life be like immediately following divorce, five years from now, and ten years from now? This exercise may seem remote because you are so caught up in the problems of the present. However, you do need to think about how you will sustain your financial security in the future.

Two of the most obvious questions are whether you will have to go to work or change your employment and where you will live. You should start *now* setting goals and objectives for yourself to be as financially independent as possible.

You should rank the order of your objectives and the rationale for how you prioritize them. You may want to write down goals, obstacles that keep you from achieving them, and your perceived needs for how to accomplish them. You may recognize a need for vocational counseling, more education, childcare while you work, or improving your employability.

ⓘ **Tip:** Your aspiration to achieve these goals will be the key to your happiness and sense of control over your future.

Your Obligation to Provide for Your Children

Be aware that, if you are parents, you not only have a moral duty to support your children jointly, but all states have laws that make child support an obligation of both parents. If you take no steps to be fully employed or seek to avoid paying child support, the court can impute income to you.

Imputing Income to You

Imputed income is income that a court assigns or credits to you for the purpose of calculating child support and spousal support. Two common scenarios in which income is imputed are when an individual is intentionally unemployed or under-employed or is being supported by a new partner. The court has considerable discretion consistent with the state and federal statutory and rule-based factors to find that a party is voluntarily manipulating his or her financial circumstances.

The court can call upon a vocational expert to evaluate your earning capacity and estimate (or impute) an amount of income you are capable of earning. Additionally, some courts have imputed income to a spouse based on assets, such as stocks, bonds, real estate, or other income-producing property. Child support guidelines permit the court to solve the problem of any parent who intentionally reduces his or her income to reduce or avoid child support (refer to Chapter 11).

⚠ **Caution:** Do not play "victim" to the court and try to convince the court you are incapable of remunerative (money-making) activities.

What Factors Will the Court Consider in Determining Whether to Impute Income?

The court makes a child support order by applying the Child Support Guidelines in your state. The court may allow for deviations if the court accepts your reasons for being underemployed or unemployed.

The court may consider the following:

- The reason and intent for the voluntary underemployment or unemployment;
- What the employment status and earning capacity of that parent would have been if the family had remained intact;
- The availability of other assets that may be used to pay support; and
- The ages of any children in the parent's household and childcare alternatives (for example, if a parent is caring for very young children, the court may consider that parent's contribution to the family to be sufficient).

Common Questions about Your Employability

Commonly asked questions about earning capacity and employability by people going through divorce include the following:

- Should I wait until my divorce is over before I get a job?
- Should I explore possible jobs but will it hurt me if I am only "looking"?
- Should I quit my job in the midst of a divorce?
- Should I make a major career change before I am divorced?
- Should I turn down a promotion or bonus so that I don't have to share it with my spouse?
- Should I refuse to do overtime even with a significant history for it?

ⓘ **Tip:** Ask your divorce attorney about your particular situation. In most cases, the court will not be in favor of a party who has deliberately lowered his or her income in anticipation of divorce.

Meeting Your Temporary Financial Needs: The Immediate Implications of Divorce

You are facing a new economic situation. In most cases, it is a time of adjustment to new financial circumstances, as well as a time to plan realistically for changes in your lifestyle after divorce. When one household becomes two, expenses increase. There are two primary ways you can cover living expenses while you are in the process of divorce.

Option 1: Continue the Status Quo

If you and your spouse can reach an agreement on how you will share expenses in the short term, then you can implement an informal arrangement. If you are used to paying all bills from a joint account, you and your spouse can agree to continue to use a joint account to support day-to-day bill paying. If you had separate accounts for expenses, then you and your spouse can agree to use your different accounts for bill paying as usual.

⚠ **Caution:** Sometimes one income is insufficient to support two households even temporarily. If you can't cover your expenses, you have serious analysis to do concerning your budget and living expenses. Some money may need to be exchanged between you and your spouse to meet ongoing living expenses and any shortfall you may have. This situation necessitates that you and your spouse agree to temporary budgets and prioritize which expenses are paid first.

Option 2: Temporary Orders

However, if you disagree over finances, you will have to go to court to ask a judge to decide how to maintain the status quo temporarily. It may be necessary to prepare and file a written motion or petition for spousal and child support, called *pendente lite* relief—meaning during the pendency of the litigation. A request for temporary support is not automatically granted. Temporary orders are designed to maintain the status quo as best as possible and spell out the "ground rules" while a divorce action is pending. A court will usually award the lower earning spouse just enough support to meet basic needs while the divorce is proceeding.

NOTE: Divorce can take years to reach the final conclusion, although most divorces are completed within one year. Be aware that temporary support does not mean you are automatically entitled to a comparable level or any support after the divorce is over.

Temporary orders deal with child custody and child support, as well as preventing parties from hiding assets, changing beneficiaries, or terminating insurance coverage. Other common temporary orders include orders for spousal support and counsel fees.

Temporary orders can address other issues, such as:

- Establishing who has possession of the marital residence,
- Establishing orders to protect all assets, and
- Awarding appraiser fees.

Temporary orders can be modified while your case is pending; they usually last until "permanent" orders replace them (or the temp orders are modified) when the divorce is final. They are designed to maintain the status quo and establish a routine that is manageable for you and your spouse until all issues can be resolved.

Having temporary orders in place can prevent a lot of tension and misunderstandings. Orders also provide one party with legal recourse against the other if one fails to comply with the order. If you don't have a court order, no other document, even one in writing, is enforceable if your spouse doesn't pay.

NOTE: You should know that temporary orders are rarely modifiable or subject to appeal pending trial. By their very nature, judges will address these issues again, as well as property distribution, at trial. Therefore, you have to make do with whatever temporary orders are granted in a highly-contested divorce.

What Do You Need to Request Temporary Financial Support?

To request interim financial support, you will need to provide evidence to support your application for an amount of support, which may include your pay stubs, bank records, credit card bills, shelter-related expenses, student loan balances, childcare expenses, and medical bills.

ⓘ **Tip:** If you are in dire need of support and your temporary support hearing is postponed, you can file an emergency motion before the court.

Are There Tax Implications If You Receive Temporary Spousal Support (Alimony)?

For payments to be considered spousal support, including temporary spousal support, a payment must meet certain IRS requirements:

- Payments must be to or for a spouse or former spouse and made under a legal order, a finalized divorce, or separation agreement.
- Payments must be made in cash (cash or checks).

- Spouses cannot be members of the same household at the time when payments are made.
- Payments are not treated as child support.
- Payments stop upon death of either spouse.

If your support payments meet the IRS definition of alimony, you may be able to deduct support payments as alimony. Your spouse (the recipient) will be required to pay taxes on these payments as income if filing separately. However, if you file a joint married income tax return, you cannot claim temporary spousal support as a tax deduction and your spouse will not include the support as income.

ⓘ **Tip:** Do not make alimony payments to a joint account if it can be avoided. This will prevent a later claim or argument that you still had access and control of the funds.

If You Receive Temporary Child Support

Child support is tax-free money. Child support is neither deductible to the paying spouse nor taxable to the receiving spouse.

Pulling Yourself and Your Family Together: Introduction of Children's Needs

At any age, divorce can be confusing for children. How you cope will affect your children. Co-parenting tips and guidance can be a huge help to you as you enter the divorce process. Children quickly pick up on your feelings of conflict and the fact that you and your spouse may have very different perceptions of your financial reality. The challenge is to not communicate negativity about economic matters, specifically about spending or housing uncertainties. By far the most dangerous risk to your children is to barter their needs for financial gain or for custody and visitation rights.

ⓘ **Tip:** It is important to be prepared to know what to say and when to say it, as well as how much information to give the children. Your attorney can direct you to mental health professionals who are specifically trained as parenting counselors and can assist you and your spouse in easing the impact of the divorce on your children.

⚠ **Caution:** It is unacceptable ethically to threaten a child custody challenge as a way to negotiate greater financial awards.

Characteristic Pitfalls of Divorce

Each divorce is different, yet each shares common ground. Custody of the children and spousal support are the most highly charged emotional topics of negotiation. Divorce can take quite a long time, and clear thinking will help you exercise control over the process and make it much less costly.

20 Common Financial Mistakes to Avoid in Divorce

1. DON'T underestimate the cost and length of the divorce process.
   DO plan early for a budget for your divorce and identify resources from which you can pay your legal and professional fees.
2. DON'T choose the cheapest means for resolving the divorce.
   DO consider the long-term consequences of your financial decisions and hire professionals who can help you make knowledgeable financial decisions.
3. DON'T expect that your spouse will pay all your divorce costs.
   DO realize that each party usually pays their own divorce fees, or the majority of them, from their income or share of the total marital assets.
4. DON'T contribute to the cost of your divorce by your negative and self-defeating behaviors.
   DO seek professional help by creating your dream divorce team: attorney, divorce financial planner, divorce coach, therapist, etc. Be realistic about the process and knowledgeable about options for an outcome.
5. DON'T tie up liquid funds and other resources that you may need to initiate the divorce process and pay for legal retainers, court fees, etc.
   DO keep a stash of cash.
6. DON'T sign long-term leases or rental agreements during your divorce or shortly thereafter.
   DO avoid long-term commitments until you know where you will want to live after the divorce. Moving twice is costly, and breaking contracts is expensive. Analyze if it is better for you to rent or buy (in the short run).
7. DON'T continue to spend to support a lifestyle that you cannot afford and incur greater debts.
   DO manage your spending so you can save something while you go through the divorce process, especially if you are unemployed or a stay-at-home spouse. You never know how bills will be paid or if you will share ultimately in the debt. Make saving a priority and reduce overhead and luxuries.
8. DON'T believe your spouse will be "proven" to be at fault for the breakdown of the marriage and that you will be vindicated by the divorce process.
   DO be aware that all states have "no fault" divorce laws, which means no one must prove fault to initiate a divorce. Fault itself must be proven and qualified by legal statutes to impact the financial outcome or to influence a parenting plan.

9. DON'T believe in the "lawyer knows best" myth by letting your attorney dictate *your* goals and your best short- and long-term outcomes.
   DO take full responsibility for making life-changing financial decisions.
10. DON'T believe you should negotiate for greater child custody for less financial security; that is, trading part of the financial settlement you are entitled to for child custody or more visitation time.
    DO be aware of your rights and entitlements under the law.
11. DON'T try to be thrifty and save money by canceling your health insurance.
    DO keep your existing health insurance policy for as long as possible and think before ending your current plan without carefully securing insurance elsewhere.
12. DON'T cancel your or your spouse's life insurance. The cost to replace it may be more expensive and more difficult to obtain in light of current health issues. A new policy may have less favorable terms.
    DO keep in mind that life insurance is required to serve as collateral for support obligations.
13. DON'T stop paying down debts.
    DO pay down a little on each credit card and loan and make payments on time. Make it a TOP priority to preserve your credit rating score and access to available credit.
14. DON'T borrow against your retirement assets—there are tax implications and possible forfeiture of employer-matching benefits.
    DO delay or tap into your retirement assets only when absolutely necessary.
15. DON'T be unrealistic about sharing your ex-spouse's future employer benefits, such as bonuses, awards, stock options, company perquisites, etc.
    DO keep the door open and negotiate to share these benefits, but do not count on them as support for your post-divorce lifestyle.
16. DON'T believe you can renegotiate the terms of your divorce *after it is final*. There are specific legal criteria that must be met to seek modification of your legal agreement.
    DO understand that the standards are high to discourage "frivolous" lawyering. Property division is a one-shot deal and cannot be modified.
17. DON'T fail to discuss thoroughly all financial items that impact your budget once you are divorced.
    DO evaluate:
    a. Gaps in health insurance (between end of COBRA and new coverage)
    b. Long-term care insurance
    c. Uninsurability and substantial out-of-pocket medical expenses
    d. Contributions during the marriage to caregiving for elderly parents
    e. Children with special needs and future planning and expenses, as well as impact on eligibility for government benefits
    f. College planning
    g. Estate planning if second families and/or remarriages are probable
    h. Living longer, finality of support, and managing assets for longevity

18. DON'T neglect to consider tax consequences of the assets you receive in a divorce settlement. Not all assets are equal; for example, a retirement account is different from a bank account. In addition, the value on paper of any asset may not be the same when you sell it.

    DO recognize that you assume the cost basis for all assets divided as marital property. All property transfers incident to divorce have no taxable impact. Cost basis is the original value of an asset for tax purposes, usually the purchase price, adjusted for stock splits, dividends, capital improvements, and return of capital distributions.
19. DON'T fail to consider the tax implications of each major decision you make in your divorce.

    DO know that the IRS is watching you.
20. DON'T neglect to plan during the divorce for how to handle post-divorce financial issues, such as transferring pension benefits, securing health insurance, and paying off debts.

    DO create a To Do list by priority of tasks you must execute pursuant to your divorce judgment and track the accuracy of all transfers. Prepare and open new accounts as needed to receive property transfers.

Chapter 4 describes the financial phases of divorce and the many tasks you will complete, both large and small. Some you will need to complete on a timeline and others as your new routine dictates. It is strongly recommended you give yourself adequate time for these responsibilities. Track all important dates, so you can hold yourself accountable to finishing tasks. Once you are done with a task, give yourself a check mark and a pat on the back. By taking one step at a time, you will ward off feeling overwhelmed.

> ⓘ **Tip:** It is a very good idea to organize and manage your To Do list in conjunction with a calendar.

4 Preparing for Your Financial Divorce

Preparation, Preparation, Preparation

The best way to prepare for divorce is to take time to understand your current economic reality, as you will soon become responsible for mapping out the rest of your life. This moment may be the first time you take a hard look at your overall financial position. And if you are not used to planning for long-term financial needs, you may feel overwhelmed, frightened, and confused about how to start.

Undoubtedly you will have many questions. How much money will you have to live on? How do you go about deciding who gets what? Who gets the antique silver your mother-in-law gave you on your wedding day? Who gets the Apple stock? The furniture? The credit card debt? How do you begin to divvy up the accumulated belongings of years of marriage?

Divorce is fraught with stress and uncertainty, which can lead you to make very poor decisions. Negotiations can become contentious, clouded, and derailed by emotion. When you are most distracted and vulnerable is when you need most a clear head to avoid common mistakes. You can start by understanding each step of the financial phases of divorce: information gathering, analysis, negotiation, decision-making, and settlement.

What Are the Primary Financial Issues in Divorce?

The primary financial issues to be decided in divorce include:

- Child support
- Spousal support (alimony)
- Assets
- Debts
- College (which will be awarded/considered in some states but not in others)

Child support and spousal support are two independent and distinct legal concepts, with each having different histories, purposes, and elements. Child support and spousal support are separately defined, calculated, and qualified by specific statutory factors in each state. These statutory factors allow for some uniformity between the states, especially regarding child support, as well as for deviations based on unique aspects of every case. All states work together to create and enforce child support orders and, to a lesser extent, spousal support orders.

In Chapter 11, I discuss child support and all children-related financial issues, which are vital to meeting your family's needs, attaining tax benefits while avoiding tax traps, and serving the best interests of your children. In Chapter 12, I discuss types of spousal support and factors that impact calculation, duration, taxes, and modification.

The division of property (assets and debts) is a fundamental part of the divorce process. You and your spouse will be required to make your inventories of assets and liabilities. You jointly, or a judge, will decide how the property will be divided. In Chapters 6 to 10, I discuss the difference between separate property and marital property, and I explain the diverse natures and characters of many types of assets and liabilities.

ⓘ **Tip:** You need to know what your state divorce laws dictate since the differences from state to state can be significant. Sometimes interpretations and applications of the state laws can even vary between jurisdictions in the same state.

What Are the Main Property Issues I Should Discuss with My Divorce Attorney?

- Equity in homestead
- Other real property
- Home furnishings
- Business assets
- Professional practices
- Professional degrees
- Retirement accounts (pension, individual retirement accounts [IRAs], 401K plans, etc.)
- Motor vehicles
- Recreational vehicles
- Personal property
- Cash and savings accounts
- Stocks, bonds, mutual funds, certificates of deposit (CDs), and money market accounts
- Vested and unvested deferred employer benefits
- Compensation for contributions as a homemaker
- Hidden assets
- Debts
- Inheritances
- Gifts
- Income tax benefits and obligations

Ownership of Property

Ownership of property refers to how the property is legally titled in someone's name. There are three ways to own property—in your own name, in joint names with others, or by contract rights. Determining ownership law in your state affects your *married or widowed* spouse's rights of ownership, rights to income from property, rights and duties of management and control, rights to make lifetime gifts, property rights in the event of death, and property rights at death. It is important to note that ownership and division of property are different in the marital context than in the probate context. This book focuses on ownership and division as it pertains to divorce in the marital context.

State property laws dictate legal forms of property ownership. Legal ownership may not limit the court's ability to award an asset to a spouse in a divorce. There are two distinct systems in the states for classifying how property will be divided in a divorce depending on whether it is marital or separate property: the equitable distribution system and the community property system.

The equitable distribution system is the most popular and 41 states use it. The term "equitable distribution" means that the court can divide the marital estate in any way it determines is "equitable." Under this system, property acquired by a married spouse during marriage is marital property even if the person holds the title of the property separately from their spouse. Legal title to property is actual ownership as it relates to third parties but does not change the court's discretion to distribute the property in an equitable fashion in the divorce. Property may be divided differently in the divorce than who is recorded on the title.

Equitable distribution states are also called "common law" states for purposes of property ownership and distribution at death. In those states, the ability to dispose property at death follows title of the asset. Elective share statutes in states are designed to give the surviving spouse a measure of protection.

Only nine states are community property states, and there are great variations between them. In a community property state, any marital property acquired by either spouse during the marriage becomes community property. Marital property is owned by both spouses equally. Community property states do not have elective share statutes because the 50/50 ownership of the community property gives the surviving spouse the needed protection. In divorce, all of the community property is divided evenly in terms of total economic value. The separate property of each spouse is distributed to the spouse who owns it. When community property crosses state lines, however, things can become complicated.

Most, but not all, states (both equitable distribution and community property states) look further to determine whether the property is marital or separate property. When you are divorcing, it is important to make sure you know how property is titled and when it was acquired and that you have identified all property before addressing how to divide it up.

Property in Divorce: What Is Marital and Nonmarital/Separate Property?

In divorce, a married couple's property is defined, under the laws of most states, as either marital or nonmarital:

- Marital: All property acquired during the marriage is presumed to be owned by both spouses. Each spouse is deemed to have an equal interest in marital assets or debts. This is true no matter how property is titled (legally owned) and no matter which spouse paid for the asset or which party incurred the debt.

⚠ **Caution:** There are some states that do not characterize property as either marital or separate, although in those states the source of the property can be important.

- Nonmarital or separate: Property acquired by either spouse before the marriage is considered to be owned individually, as is any property received through a gift, award, or inheritance as long as it remains separate and has not been commingled in any way.

⚠ **Caution:** Claiming property acquired *during the marriage* as separate can be complicated; state laws vary a lot in what is considered separate property. Certain circumstances may change the nature of property and how it is treated in divorce. For example, the co-mingling of assets over time makes it difficult to sustain as separate property.

NOTE: When a divorcing couple cannot agree on who gets what property, state law creates rules or guidelines for how the court will allocate it for them.

Dividing Marital Property in Divorce

As stated previously, all states distribute marital property using the equitable distribution or community property approach. It is important to understand that:

- State divorce laws differ in how they treat certain circumstances that may change the nature of the property and how it is treated in your divorce,
- Rules vary widely among the different states, and
- There are exceptions to the general rules that are unique to the events of your divorce.

Most states (41 states) follow the equitable distribution approach for distributing assets in a divorce. In equitable distribution, marital property is divided equitably (not necessarily equally) between you and your spouse.

In community property states (nine states), marital property is divided equally (50/50); you and your spouse will each end up with 50 percent of its total economic value.

NOTE: Different community property states have different laws.

In all states, there is a time frame with *two operative dates* used to determine what property is to be divided:

1. The first date is the date of the marriage, which is the point after which acquired property, unless excluded, will be considered marital.
2. The second date is the date after which acquired property will no longer be considered marital property. *The cutoff date is a date to be determined (see Chapter 2).*

Once the property is classified as marital or nonmarital, you and your spouse negotiate a percentage or dollar value of the marital property (assets and debts) and then divide it. The division of property could be 50/50, 60/40, 70/30, or even all for you and nothing for your spouse (although this would be very unusual).

If you cannot agree, the court can consider a variety of factors and need not weigh the factors equally, along with any other evidence in your case. The court has the flexibility to consider the financial situation of both you and your spouse after the divorce, which makes the resolution of property issues less predictable than if you and your spouse had jointly resolved them.

> ⓘ **Tip:** The court has the discretion to consider any factors related to your unique situation in both equitable distribution and community property states.

Changing Your Property Award

Most property decisions are a one-shot deal and can be nearly impossible to change through either modification or appeal. The legal hurdles are very high to revisit, undo, appeal, or modify property division after you divorce.

If you or your spouse disagrees with the final property division in your judgment, you can appeal the decision within the specific time frame established in your state. This time limit can be very limited and short, typically one month. You may appeal all or part of the judgment. The appeal is based only upon the trial court's existing record, which means you cannot bring up new evidence.

The appeals court in your state will have certain standards they will use when reviewing the trial court's decision, such as to determine if (1) the trial court abused its discretion in the division of property and if this (2) materially affected a just and right division of the marital estate.

An "unjust" judgment is very different than you simply not liking the outcome. It is unusual for an appeals court to overturn a judge's decision in a divorce case.

There are a couple of reasons why people may ask a divorce court to reconsider a debt and asset division decision. However, as with an appeal, dissatisfaction with the property division alone isn't enough. When seeking reconsideration, you have to prove fraud, duress or coercion, or a mutual mistake. Courts regularly deny post-divorce modification of property division orders in order to achieve an important goal—giving divorcing couples finality.

NOTE: You cannot appeal your judgment if it is based on a settlement that both you and your spouse have already agreed to.

If your divorce was decided in an arbitrator's award, you can usually appeal within 20 days. This appeal is *de novo*, meaning that all your divorce issues will be reconsidered from the very beginning.

Is There a Tax Impact on Dividing Marital Property?

While you are married, all property transfers between you and your spouse typically qualify for the unlimited marital deduction and will not have any negative tax impacts. In divorce, transfers between you and your spouse before or incident to your divorce will not have any unfavorable tax impact.

Under the general rule of Section 1041(a) of the Internal Revenue Code, a transfer of property to a former spouse incident to divorce will not cause the recognition of gain or loss. A transfer of property is incident to a divorce if the transfer occurs within one year after the date on which the marriage ceases or is "related to the cessation of the marriage," which requires that the transfer: (1) is pursuant to a divorce or separation instrument, and (2) occurs not more than six years after the date on which the marriage ceases.

NOTE: As the recipient spouse, you will assume the same cost basis and holding period for the asset as what your transferring spouse had before the transfer. Cost basis is usually the original purchase price that is adjusted for stock splits, reinvested dividends, capital improvements, etc.

ⓘ **Tip:** If you transfer your IRA directly to your spouse's new or existing IRA, you will not incur any taxes or penalties on the transfer; it will not be deemed a withdrawal.

What Is Equitable Distribution?

How does a court establish a fair and equitable division of marital property? The court may consider a set of statutory factors when naming a "just and right" division of marital property. A court will consider the amount of a spouse's separate property when determining how to divide the marital property. Fairness is the prevailing guideline. Equitable does not mean equal.

These factors vary from state to state and may address:

- The financial condition and earning power of you and your spouse
- The value of each spouse's separate property, including a spouse's business, business interests, retirement plans, 401K plans, stocks, bonds, etc.
- Size and liquidity of the marital estate
- The degree to which each spouse contributed to the acquisition of marital property
- The degree to which each spouse contributed to the education and earning power of the other spouse
- Probable future financial needs and liabilities of each spouse
- Anticipated inheritances
- Marital fault such as wrongful dissipation of assets, abuse, and adultery
- Duration of the marriage
- The ages and overall health of each spouse
- Premarital and postnuptial agreements
- Spousal maintenance or alimony obligations

What Is Community Property?

A community property approach divides all marital property equally between you and your spouse so each spouse ends up with 50 percent of total economic value. With a community property scheme, judges won't analyze which spouse deserves more property. They simply ensure that property division is equal. Spouses typically get to keep their separate property.

Community property is property that your spouse or you both acquire during your marriage while you and your spouse are domiciled in a community property state, including

- All earnings during the marriage
- All property bought with those earnings
- All debts accrued during marriage
- All assets transferred or gifted to the other spouse of the community property
- All commingled assets
- All property that cannot be identified as separate property

What Is Separate Property?

In states that recognize a distinction between separate and marital property, separate property is that which is deemed to be in the entire interest of one spouse. Categorizing it as such affects the property distribution in a divorce. There are some differences in how separate property is defined in different states, but the same general rules apply.

Separate property is defined as:

- Property that you or your spouse owned separately before your marriage
- Property that you or your spouse received separately as a gift or inheritance during your marriage (and kept separate)
- Money earned out of state in a noncommunity property state if you are a resident in a community property state
- Property that you or your spouse bought with separate funds, or acquired in exchange for separate property, during the marriage
- Property that you and your spouse converted from community property to separate property through an agreement valid under state law (e.g., a prenuptial or postnuptial agreement)
- The part of a property bought with separate funds if a part was bought with community funds and a part with separate funds.

Can Separate Property Become Marital Property?

Separate property can become marital property depending on how you hold its title, use the property during your marriage, or if it is mixed with marital property. Commingling or "transmutation" happens when separate and marital property becomes mixed to such a degree that each cannot be identified and separated for purposes of classification or distribution. When it becomes too difficult to unwind and you lack clear evidence, a judge will be inclined to call it all marital.

For example, if you used the money you had before the marriage to buy a house for both of you, that money, and thus the house, might become marital property. If you and your spouse regularly use property acquired by one party before the marriage for the joint benefit of your family, it is more likely to be available for consideration in dividing property.

If you inadvertently commingled funds but never intended to share them with your spouse, some courts may hold that only a portion, or none, of the commingled funds may remain separate property. The burden of proof is generally on the spouse seeking to undo the transmutation.

There is also a thing called reverse transmutation that occurs when you and your spouse both agree to transmute marital property into separate property. This change usually happens if there is a gift from you to your spouse and also when legal title of an asset has changed from joint to single ownership. In a dispute, there must be clear and convincing evidence that both you and your spouse intended for that marital property to become separate property because you both had an interest in it.

State laws determine how inheritance is treated once it is shared, and the rules vary tremendously among states. If you received an inheritance before the marriage and it was safeguarded with a prenuptial agreement that is found to be valid and enforceable, it remains separate.

Who Gets Appreciation and Interest on Separate Property?

Appreciation

Property appreciation is the growth in value over time. There are two kinds of appreciation in value: active and passive. A court will make the distinction between active and passive appreciation when dividing a significant increase in the value of an asset arising from one spouse's contributions.

Active appreciation, which results from ongoing efforts, is typically marital property. *Passive appreciation*, which results from inflation and regular market forces, is ordinarily separate.

In community property states, property is classified under the inception of title rule, which means it is identified by when the title was received. This initial classification is retained to include all subsequent appreciation, regardless of cause. If it is separate property, the appreciation of it during the marriage is deemed separate.

> ⓘ **Tip:** There are always exceptions. If you are seeking to call it community property, you must prove commingling of assets or establish a community property interest (your contribution to it).

In equitable distribution states, when separate property increases in value (appreciates), some or all of that appreciation can be classified as marital property. Not all appreciation of separate property, however, is marital. A nontitled spouse has an interest in the active appreciation of marital property. Passive appreciation occurs when neither the titled spouse nor the nontitled spouse has made any active contribution that caused the asset to appreciate.

Courts recognize that a variety of factors come together in a marriage, and judges vary in their rulings. A judge may determine that appreciation was active if:

- The separate property increased in monetary value over the course of the couple's marriage,
- Both parties either directly or indirectly contributed to the appreciation, and/or
- The appreciation was at least partially caused due to the spouse who does not own the asset (such as a stay-at-home parent).

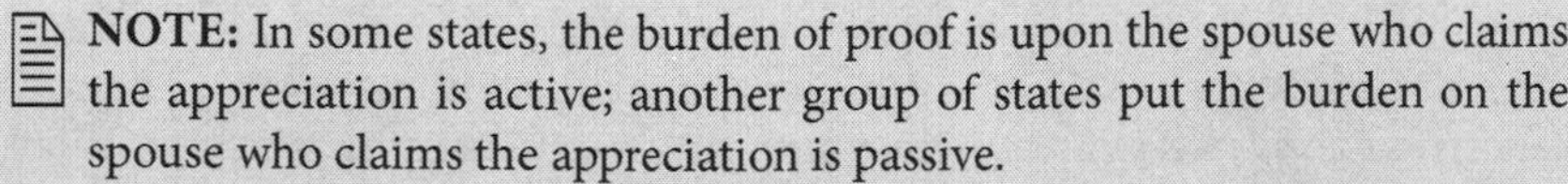
NOTE: In some states, the burden of proof is upon the spouse who claims the appreciation is active; another group of states put the burden on the spouse who claims the appreciation is passive.

Active and passive appreciation is a complex concept that is difficult to define and quantify. Courts take different views on appreciation, on how to classify interest from separate property, on how to determine the transmutation of property, and on how to demonstrate the contributions of a nonworking spouse or a stay-at-home parent. Discussing any form of appreciation with your divorce attorney is important.

What If You Used Marital Funds to Pay Down Your Spouse's Debt on Separate Property?

The doctrine of recoupment is related to separate property appreciation. Suppose you and your spouse used marital funds to pay down a separate debt; i.e., a debt that existed before the marriage. In some states, the nondebtor spouse may have a claim to "recoup" or get back an equitable portion of those funds usually expended from property division.

What Happens If You Use Nonmarital Funds to Pay Off Marital Debts?

If you use nonmarital funds to pay off a marital debt, your separate funds could lose their distinction.

ⓘ **Tip:** Use only your nonmarital property to purchase other property that you want to be considered nonmarital property.

 **NOTE:** Do not assume a property or business you owned prior to marriage remains a nonmarital asset entirely after marriage.

What Happens If You Move from a Community Property State to a Noncommunity Property State?

In general, property acquired as community property in a community property state is *not* automatically converted into noncommunity property when moving to a noncommunity property law state. Community property may retain its characterization when you and your spouse move from a community property state to a noncommunity property state.

What About Moving from a Noncommunity Property State to a Community Property State?

If you acquire separate property in a noncommunity property state, then that property is considered your separate property. If you then move with your spouse to a community property state, the property remains characterized as separate. It is not necessarily automatically converted to community property because you move to a community property state.

NOTE: Basically, separate and community property retain their characterization when you move to a state with different marital property laws. However, you should check with your divorce attorney to ask about "quasi-community property" rules (property acquired by a couple living in a common law state that would have been shared property if they were living in a community property state).

Commonly Asked Questions

Is it considered abandoned property if your spouse walked out on you?

No, your spouse remains an owner of marital assets.

Can we still own the house jointly after divorce?

Yes, many couples divorce and retain joint ownership of property. Some do it indefinitely (by changing the legal title after divorce). Others do it until the house can be refinanced or sold (see Chapter 10).

Who gets the car?

People argue over vehicles in too many divorces: whose is oldest, whose is driven by whom, whose needs major repairs, etc. Contrary to common belief, vehicles and other property are not necessarily granted to the spouse who holds an individual title. Vehicles, just like other assets, will be allocated according to divorce laws for community or marital property. Your first efforts should be to know the value of the car. You can find car values in automotive industry Blue Books or by visiting several reputable used car dealers. Leased vehicles may have little value.

How do you split up personal household items?

Household items, as well as valuable collectibles, should be divided in agreement between the spouses. It is not unusual that spouses may find the exercise of splitting up personal and household effects to be emotionally volatile. Various strategies can be employed to help resolve what's best for the interests of both spouses to determine division without outside intervention.

5 The Financial Phases of Divorce

In divorce, your financial life will be carefully scrutinized, debated, dissected, and questioned by your spouse, legal professionals, and potentially a judge. Your divorce will be nearly impossible to obtain without complete financial disclosure and skilled negotiations. You will set the best foundation for the legal settlement if you take the time to prepare and present your financial information accurately.

You will be required to provide a formal personal Net Worth Statement (called a Financial Affidavit or Case Information Statement) of your income, expenses, assets, and debts that you will submit to the court under oath. You must attest to its truthfulness. This document, along with your divorce agreement, is not only an *essential planning tool*—it is the single most important piece of financial disclosure you can provide to the court.

A Financial Affidavit forms the foundation of the court, making its requisite finding that the divorce agreement is fair and reasonable. When considering your divorce, your statement shows how much you stand to keep, gain, or lose. It is *the controlling* document in divorce and for post-judgment orders.

You want to do your very best at the outset to make certain that the information contained in the Financial Affidavit is accurate, because any misrepresentation has the potential to cast you in an unfavorable light and, in some instances, can form a basis for the court to reopen a judgment. Opening up your divorce agreement at a later date to renegotiate financial issues is tough, expensive, and exhausting.

What can you expect? When do you gather and organize your financial information?

What if you don't have access to financial records? When do you analyze your information produced by your spouse? When do you start to negotiate? How do you reach an agreement?

Here is an overview of the multistep process of the financial phases of divorce.

What Are the Financial Phases in Divorce?

There are six financial phases of divorce, usually consistent with any legal process you are in, be it mediation, collaborative, or litigation. Each financial stage has its own set of tasks and a timeline that are assigned by the court, your divorce attorney, mediator, or by "necessity."

Each phase sets forth specific tasks to be performed.

DIVORCE FINANCIAL PLANNING FLOW CHART FOR THE CLIENT

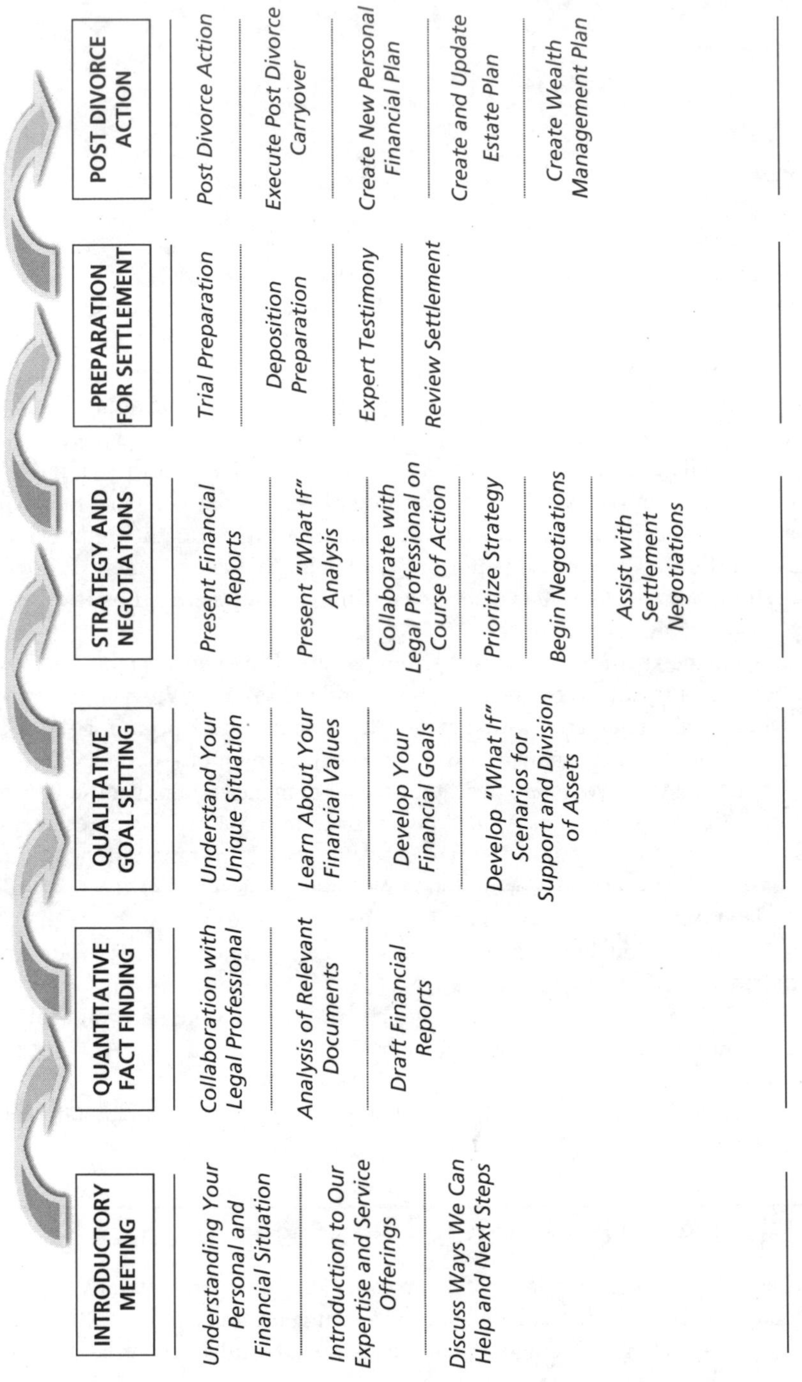

INTRODUCTORY MEETING	QUANTITATIVE FACT FINDING	QUALITATIVE GOAL SETTING	STRATEGY AND NEGOTIATIONS	PREPARATION FOR SETTLEMENT	POST DIVORCE ACTION
Understanding Your Personal and Financial Situation	*Collaboration with Legal Professional*	*Understand Your Unique Situation*	*Present Financial Reports*	*Trial Preparation*	*Post Divorce Action*
Introduction to Our Expertise and Service Offerings	*Analysis of Relevant Documents*	*Learn About Your Financial Values*	*Present "What If" Analysis*	*Deposition Preparation*	*Execute Post Divorce Carryover*
Discuss Ways We Can Help and Next Steps	*Draft Financial Reports*	*Develop Your Financial Goals*	*Collaborate with Legal Professional on Course of Action*	*Expert Testimony*	*Create New Personal Financial Plan*
		Develop "What If" Scenarios for Support and Division of Assets	*Prioritize Strategy*	*Review Settlement*	*Create and Update Estate Plan*
			Begin Negotiations		*Create Wealth Management Plan*
			Assist with Settlement Negotiations		

Phase 1: Fact Finding and Financial Gathering

- ❑ Compile, organize, and make an inventory (list) of all your financial information
- ❑ Identify what is missing or gaps in information
- ❑ Make a list of your financial questions for further investigation

Phase 2: Pre-Divorce Financial Review

- ❑ List and value your assets and debts
- ❑ Estimate your immediate needs
- ❑ Prepare your Net Worth Statement (Case Information Statement, Financial Affidavit, etc.)
- ❑ Develop a realistic budget
- ❑ Discuss your financial priorities and concerns

Phase 3: Personal Long-Term Financial Planning

- ❑ Determine your credit rating and correct any credit mistakes in your history
- ❑ Establish credit in your name
- ❑ Estimate your earnings potential
- ❑ Estimate career training costs and timeline for getting a job
- ❑ Estimate college and educational costs
- ❑ Estimate work-related childcare costs
- ❑ Estimate your ability to set aside savings and build retirement savings
- ❑ Analyze your insurance needs and costs
- ❑ Identify short- and long-term major expenditures
- ❑ Analyze buy-versus-rent decisions for post-divorce and financing options

Phase 4: Divorce Settlement Analysis

- ❑ Compare after-tax cost of assets
- ❑ Evaluate character and risk of assets and debts
- ❑ Prioritize how debts will be paid off
- ❑ Quantify any damages or dissipation of assets
- ❑ Estimate support needs
- ❑ Estimate capacity to pay support
- ❑ Analyze annual income versus weekly/monthly cash flow for both parties
- ❑ Analyze long-term cash flow and net worth for both parties
- ❑ Evaluate inheritances or gifts

Phase 5: Negotiations and Settlement

- ❑ Review after-tax proposed settlement proposal
- ❑ Compare and contrast settlement proposals
- ❑ Negotiate alternative settlement proposals
- ❑ Reach a settlement or prepare for trial

Phase 6: Post-Divorce Financial Management and Carryover

- ❑ Oversee asset transfers
- ❑ Set up budgeting and money management systems
- ❑ Manage investments
- ❑ Update estate plans
- ❑ Monitor results

> ⓘ **Tip:** Stay financially focused. Fundamentally, you have to learn how to deal with money and separate yourself emotionally and financially from your spouse.

What Should You Do First?

Gathering Your Financial Information: The Discovery Process

The first step is to collect and organize as much financial data as possible. At the outset of every divorce, your divorce attorney will give you a checklist of financial information and documents to gather, organize, and compile; your spouse will have to do the same.

This step is the discovery phase of divorce that is started at the beginning of the divorce process. Both you and your spouse will be exchanging, through your respective counsel, detailed information related to your own financial and personal situations, including the extent of your property ownership, debt, and income. A married couple's assets and property are generally divided into two categories: marital (also referred to as joint or community depending on where you live) or separate property (see Chapter 3).

> ⓘ **Tip:** Both you and your spouse are entitled to full disclosure.

By examining this information, you, in consultation with your divorce attorney (or in consultation with your mediator if you and your spouse are in mediation), can begin to understand and then negotiate how to divide up property fairly and how to deal with divorce-related issues such as child support and spousal support.

You will be required to provide copies of financial documents to back up and confirm the accuracy of the information contained in your Financial Affidavit. It will save you time and money by doing as much as you can do by yourself as early as possible: list sources of income, from which accounts you spend money, your assets, and your debts. This is true no matter which legal process you pursue.

Make a list of all the documents you can find, record their date, and enter a zero for whatever is missing. For any financial information you do not have, make a note as to who may have it or how you can get it. This list is called a working inventory. You can find a lot by searching around your home and/or contacting your CPA, banks, credit card companies, utilities, insurance providers, pharmacy, lenders, etc., to request past statements.

⚠ **Caution:** It is critical that you do not place yourself at any risk to obtain this information or that you hide or destroy documents or are dishonest in this effort.

Discovery Can Be Formal or Informal

The discovery phase can be informal or formal depending on the legal process. In mediation and collaborative law, discovery is not compelled and rests on the premise of honest and transparent voluntary disclosure. However, discovery is still consistently expected by most professionals.

In litigation, the discovery process is compulsory disclosure and may include the following:

- Disclosure—Both parties request certain items from each other and set a deadline (i.e., 30 days) for a response.
- Interrogatories—This is a list of questions prepared by your divorce attorney that is sent to your spouse and their divorce attorney. Your attorney is limited in how many questions can be asked, and the response time is a specific number of days.
- Request for Admissions of Fact—This written list of facts is directed at the other party. The other party must admit, deny, or object to the substance of each fact. Statements that are admitted do not have to be proven at trial.
- Request for Production—This is a written request to the other party used to obtain financial documents, such as bank statements, credit card statements, statements of income, receipts, or any documents that are required in your case.
- Depositions—This is a sworn testimony in writing, usually transcribed by a court reporter, that you or your spouse may be involved in if there are conflict or discovery issues. Anything said during a deposition can be used in court should an agreement not be reached.
- Subpoena—This is a document that requires its recipient to appear in court as a witness or requires the submission of evidence, as records or documents, before a court or other deliberative body.

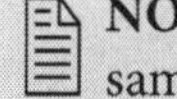

NOTE: In this section, I have included worksheets to help you. Below is a sample financial checklist of documents exchanged between attorneys in the discovery phase.

Sample Financial Checklist of Documents

- Tax returns
  - At least three years of prior federal and state personal income tax returns
  - At least three years of prior federal and state business income tax returns
  - Copies of any gift tax returns
- Proof of income
  - Year-end pay stubs, current pay stubs, and W-2 forms

- Business financial statements
    - Balance sheet or list of assets and liabilities—for year-end and current month
    - Profit-and-loss statement (income and expenses) or cash flow statement—for year-end and current month
    - List of business accounts (if the owner of the business) and business financial records, credit cards, check registers, etc.
    - Chart of interrelated business interests by ownership or other
- Records of any other income received
    - Dividends, interest, K-1 income, rental/lease arrangements, investment property, pension income, Social Security, annuities, profit-sharing plans, etc.
- Records regarding monthly expenses
    - Copies of receipts, billing statements, cash withdrawals, etc.
- Employee benefits
    - Statement of employee benefits and perquisites
    - Deferred compensation benefits as of year-end and all vesting schedules
- Prenuptial and postnuptial agreements
- All documents relating to any prior divorce settlement(s)
- Wills and trust documents (for beneficiary interest)
- Statements and documents of:
    - At least past 12 months for all bank, credit union, brokerage, mutual fund company, savings, and money market accounts, with copies of scanned checks and check registries
    - At least past 12 months for all investments (public and private, real or financial) or a list of individually held investments/securities (stocks, bonds, CDs, etc.)
    - Business accounts (if the owner of the business) and business financial records, credit cards, check registers, etc.
    - At least past 12 months for all credit cards
    - At least past 12 months for all retirement, profit sharing, and IRA accounts
    - Current pension statements and pension plan policy books (defined benefit plans)
    - Recent valuations or appraisals of your financial assets: house, real estate, collectibles, vehicles, furniture, antiques, etc.
    - Current cash value and surrender value of any life insurance
    - Current annuity statement
    - A list of children's accounts, trusts, etc.
- Insurances
    - Current insurances, policy statements and explanation of benefits:
        - Medical
        - Dental
        - Optical
        - Life

        - Disability
        - Auto
        - Homeowners
        - Renters
        - Long-term care
        - Liability, umbrella, and valuables policies
- Real estate records for all properties owned (whole or partial), including principal residence, second home, and investment properties
    - Original mortgage/deed of trust
    - Copy of note
    - Purchase agreement
    - Uniform residential/commercial appraisal reports
    - Rental/lease agreements
    - Refinance agreements
    - Home equity line of credit (HELOC)
    - Any secured liens
- Information on debts and liabilities
    - List of outstanding debts:
        - Credit cards, bank loans, student loans, loans against retirement plans, personal loans to business (if owned), personal loans, unpaid bills, etc.
        - Copies of loan applications, promissory notes, guarantees, collateral pledged, etc.
- Other documents
    - Credit reports on both spouses
    - Frequent flier miles, reward points, timeshare allowances, etc.
    - Safety deposit box contents
    - Titles to vehicles
    - Any other information you think is relevant

What Do You Do with All Your Financial Stuff?

How to Prepare a Net Worth Statement

In divorce, custody, and legal separation cases, spouses must provide accurate financial information to the court. The court requires your financial information to make orders about child support, spousal support (alimony), and property division. The forms vary from state to state.

Depending on its name in your state, this form is called a Personal Net Worth Statement, a Financial Affidavit, a Case Information Statement, a Domestic Financial Affidavit, or a Financial Declaration. It is a *comprehensive financial snapshot* of an individual's financial health at one particular point in time. It is a summary of what is owned (assets) less what is owed to others (debt), and it also sets forth all your sources of income minus all your spending.

A personal Net Worth Statement has two parts:

1. Total assets minus total liabilities
2. Total income minus total expenses

Properly preparing a Net Worth Statement can be anything but simple. For many, knowing how important it is for temporary spousal support, temporary child support, and the final divorce agreement, as well as for post-judgment appeals, makes the task all the more intimidating. Seek professional help to get it done correctly and expediently.

Completing the Different Sections of Your Net Worth Statement

The Personal Background Section

Most Net Worth Statements have a personal information or background section. This section will require the names and ages of you, your spouse, and your children, as well as any other relationships. You also include information about your current employer, job address, and title. Some states may require you also to disclose your educational background, professional licenses, health status, and the date and place of your marriage.

The Income Section

When filling out your Net Worth Statement, you will need to state your income from all sources, including your primary job as well as part-time or side jobs. You will also need to report any income you receive from unemployment; Social Security; disability; rental income; consistent gifting from others (i.e., relatives and friends); distributions from trusts/accounts; or funds from retirement accounts, annuities, and pensions.

You will also include all taxes and deductions (both mandatory and discretionary) taken from your paycheck or compensation. If you are self-employed, you will be required to provide business tax returns and any other proof of income. If you are unemployed or disabled, you will need to provide copies of your state unemployment or disability checks.

The Expense Section

In the next part of the form, you will list all your monthly or weekly expenses. Your Net Worth Statement discloses everything about your family's finances and represents what it costs you to live. It is a complete list of your expenses, including those you pay in full and those you share or pay partially.

⚠ **Caution:** Tracking and calculating expenses are the most tedious and challenging tasks required for completing the form.

You will need to provide a detailed accounting of your spending by category and dollar amount on such things as mortgage or rent, utilities, food, clothing, travel, and entertainment. Itemize all bills; for expenses that are not the same every month, find the average by adding together a year's worth of bills and dividing the total by 12. Be sure to count and allocate how you spend cash. Remember, you are helping the court to better understand not only the ordinary and necessary living expenses of you and your children, but also your unexpected, occasional, seasonal, and nonrecurring expenses.

If you are a parent requesting child support, you will need to provide a lot of information regarding your children. You will need to explain where they live, if they work, whether they attend college, and whether they have special needs. You should include any child-related expenses that you incur so you can go to work, such as before- and after-school programs, childcare, and babysitters.

Some forms allow for footnotes or comments. Adding comments can be helpful if you expect your income or expenses to change soon. Resist the urge to guesstimate a response because most people *vastly underestimate their spending* and end up way off the mark, which ultimately can do more harm than good. Do not try to artificially balance your financial form with income equals expenses. Most people have expenses that usually outpace their earnings.

> ⓘ **Tip:** You must pay attention to detail. Remember the "little" expenses can add up significantly, and errors and omissions could affect the financial outcome of your divorce agreement.

Assets and Liabilities Section

This section of the form is where you list all of your assets and debts. Assets are what you own, and liabilities are what you owe to others. Assets minus liabilities equal your net worth. If you have a negative net worth (debts greater than assets), it is time to take dramatic action to get out of debt.

Assets include checking and savings accounts, brokerage accounts, retirement accounts, pensions, stocks, bonds, private equity investments, and tax refunds. Assets also include businesses, real property, vehicles, boats, art, and jewelry. Debts include credit card debts, car loans, personal loans, student loans, tax liabilities, and unpaid bills. If you have any insurances, you will need to provide policy information for health, life, and automobiles. Details of assets and liabilities are further described in Chapters 6 to 10 and Chapter 13.

Attestation to Accuracy

Both you and your spouse are required to swear, under penalty of perjury, that the information you provide is true and accurate to the best of your knowledge. An affidavit is notarized to prove its authenticity. If your financial circumstances change or if your case lasts at least several months and data become stale, it is possible you will need to update your Net Worth Statement even after it is filed with the court.

> ⓘ **Tip:** If you are uncertain about what to include or how to value something, ask your divorce attorney.

It should not be surprising that Net Worth Statements are frequently inaccurate, inflated, and not verified. A forensic accountant may be helpful to get the correct numbers and ensure discovery is complete.

What Is a Lifestyle Analysis?

The Net Worth Statement is also a tool used for lifestyle analysis, which is a process of tabulating and analyzing the income and expenses of both parties over a certain period to determine the standard of living of the parties.

The marital standard of living is *the benchmark* used by the court for determining spousal support. It is increasingly becoming *an essential component in the changed circumstances analysis,* which is when the court reviews an application for modifications to spousal support (alimony).

Consequently, methods to present your marital lifestyle should be clear and unambiguous and should provide an analysis of a "baseline," such that the family expenditures of everyday life are enumerated and described. The concept is simple, but the execution is not.

The analysis attempts to quantify a spouse's living expenses and compare them to known sources of income. If there are differences between known sources of income and spending, there may be concealed income or debts.

The goal is to compute the cost of your lifestyle before separation and determine if reported income sufficiently supported your lifestyle during marriage. It will either confirm or refute claims made by you for support purposes and may have a substantial impact on the property division. If controversial, a forensic accountant may be needed to review, audit, and compile an analysis of all spending records of the parties.

NOTE: A lifestyle analysis influences support calculations and possibly property division.

ⓘ **Tip:** The purpose of a lifestyle analysis is to evaluate the finances of each party post-separation to prove a spouse's financial needs following divorce.

Even after you have compiled all this information, there may still be some unknowns at the end of the day where common-sense assumptions using estimates can be made. Considering historical patterns and significant changes in spending is important.

Common problems arise when one party, in contemplation of divorce, unilaterally alters the status quo spending practices of the family. In these situations, it is advisable that you exclude time periods from the analysis if the spending is wholly inconsistent with the historical marital standards. Alternatively, you could just extend the period of analysis and document all deviations in spending.

> ⓘ **Tip:** An important consideration is whether family expenses are paid by another entity, such as by a relative, a family business, or trust. These payments need to be captured, calculated, and added to the family's spending and disclosed as such.

Courts in various states attempt to establish the lifestyle enjoyed during the marriage *as a reference point* to determine whether the parties *will be able to live the same or a reasonably similar lifestyle after divorce*. There is no guarantee that both spouses will have sufficient means or capacity to support the same lifestyle following divorce as the one they enjoyed as a married couple.

Even in uncontested divorces, courts may ask the question as to whether the parties believe they will continue to enjoy the same or comparable lifestyle they enjoyed during the marriage. In essence, the court seeks your acknowledgment of all of the facts and circumstances surrounding your settlement agreement. In the event you do not believe that you can continue to live the same or similar lifestyle enjoyed during the marriage, the court will need to explore why you feel this way and may refuse to proceed with the divorce.

> ⓘ **Tip:** A lifestyle analysis often helps you get a better grasp of the truth about your prior, present, and future lifestyle. It helps you to be realistic and to manage your expectations in divorce.

> **NOTE:** Below are some pointers for how to complete the Net Worth Statement sections for assets and liabilities, followed by a sample of a basic Net Worth Statement. Pointers for how to prepare a lifestyle analysis are included after the sample Net Worth Statement.

The following chart is a sample of a basic Net Worth Statement, followed by pointers for how to complete the sections for assets and liabilities on the Net Worth Statement and how to prepare a lifestyle analysis.

COURT DOCKET NUMBER		**COURT OF YOUR STATE**
NAME	PLAINTIFF'S NAME	: J.D. OF JURISDICTION
V.		: AT
NAME	DEFENDANT'S NAME	:

DEFENDANT OR PLAINTIFF'S FINANCIAL AFFIDAVIT

I, ____________________, being duly sworn, do hereby depose and say that the following is a statement of my monthly income, monthly expenses, assets and liabilities:

I. INCOME

A. <u>From Employment</u>

The Defendant or Plaintiff is employed as

Gross Monthly Income (Wages)

Less:		
Federal Withholding		
FICA		
Medicare		
State Tax		
Other Mandatory Deductions	______	$0.00
Self-Employment Income		
Bonus		
Commisssions		
Overtime		
Less Estimated Taxes	______	$0.00

B. Other Income

Contribution from Spouse		
Interest/Dividends		
Rental Income		
Pensions and Annuities		
Royalties		
Fringe Benefits		
Trust Distributions		
Veterans Benefits		
Social Security		
Disability or Workmans Compensation		
Unemployment Benefits		
Public Assistance		
Other Income		
Less Estimated Taxes	______	$0.00

TOTAL NET MONTHLY INCOME $0.00

II. EXPENSES

A. Shelter

Mortgage or Rent

Real Estate Taxes

Homeowner's Assessments or Fees

Homeowners Insurance

Water

Electricity

Telephone

Heating Oil Fuel

Gas / Propane

Furnace (repair and cleaning)

Garbage Collection

Household Maintenance

Yard Maintenance & Garden

Snow Plowing

Furniture, Appliances, Warranties

Alarm System

Cable TV, Internet

Water and Sewer

Pool Maintenance & Supplies

Household Supplies

Housecleaning

Other Utilities

Other ________ $0.00

B. Food

Groceries

Work Lunches & Fast Food Take Out

Restaurant ________ $0.00

C. Medical/Dental

Medical Insurance Premium

Dental Insurance Premium

Optical Insurance Premium

Unreimbursed Medical

Unreimbursed Dental

Unreimbursed Optical

Drugs/Medication
Therapy
Nutritional Supplements & Vitamins
Health Related Other ________ $0.00

D. Transportation

Car Loan/Lease
Personal Property Tax
Auto Insurance
DMV Fees (License & Registration)
Tolls/Parking
Maintenance/Repairs
Gas/Oil
Car Washes
Public Transportation
Other ________ $0.00

E. Clothing

For Self
Shoe Repair/Tailor
Accessories
Laundry
Dry Cleaning/Storage ________ $0.00

F. Children's Expenses

Child Care
Baby Sitters
Tuition (preschool, private, college)
School Room and Board
Camp & Clubs
School Books, Supplies, Computers
School Sponsored Activities
School Transportation

School Lunches
Tutors
Clothing
Personal grooming
Cell Phone
Allowance
Sports Activities, Equipment and Fees
Lessons & Extracurricular Activities
Entertainment
Gifts
Toys/Books/Videos
Travel
Unreimbursed Medical
Unreimbursed Dental
Unreimbursed Optical
Orthodontics
Medication
Therapy
Other ________ $0.00

G. Miscellaneous (Personal)

Bank & Credit Card Fees, Charges
Cell Phone
Cigarettes, Alcohol
Club Dues & Membership
Computer, Supplies, Software
Charity
Religious Organizations
Education Classes
Employment Uniforms
Employment Unreimbursed Travel
Employment Unreimbursed Education
Professional Licenses

Entertainment
Gifts
Hobbies
Life Insurance Premiums
Liability Insurance, Umbrella Insurance
Lottery
Office Supplies, Books, etc.
Payment on Recurrent Debt
Personal Grooming
Personal Property Insurance (valuables)
Pet Care
Professional Fees (legal, advisor, tax)
Subscriptions
Sports and Fitness
Travel
Vacations
Other: Visitation Travel Expenses
Other: Alimony
Other: Child Support
Other ________ $0.00

TOTAL MONTHLY EXPENSES **$0.00**

III. ASSETS

A. <u>Real Estate</u>	VALUE	TITLE	YOUR EQUITY
Marital home Property Address			
Fair Market Value			
Less Mortgage			
Less Second Mortgage			
Less Home Equity Line of Credit			
Equity	0.00		$0.00
DATE OF ACQUISITION			
SOURCE OF FUNDS			

<u>Other Real Property</u>		
Vacation Home		
Undeveloped Real Estate		
Timeshare		
Rental Property		
Less Debt	0.00	$0.00
DATE OF ACQUISITION (FOR EACH)		
SOURCE OF FUNDS (FOR EACH)		
B. <u>Bank Accounts</u>		
Checking		
Money Market		
Savings		
DATE OF ACQUISITION (FOR EACH)		$0.00
SOURCE OF FUNDS (FOR EACH)		
C. <u>Motor Vehicles</u>		
Year and Model		
Value		
Less Loan		
Equity		$0.00
DATE OF ACQUISITION (FOR EACH)		
SOURCE OF FUNDS (FOR EACH)		
D. <u>Brokerage Accounts</u>		
Cash		
Portfolio Value Held In Brokerage A/C		
(includes stocks, bonds, ETFs, mutual funds, alternatives, etc.)		
Less: Margin Loan		
		$0.00

DATE OF ACQUISITION (FOR EACH)
SOURCE OF FUNDS (FOR EACH)

E. Stocks, Bonds and Other Securities
(Individually Owned Securities) ________ ________
$0.00

DATE OF ACQUISITION (FOR EACH)
SOURCE OF FUNDS (FOR EACH)

F.	Life Insurance	Face Value	Surrender	Equity
	Company Name & Policy No.			
		________		________
				$0.00
	Annuities	________		________
				$0.00

DATE OF ACQUISITION (FOR EACH)
SOURCE OF FUNDS (FOR EACH)

G. Business Interest
Appraised Value Less Debt ________ ________
DATE OF ACQUISITION (FOR EACH) $0.00
SOURCE OF FUNDS (FOR EACH)

H. Trademarks, Patents, Goodwill ________ ________
DATE OF ACQUISITION (FOR EACH) $0.00
SOURCE OF FUNDS (FOR EACH)

I. Miscellaneous

Antiques
Artwork
Collectibles
Jewelry
Boat, Plane, Trailer, etc.
Furniture/Furnishings

Tax Refund
Tax Loss Carryforwards
Frequent Flier Points, Rewards, Miles
Personal Loan (you as lender)
Prepaid Debts or Commitments
Lawsuits
Other

________ ________
$0.00

DATE OF ACQUISITION (FOR EACH)
SOURCE OF FUNDS (FOR EACH)

TOTAL CASH VALUE OF ALL ASSETS **$0.00**

IV. MEDICAL INSURANCE

Insurance Company:
Group Number:
Names of Insured:

V. DEFERRED ASSETS

A. Retirement Plans
401(k), 403(b), 457, profit sharing plans
SEP, SARSEP plans

________ ________
$0.00

DATE OF ACQUISITION (FOR EACH)
SOURCE OF FUNDS (FOR EACH)

B. Defined Benefit Plans
Qualified Pension

________ ________
$0.00

DATE OF ACQUISITION (FOR EACH)
SOURCE OF FUNDS (FOR EACH)

C. Individual Retirement
Traditional IRA

ROTH IRA

SEP IRA

Simple IRA

$0.00

DATE OF ACQUISITION (FOR EACH)

SOURCE OF FUNDS (FOR EACH)

D. <u>Nonqualified Plans</u>

<u>TYPES:</u>

Deferred compensation plans (stock options, restricted stock, performance units, restricted stock units)

Executive bonus plans & supplemental plans

Group carve out plans

Split dollar life insurance plans

$0.00

DATE OF ACQUISITION (FOR EACH)

SOURCE OF FUNDS (FOR EACH)

TOTAL DEFERRED ASSETS **$0.00**

VI. LIABILITIES

Credit Card Balances

Unpaid Bills

Installment Loans, Promissory Notes

Taxes Owed, Liens, Penalties

Pledges or Commitments

Student Loan

Other

$0.00

TOTAL LIABILITIES **$0.00**

VII. SUMMARY

TOTAL MONTHLY INCOME **$0.00**

TOTAL MONTHLY EXPENSES **$0.00**

TOTAL ASSETS	**$0.00**
TOTAL DEFERRED ASSETS	**$0.00**
TOTAL LIABILITIES	**$0.00**

VIII. Certification

The foregoing is a true and complete statement of my current financial status and condition as nearly as I am able to estimate same with the information available to me.

____

Subscribed and sworn to before me this _____ day _____ year

____

Commissioner of the Superior Court

THIS IS TO CERTIFY THAT A TRUE COPY
OF THE FOREGOING WAS MAILED, POSTAGE
PREPAID OR HAND DELIVERED, TO THE
FOLLOWING COUNSEL AND PARTIES
OF RECORD ON THE ABOVE DATE.

Notes about How to Prepare a Net Worth Statement

1. **Property:** You will need to document your assets and liabilities. You will have to identify whether you acquired property and debts before or during the marriage and which are marital or separate.
2. **Assets:** Remember paper value is not the same as real value. Different assets are taxed differently depending on their nature and how long you have owned them. Some assets will have to be appraised, such as real property, collectibles, or your own business. In Chapter 6, I discuss the distinctions of various assets and debts and the decisions you face when dividing marital property. For each asset, you will
   - Estimate the value of each asset you own jointly and separately, using any of the appropriate methodologies below:
     1. Current value (current balance in bank account),
     2. Market value (what could you sell it for),
     3. Appraised value (objective third-party assessment of market value),
     4. Replacement value (insured value), and
     5. Purchase value (if quite new or unknown how to value).
   - List the source of each asset (i.e., where the money came from to purchase it)
   - List the date of acquisition or purchase
   - List the value of equity (asset minus debt equals equity)
   - List the legal title to each asset (you or your spouse may have ownership interest in it)

1. Joint tenancy: Co-owners of a property who own equal shares, with the share of each passing to the other or others in death, which is called the "right of survivorship."
2. Tenancy by entirety: An interest in property that can be held only by a husband and wife in which each party has a right of survivorship over the property and which neither party can terminate without the consent of the other; this is a form of concurrent ownership that can only exist between a husband and wife.
3. Tenancy in common: Each owner of an estate or property is regarded by law as owning a distinct, separately transferable interest.

- Community property: Property owned jointly by a married couple that is divided equally; after divorce, it cannot be held as community property.
- Separate title: The property held in only one name—yours or your spouse's, but you can prove ownership based on financial contributions.

3. **Liabilities:** This includes all debts.
   - For each liability, you will list
     1. All debt (other than those attached to assets),
     2. Current balances owed,
     3. Original loan amounts,
     4. Dates made,
     5. Interest rates,
     6. Terms of loans,
     7. Monthly payments due, and
     8. Sources of debt payments (from which accounts payments are made).
   - Sometimes you may wish to describe the purpose of debt, why it was incurred, and how it supported your lifestyle, family expenses, etc.

Notes about How to Prepare a Lifestyle Analysis

1. **Income**
   a. Determine what period of 12 months best reflects your "normal" lifestyle standard; it should be within six months of your filing or separation date.
   b. Total all income and expenses for this 12-month period and average the total over 12 months to enter a monthly figure.
   c. Determine where all the money came from. Sift through records and document your findings thoroughly to make it credible. For defining income, a court has the discretion to consider all sources for purposes of child support and alimony.
   d. Determine which accounts you use when you spend money. Do you just spend your income? Do you borrow or use credit cards? Do you sell assets or property? Do you draw more from a business when needed? Your cash flow may not be the same as your income. Cash flow is how money comes in and out. Identify all sources of spending:
      - Earned income
      - Credit cards
      - Bank accounts (checks and ATM withdrawals)

- Savings accounts
- Investments (dividends, interest, and liquidations)
- Retirement accounts
- Loans (HELOC, personal, college, etc.)
- Gifts and inheritances
- Trusts
- Business (paid for by business)
- Third-party payors (parents, friends, siblings, etc.)

2. **Expenses**
   a. What are all the things you spend money for? You should include all expenses *except* any relating uniquely to your spouse. If you are unsure as to what spending includes her or him, list the items on a separate paper and ask your divorce attorney. Segregate spending by type of expense in different categories. Feel free to edit and revise categories.
   b. If expenses are different substantially than in prior years, make an attachment for footnotes. You can use footnotes to provide details about how you calculated monthly numbers and which expenses you lumped together. For example, if you include divorce therapy for the children (a new expense), you can explain with a footnote how often, at what cost, for how long, and for how many children.

ⓘ **Tip:** The nature (ordinary, nonrecurring, seasonal, or major), frequency (annual, biannual, etc.), and amount of expenses will help you to detect patterns of spending. These patterns may be previously unknown to you, and this exercise allows you to grasp improved control over it.

   c. To allocate cash withdrawals from ATM or checks written to cash, keep a cash diary for three weeks (at least) to track all spending. Write it down, and if this is representative of your daily spending, extrapolate it to 12 months for total cash withdrawals over the 12 months.
   d. You will need to break out in detail all credit card spending and categorize expenses. Include the minimum or actual monthly payment you make in the liability section of your Net Worth Statement along with the balance of any debt outstanding on the credit card.
   e. Be sure you identify any unusual or atypical expenses relating to only your current situation while going through a divorce, such as your rent, new furniture purchases, etc.
3. **The MOST important part is to be accurate** and to portray your financial profile in a way that is most telling of your needs. It also is a somewhat subjective exercise as to how to allocate some expenses relating to family, children, or the house. A little finesse is required to recognize which expense you should prioritize and what is the "most acceptable" kind of expense your spouse would pay for.
4. After you make a draft, go over it with your divorce attorney and a divorce financial planner to address any questions you may have had in preparing it.

Why You Must Have a Divorce Financial Planner: The Only Expert Who Can Help You Pull Together All the Pieces of the Financial Puzzle

How do you know how much you will need? How do you know how much you want? How can you get what you need and want? A genuine and accurate lifestyle analysis is a vital and valuable tool that gives you a strategic advantage when you know your financial situation. Using your information in combination with your spouse's financial data lays the groundwork for consideration of various scenarios for support and property division as well as lifestyle changes necessitated by the transition.

It is probable you can benefit from focused financial expertise and guidance to help you raise the appropriate questions and find practical solutions. One of the key resources available to you and your attorney is a divorce financial planner.

A divorce financial planner is a fee-only financial expert who has received specialized training and has interdisciplinary knowledge of the divorce legal landscape and comprehensive personal finance. **A divorce financial planner cannot provide any legal advice but adds essential value for you and your attorney concerning financial analysis, strategy, projections, and opinions.**

How Will a Divorce Financial Planner Benefit You in Divorce?

A divorce financial planner adds value by helping to calculate and resolve critical decisions such as

- How to set new financial goals and prioritize them
- Analyzing if you should you buy or lease a new car
- Analyzing how much house can you afford
- Figuring out how you can refinance your mortgage
- Figuring out how to pay off your debts
- Figuring out how you can get off of joint debts
- Figuring out how to improve your credit rating
- Determining the best way to establish credit in your name
- Determining which assets you should ask for in your divorce
- Figuring out how to get cash from retirement accounts without penalty
- Determining what kinds of investments you are receiving and whether you should make any changes
- Determining the tax implications for selling the assets you receive in your divorce settlement
- Determining who will help transfer and track assets
- Figuring out how to open new investment accounts
- Determining how to project your future costs of living and what happens if your income falls short of expenses

- Analyzing if you need to buy or change insurances (home, auto, umbrella, etc.)
- Figuring out what you should do for new health insurance (private or COBRA)
- Determining how you will pay for college
- Analyzing whether it is too late to catch up in savings for retirement
- Figuring out how to estimate taxes post-divorce
- Determining whether you should buy long-term care insurance
- Analyzing who claims the children on their taxes
- Figuring out what to do if you find out post-divorce that your spouse hid assets
- Figuring out who should follow up on the QDRO to be sure you get your portion of your ex-spouse's qualified retirement plan
- Determining who will help you track when assets vest in the future and when you are supposed to receive them
- Analyzing if you should accept a lump sum settlement or periodic spousal support

Ultimately, a divorce financial planner aims to educate you, manage your expectations, give you peace of mind that the settlements are practical, and increase your satisfaction by reducing stress.

What Does a Divorce Financial Planner Do?

A divorce financial planner wears many hats: advocate, expert, neutral, and coach. You determine the scope of their engagement; it also depends on the complexity of your case and on the legal process you choose: mediation, collaborative, or litigation. A divorce financial planner performs the following tasks:

- Fact finding and investigation (discovery)
- Lifestyle analysis
- Net Worth Statement preparation
- Detailed list of marital and separate property (assets and liabilities)
- Child and spousal support (capacity to pay and needs analysis)
- Financial valuations
- Financial forensics (a record of where all the money is/went)
- Tax analysis
- Pension valuations
- Different scenarios for settlement
- Future cash flow projections
- Expert testimony
- Post-divorce carryover

A Financial Neutral Third Party

A divorce financial planner takes on the role of a neutral third party in the legal context of a mediation, arbitration, or collaborative divorce. Here, you agree that their role is clearly defined. For example, he or she will:

- Provide both you and your spouse with ongoing financial education, guidance, and analysis throughout the divorce process.
- Assist with the gathering, analysis, and preparation of financial documentation of income, assets, debts, and expenses.
- Perform financial projections based on different scenarios for settlement.

You will be supported and guided by the divorce financial planner to identify issues and consequences and define your potential choices that will promote mutually satisfactory and desired outcomes for your family. As a neutral participant, a divorce financial planner may not advocate, take sides, or testify for either spouse.

However, in mediation or the collaborative process, you may perceive an imbalance of power or knowledge about financial issues that impedes the process. In this circumstance, a divorce financial planner can be brought in to work with the more vulnerable spouse to level the "playing field" with the consent of both spouses. With this added professional, you receive all the appropriate information, education, and "hand-holding" support you may need to move forward to make final financial decisions with greater confidence.

Your Financial Advocate

As a financial advocate, a divorce financial planner serves your best interests by providing financial expertise during the divorce process. You or your divorce attorney feel it is necessary to have a financial expert perform specific tasks that comprehensively address financial issues and risks to supplement your attorney's legal efforts. These tasks may include discovery, analysis, tracing, strategy, negotiations, and projections. You rely on the expertise of the divorce financial planner to achieve solutions unique to your case that result in an attainable and practical outcome.

It is usually best to engage a divorce financial planner as early as possible in the process. Often, you will find that the initial scope of tasks expands for the divorce financial planner over time based on necessity and new case developments. A divorce financial planner is the only financial professional who is intensely involved in your divorce but is also looking to the future, helping you create new budgets and financial goals and providing post-divorce carryover to help you implement the terms of your agreement.

A Testifying Expert

Your divorce attorney can hire a divorce financial planner to serve as a financial expert in court by providing an unbiased, objective opinion on a particular topic. The divorce financial planner must go through the rigorous process of qualifying as an expert in the eyes of the law and court, and she or he must testify about their area of competence and respect strict rules for proper testimony. Your divorce financial planner may be deposed by the opposing side when disclosed as an expert witness or fact witness in the case.

How Does a Divorce Financial Planner Work with You and Your Divorce Attorney?

A divorce financial planner supplements and adds value to the legal process by collaborating with you and your attorney. Typical tasks performed include:

- Organizing and compiling accurate and full disclosure of financial information
- Eliminating costly financial errors by providing detailed and precise financial reports
- Assisting with discovery and forensic analysis of money/asset movements
- Identifying financial fraud, dissipation of assets, or transmutation of assets before or during the divorce process
- Preparing questions about financial issues for deposition/interrogatory
- Managing the client's financial expectations
- Helping the client understand various financial decisions and consequences
- Helping the client to understand the risks of going to trial
- Helping the client to understand the settlement proposal/outcome
- Testifying as an expert witness in court
- Providing assistance post-divorce to client to implement terms of judgment

Summary of the Role of a Divorce Financial Planner

Overall, a divorce financial planner is trained specifically to provide focused expertise in all divorce financial-related issues. Every divorce is different, and you should weigh carefully all of your financial options. Being informed early in the process may help you avoid the risk later of going to court and having a judge make the final decisions about you, your children, your property, your money, and how you live your life.

By bringing this professional on your team, you will benefit from understanding both the short- and long-term consequences of your decisions and final outcome. A divorce financial planner can help you in any legal setting to make fully informed decisions in divorce with confidence and peace of mind.

How Can You Find a "Good" Divorce Financial Planner?

The best way to find a divorce financial planner is to ask for referrals from friends, divorce attorneys, and other professionals. One can also go online and search the website of the Association of Divorce Financial Planners, a not-for-profit national organization that lists divorce financial planners geographically (divorceand finance.org). Other websites include FPAnet.org (for certified financial planners) and

Institutedfa.com. You should interview potential candidates about their experience, types of divorce cases they have been involved in, and about their credentials and training.

When Should You Hire a Divorce Financial Planner?

You should consider hiring a divorce financial planner at any time when divorce is contemplated, before, during, or after divorce (for post-judgment implementation). The tasks which a divorce financial planner may perform are specific to each case and the stage of the divorce process. Services are geared to the complexity, size, and nature of the specific case. Different cases call for different tasks.

Generally speaking, it is best to hire one as early in the process, sometimes before hiring a legal professional, to gather, organize, and compile pertinent financial information. Not being adequately prepared to deal with the financial issues in divorce has long-lasting financial consequences.

What Will It Cost?

A divorce financial planner charges an hourly fee. Each professional charges their rate based on their experience and knowledge. Fees may range anywhere from $50 to $500 per hour. Typically, their hourly fees are less than those of legal professionals. Fees may also vary depending on the legal process: mediation, collaborative, or litigation. In the context of mediation and collaborative divorce, if the divorce financial planner acts as a neutral professional, then both parties use only one person, and fees are reduced by being consolidated.

Do You Need a Divorce Financial Planner If You Already Have an Accountant or Investment Advisor?

A divorce financial planner is a financial expert in comprehensive personal financial planning and in the context of how these financial issues are examined and resolved in a divorce. A divorce financial planner is familiar with historical, current, and projected areas of personal finance that cover budgeting, investments, taxes, retirement planning, college planning, employee benefits, estate planning, and insurances. They focus on the present and on the future to provide assistance for helping a client move forward past their divorce. Many times, they can address all aspects of each personal decision to help with strategy, negotiating, and testifying for clients in divorce.

A divorce financial planner is a unique financial expert who understands the divorce process and the psychological needs of the client, possesses unique planning software for divorce, and is used to working as a team member in divorce.

Other financial professionals do not necessarily have the interdisciplinary knowledge of divorce laws and finance. Their focus is narrower and often subjective (rather than objective) because of traditional relationships with you or your spouse.

Financial Planning Tips for How You Can Become Financially Self-Sufficient and Positive

Adopt Positive Behavior Goals

1. Spend less than you make
2. Know where your money goes
3. Save more than you splurge—build a nest egg and invest!
4. Don't be afraid to ask for help
5. Know how you will pay for everything
6. Review your credit report at least once a year
7. Build an emergency fund
8. Beware of scams
9. Learn about investments
10. Don't be consumed by your financial fears

If You Are a Chronic Overspender

1. Foster a positive attitude
2. Forego judgment
3. Redirect your focus to the impact of overspending

Eliminate Negative Language

1. Stop saying "I can't," "I have to cut back," and "I have to cut out."
2. Replace this language with, "I can," "I have a choice," and "I am in control."

Take Action Steps

1. Keep a spending diary
2. Identify goals for each kind of spending; break it into small steps
3. Revise spending goals when needed and monitor regularly
4. Pat yourself on the back when you achieve each goal, no matter how small
5. Celebrate a sense of achievement and make it visible—make yourself a sign, tell friends and family, etc.

6 What If I Don't Know . . . ? How Do I . . . ? The Unknowns That Keep You Awake at Night

You Don't Have Enough or Accurate Financial Information

Gathering financial information in a timely fashion to prepare your Net Worth Statement can be tricky as well as stressful. What if you do not have all the information you need or your numbers conflict with those in the Net Worth Statement prepared by your spouse?

You can do some sleuthing on your own. Follow these steps below to help find what you should be looking for.

1. **Review your income tax returns, K-1s, and 1099s**. Tax returns, especially a couple of years' worth, can reveal a lot of information. It is like looking for buried treasure. Look for:
   a. Income from wages: It may be possible to discover previously undisclosed businesses or consulting jobs, contributions (as deductions from taxable wages) to retirement plans, exercise of deferred compensation, fringe benefits, etc.
   b. Tax-exempt interest income: This may reveal other investment assets.
   c. Itemized deductions on Schedule A: This reports an itemization of expense deductions in seven categories instead of taking a standard exemption deduction on your taxes. Look at medical and dental expenses, local and property taxes, mortgage interest, charity, theft losses, job-related expenses, and miscellaneous (safety deposit box, tax prep fees, investment fees, etc.). Compare these numbers to what you know about your real estate taxes, mortgage interest, personal property taxes to reveal the existence of any undisclosed real estate, mortgages, or other assets.
   d. Dividends and interest on Schedule B: This reports interest and dividends earned or accrued. Look at which banks report interest and

which brokerage accounts report dividends. Pay attention to any foreign accounts or trusts.

e. Capital gains and losses on Schedule D: This reports profits and losses from the sale of investments (capital assets). Look at which stocks produced capital gains, if any businesses or properties were sold, and if there is any loss carried forward for future years. Where did the sales proceeds go?

f. Supplemental income and loss on Schedule E: This reports income from rental properties, royalties, partnerships, S corporations, estates, and trusts. This information can reveal undisclosed personal and business assets.

2. **Conduct a public records search** under your spouse's name to see if he or she owns any real property that wasn't disclosed. Go to your town hall to ask who holds the title to your marital home and automobiles.
3. **Review any joint bank account statements** to see if there are any unusual cash withdrawals, large checks made out to cash, wire transfers, or canceled checks made out in large amounts to unknown parties.
4. **Review any credit card statements** for substantial purchases that have not been disclosed.
5. **Run a credit report** from all three credit agencies on yourself and your spouse (if possible). Credit reports provide you an opportunity to correct errors, track spending sources, and discover any debts previously unknown to you.

You Cannot Put a Dollar Value on Your Contributions and Sacrifices

During your married life, you may have made contributions or sacrifices that are difficult to value in dollars. Nonetheless, what you did resulted in the building of an economic partnership called a marriage. Divorce attorneys may be reluctant and find it very problematic to assign a monetary worth to these nonmonetary items.

These issues could include:

- Community stature as a couple (charity involvement, celebrity status, and/or corporate life)
- Serious health problems, dysfunctions, or addictions
- Prior and repeated threats of divorce, coercion, and loss
- Unbalanced economic history during marriage
- Excessive business travel or frequent relocations that caused financial losses or career interruptions
- Shared increase in value of a family-owned business through the labor of both spouses
- Benefits forfeited to marry your current spouse (pension, Social Security, or alimony)
- Putting your spouse through school
- Delaying or not having children
- Caregiving for your in-laws

State laws vary, but for the most part mainstream financial settlements in divorce largely exclude any specific valuation of particular marital conduct. The interchange or "sacrifices" you made during a marriage may not be reflected to the degree you would hope for as measured by your financial results.

However, you should NOT be dissuaded from speaking up. Depending on your state, courts will sometimes give thoughtful recognition to the concept of joint enterprise and noneconomic contributions of a homemaker in both the award of alimony and property distribution.

You Think Your Spouse Is Dissipating or Spending All Your Money

Dissipation is broadly defined as the squandering of money, energy, or resources. It is the wasting, destruction, or getting rid of marital property without the approval of the other party. It is a remarkably broad term. Courts allow leniency regarding intent and have the discretion to consider whether "foolish," "speculative," "rash," and/or "frivolous" expenditures demonstrate dissipation.

The party claiming dissipation must allege it and bears the burden of proving that it occurred. The other spouse who spent the money must show that the challenged spending was appropriate and was not intentional misconduct. Examples of dissipation include a gambling problem, addictions, failure to preserve a marital asset (letting a house go into foreclosure), spending money on a third party (extramarital affairs), distributing assets to adult children from a previous marriage, self-serving spending on frivolous or wasteful tangible assets, or use of community property for personal benefit when a divorce is imminent.

In some jurisdictions, once you file for divorce, automatic orders are imposed on finances that prohibit dissipating, selling, transferring, encumbering, or wasting marital assets during the pendency of the divorce. Automatic orders ensure that the property of the marital estate remains intact so that the court may equitably or equally divide it. In reality, dissipation does occur during a divorce, even under automatic orders or an injunction, when a party fails to comply. If dissipation takes place after the filing for divorce, you can raise the argument that you have been deprived of marital assets and request an unequal division of the marital property before the court.

Your Spouse Poorly Managed Your Money and Lost It All

Most courts agree that negligent mismanagement of marital property does not constitute dissipation of marital assets. Because money is the primary point of conflict in the majority of marriages, arguing over how your spouse poorly managed or spent it is to be expected. The blame game can be a real problem, but much depends on how and if differences were resolved during your marriage.

There is no clear rule for defining dissipation versus mismanagement of resources because courts hold that the outcome of the dissipation issue often depends on the particular facts and circumstances surrounding the conduct. Courts consider whether the expenses were unreasonable in light of the parties' marital estate, standard of living, and routine expenditures relating to the necessities of life.

Finally, courts will consider whether the accusing spouse objected at the time of the outlay or action. The general rule is that consent is a defense to dissipation. So if you objected to your spouse's actions and she or he took action in disregard of your protestations, you may be more credible. Courts typically do not recognize improper financial acts that occur during the marriage that predate the breakdown of the marriage.

You Think Your Spouse Is Hiding Assets and Money

It is common for one spouse to manage the big picture finances for the long term while the other manages the day-to-day finances. The spouse who is the higher wage earner or the business owner usually has greater liquid assets and is therefore more sophisticated and has a deeper knowledge of the couple's finances than the other. The result is that this spouse has an unfair advantage in divorce concerning the investment and control of cash flow and assets. Capitalizing on this strength could escalate to the level of fraud by the "money manager" spouse.

What can you do if you think your spouse is delaying the discovery process, not reporting real income, or hiding assets? Your best defense always is to wipe out any advantage your spouse may have. The best way to find hidden assets is to prevent them from becoming concealed in the first place.

Some spouses do attempt to deflate income or hide assets, before or during a divorce, to avoid sharing it with their soon-to-be ex-spouse. Your spouse may try to shelter income from you (and the court) by deferring salary, commissions, and bonuses. Your spouse could underreport self-employment income and other financial perks or investment returns. Further, your spouse could overstate his or her expenses, such as overpaying or prepaying taxes, creditors, and college savings accounts or making phony loans to friends or family.

Hiding assets is defined by actions your spouse takes to transfer assets from joint accounts to individual accounts or to third parties or to simply waste them. It is not common to hide significant assets. Squirreling away emergency funds or small cash is typical. Hiding more substantial assets is relatively difficult with the explosion of information on the Internet, sophisticated forensic investigation methods, and required public disclosure of publicly owned businesses.

Discovery is a powerful legal tool in all states to help you find hidden income or assets. It is risky to try to hide assets or intentionally reduce income in divorce because there can be severe penalties. The court will be displeased with a deceitful spouse and may impose monetary sanctions as well as affect the ultimate disposition of marital property against a dishonest spouse.

Sleuthing Tips If You Are Asking for "Show Me the Money"

- What assets are you are trying to find?
  - Unreported income
  - Imputed income
  - Unknown assets
  - Misappropriation of assets
  - Assets transferred in contemplation of divorce
  - Assets transferred during divorce
  - Unknown business entities
- What documents will you need for what you are trying to find?
- What are some common discovery techniques?
- How do you gain access to the information you need?
- Who do you need to hire to find what you think is hidden?
- What if the assets are foreign or hidden overseas?

Do You Have Reason to Be Suspicious?

Are you suspicious with good cause? Observe your spouse's behavior. Attempt to engage your spouse in sharing of financial information and to communicate about your money situation. Stay focused on what you know about and assess how to benchmark your financial situation. If red flags pop up and you perceive noticeable changes in the status quo, you may have good reason to be distrustful. Timing is everything, and you want to detect schemes to hide money or manipulate financial information before they happen.

There are many ways individuals can move assets into the hands of a third party or hide behind false documents and techniques. If you have doubts, you should ask yourself about opportunities your spouse has to hide income, assets, or a lifestyle.

- Is there a business? Is it a cash business? Is it a family business?
- Is there a subchapter S corporation?
- Is there a privately held company or limited partnership?
- Has your spouse recently changed jobs and received severance packages or been given sign-up incentives?
- Is your spouse's business engaged in any mergers, acquisitions, or private buy-outs?
- Has your spouse made any unusually large business purchases that could mask the purchase being for personal items?
- Are your assets and spending significantly more than would be expected when compared to your reported income? (Refer to your lifestyle analysis.)
- Does your spouse deposit a separate paycheck into a separate account?
- Does your spouse get an automatic transfer of funds or an allowance?
- Does your spouse have bank and credit card statements mailed to his or her employment or another address?
- Are there large amounts of cash floating around?
- Do both of you have a professional relationship with your accountant and financial planner or just one?

- Has your spouse ever been dishonest on prior tax returns?
- Does your spouse have multiple business entities for tax purposes?
- Does your spouse travel internationally and engage in business abroad?

Places for Hiding Assets

There are as many methods for concealing assets as the number of personalities of the individuals involved. Nevertheless, with thorough discovery and meticulous investigation, you can uncover a lot of information and relevant evidence.

Common Types of Hidden Assets and Hiding Places

- Any asset held under your spouse's name, aliases, friends, relatives, partners, etc.
- Home mortgage pay-downs (depletes cash but retains value)
- Whole or universal life insurance (cash value)
- Savings bonds, bearer bonds, and traveler's or cashier's checks
- Dissolved corporations (bank accounts and capital accounts)
- Transfers to children's accounts (529 plans, trusts, and UGMAs)
- Family or third-party trusts and domestic asset protection trusts
- So-called debt repayments to a friend, relative, or partner for phony debt
- Offshore corporations or dead shell corporations
- Stockbroker accounts
- Collectibles
- Safe deposit boxes
- Offshore foreign bank accounts and foreign investments
- Sweetheart lawsuits (a bogus liability intended to run interference against legitimate claims of a divorcing spouse)
- Overpayments to the IRS
- Overpayments to credit cards

Searching for Hidden Assets and Income

When searching for hidden assets and income, here are some good indicators that something is amiss:

- The values of your assets look lower than you remember
- Your spouse's income looks low (your spouse can defer income to executive supplemental plans and both qualified and nonqualified deferred compensation benefits or collude with an employer to delay income)
- Your spouse is reluctant to share information with you
- Your spouse travels frequently and abroad
- Your spouse makes new efforts to give gifts to family members, to establish trusts, or buy real estate held by a third party
- Your spouse incurs new expenses paid on behalf of the family, relatives, friends, etc.
- You note inconsistencies on your spouse's social media accounts, browser history, and smartphones (be aware that not all data or evidence are admissible in court and may or may not be used in your divorce case)

- Your income tax returns on a year-to-year basis are substantially incomparable and are prepared each year by different CPAs
- Your spouse is skimming cash from a business
- Loan applications differ substantially from other information you were told or given or as stated on tax returns

How to Follow the Money

A detailed forensic review of all money flows can prove invaluable in identifying situations where one spouse has committed fraud in anticipation of divorce.

Key professionals for helping you find hidden assets include:

- A divorce financial planner and/or forensic investigator (e.g., a financial, accounting, or computer expert)
- A private investigator
- An attorney

There are multiple methods for uncovering hidden assets, irregularities, undiscovered liabilities, and financial abuse that include the analysis of individual income tax returns, business records and business tax returns, bank loan applications, and financial accounts. The principal methods include the following:

- The Cash T method—Compares cash received to the amount of cash spent and is used to determine if an individual had understated income.
- The Net Worth method—Calculates total assets and liabilities of an individual and is compared over several time periods to income.
- The Bank Deposit method—Analyzes total deposits during the year and compares it to total expenses to determine any unknown sources of funds.

Usually, a forensic examination by a forensic expert is recommended by an attorney when one spouse is actively involved in running a closely held business or is a single-owner business. This recommendation also serves to protect your attorney from any future malpractice claim because, in this scenario, the potential to manipulate income and hide assets is unlimited.

It is important to bear in mind that the cost benefit of a forensic review must be worthwhile before you perform an investigation. That is, you should expect to recover more than what you pay to find it.

Every Act Has a Consequence: The IRS Is Watching

Once a forensic investigation is begun, both you and your attorney will have knowledge that could become public in divorce. This revelation means that by following the right process, anyone can find your records.

While a forensic investigation can be extremely beneficial to you, it also may lead to serious income tax consequences. The extent of misconduct includes activities, such as the following:

- The discovery of unreported income
- Taking substantial cash from the business
- Intentionally reducing the profitability of the business
- Making inappropriate transactions with third parties
- Concealment of and unreported foreign assets
- Having the business pay for many personal expenses that are more than normal or reported for taxes; typical nonbusiness expenses could be
  - Paying salaries to "ghost" employees
  - Social and health club expenses
  - Auto and boat expenses (including insurances)
  - Nonbusiness travel and entertainment
  - Rent on nonbusiness property and equipment
  - Personal computers and family cell phones

What Happens When You Find Undisclosed Assets During Divorce?

There may be consideration of not only civil penalties, but also criminal penalties. Civil penalties can be that the asset-hiding spouse is assessed court costs, ordered to pay the legal or investigator fees incurred by their wronged spouse, and their prenuptial or postnuptial agreements are voided.

Far worse are criminal penalties. Depending on the laws of your state, your spouse could be held in contempt of court or charged with a misdemeanor, which can result in fines and even jail time. If your spouse lies about his or her assets in court, they can be charged with perjury under oath for falsely testifying. The court could also prosecute your spouse with fraud, a criminal act that incurs penalties of restitution and jail time.

It is much more formidable when there are foreign asset protection trusts or foreign assets. So long as the title to the asset is placed in the name of a trust, the trust has ownership of the asset. Some assets may be impossible to locate when titled in the name of such a trust that has not been disclosed voluntarily.

These trusts are established under the laws of foreign countries that may or may not have treaties with the United States, and thus U.S. laws do not apply. Even if the foreign jurisdiction does recognize U.S. law, the validity of your divorce judgment and your cause of action for fraudulent conveyance of assets, the statutes of limitations on those causes is usually very short (six months) and missed more often than not. Rarely, it is fruitful to undertake legal actions to recover assets in foreign jurisdictions.

What Happens If Hidden Assets Are Found Post-Divorce?

Your ex-spouse remains vulnerable if proof later comes to light about hidden assets. Most divorce decrees incorporate a clause requiring full disclosure of assets. But even if yours does not contain such a clause, you are still protected if hidden assets are later discovered. The innocent spouse can petition the court to reopen the divorce settlement, which might result in similar penalties to the perpetrator as if the concealment had been discovered during the divorce. You, as the innocent spouse, can also file civil charges against your asset-hiding ex-spouse and request monetary and punitive damages.

Your Spouse Is Considering Bankruptcy and Divorce

Many people cite divorce as a leading cause for their bankruptcy filing. The goal of most individuals filing bankruptcy is to obtain a discharge of personal liability for unsecured debts. The idea is to get a fresh start and to wipe out debts. For those divorcing or divorced, the bankruptcy issues usually fall into three categories:

(1) The payment of child support and spousal support after a bankruptcy has been filed;
(2) The enforceability of a property settlement agreement after a bankruptcy has been filed; and,
(3) Payment of joint debts if only one spouse files for bankruptcy.

The Pros for Filing Bankruptcy During Divorce

Planning ahead can make both your bankruptcy and divorce less complicated and maybe even more cost-efficient. Whether you should file joint bankruptcy before or after a divorce depends on where you live, how much property and debt you have, and what type of bankruptcy (Chapter 7 or Chapter 13) you wish to file. Joint bankruptcy petitions have advantages and disadvantages. Filing for joint bankruptcy before a divorce can simplify the issues regarding debt and property division because there is less to argue about and less to divide.

It is imperative before filing for joint bankruptcy to find out the means tests and other eligibility issues for which type of bankruptcy you file. Your state may allow exemptions to protect a certain amount of equity in various assets you own with your spouse. Some states allow you to double the exemption amounts if you file jointly. The most common exemptions are equity in your home and automobile.

The Cons for Filing Bankruptcy During Divorce

But what if only your spouse is filing for bankruptcy? If your spouse wants to file alone and you are contemplating divorce, this means you, the nonbankrupt spouse, remain wholly liable for your share of joint debts and are left with little property.

If one spouse files bankruptcy during an ongoing divorce, the automatic stay will put a hold on the property division process until the bankruptcy is completed. That means that your divorce cannot proceed until the bankruptcy is completed. Bankruptcy trumps divorce.

Lastly, the bankruptcy court takes a dim view if the nonbankrupt spouse is merely holding property or has received property from the bankrupt spouse within one year of filing bankruptcy. In this case, the transaction is considered fraudulent, and the property will be turned over to the bankruptcy trustee.

Bankruptcy When Already Divorced

Bankruptcy courts deal with the competing concerns of giving bankruptcy debtors a fresh start and the payment of marital obligations and support. It is relatively difficult to discharge divorce-related debts in bankruptcy. Both spousal support and child support payments and certain property settlements are given protection and must be paid as agreed upon in both Chapter 7 and Chapter 13 bankruptcies. Additionally, if you are awarded legal fees as additional spousal support, this will be nondischargeable debt. These obligations continue and are not affected by the bankruptcy. However, wage garnishments to collect past due support may be "stayed" or blocked during the bankruptcy filing, and in most cases, motions for an increase in child support will not be heard in family court until the bankruptcy case is finished.

Beyond spousal support and child support, the federal bankruptcy court is not necessarily bound by a state court's designation or language in a divorce decree referencing that debt is support or property settlement. The bankruptcy court can look behind such language to determine the real nature of the debt as well as distinguish differently in Chapter 7 or Chapter 13 cases regarding debts, domestic support obligations, and property settlements. This distinction in determining dischargeability of debts can be critical.

If your ex-spouse files for bankruptcy and you own joint credit card debt, his or her share of paying off debts may be discharged by the court. If your ex-spouse is given bankruptcy relief, the credit card company can and will "go after" you, the spouse who did not file for bankruptcy, for the entire amount owed. The credit card company has only one objective, and that is to collect money.

As an added layer of protection, a divorce judgment should always include a hold-harmless indemnity clause that creates a separate obligation between former spouses. The hold-harmless obligation creates a new liability independent of the pre-existing liability to the third-party original creditor; this is like a promise of "I'll protect you." A typical provision requires each spouse to hold the other harmless from the debt assigned to that spouse. The primary problem with an indemnity is that it is binding only between former spouses, not on third parties. Indemnities are helpful but incomplete. They are nondischargeable in Chapter 7 bankruptcy but can be wiped out in Chapter 13.

The Different Kinds of Bankruptcy

Chapter 7: This is liquidation bankruptcy, where the debtor does not pay anything back to creditors. The principal advantage is that the debtor comes out without any future obligations on discharged debts. This bankruptcy does *not* discharge or wipe out most taxes, most school loans, child support, or spousal support. You can keep the property on your state's exemption list.

Chapter 13: The debtor must pay all or part of total debts from future income over a period of three to five years through a payment plan. Some debts may be wiped out or discharged in full. However, most long-term debt and home mortgages must be paid in their standard monthly payments either through or outside a payment plan. In most cases, the debtor can retain all assets provided payments are made on time and as required.

Chapter 11: Chapter 11 is used by large businesses to reorganize their debt and continue operating.

You Have a Prenuptial or Postnuptial Agreement

A prenuptial agreement is a private written contract created by two people *before* they are married. A prenup lists all income sources and property each person owns (as well as any debts) and specifies what each person's property rights will be if they divorce, become disabled, or die. It seeks to avoid court involvement in determining which property belongs to which person.

A postnuptial agreement is a private agreement signed *after* the couple is married. It dictates how the couple's financial affairs and assets will be divided in divorce or separation. The intent is to try to "fix" something that has gone wrong in the marriage so the marriage can continue or to ease the transition to divorce if it becomes inevitable.

Both types of agreements can also act in conjunction with an estate plan to define ownership in the event of either parties' death or disability. Both prenuptial agreements and postnuptial agreements are legal contracts and enforceable under the law. The rules vary from state to state, but in general, parties to these agreements must make a knowing waiver of the marital rights; it must be fair and reasonable at the time it was entered into and when it comes into play. There can be no coercion or duress, unconscionability (include terms that are extremely unjust or one-sided), or fraud. Both types of agreements should be as specific as possible, except you cannot limit anything to do with children, such as child support and visitations, now or in the future. The content of a prenup or postnup can vary widely.

Postnups are still evolving in law, growing in popularity, and vary from state to state. It is important for couples to know the factors for enforceability and that it is not motivated by one spouse threatening divorce that then uses it to get better terms from an imminent divorce.

In divorce, prenups and postnups are challenged and have to be addressed before the divorce can proceed. You can sometimes adjust the agreements to be more favorable on points where you mutually agree or consent if you have to invalidate it completely. Full disclosure of assets and liabilities are required to make a prenuptial or postnuptial agreement valid.

If you want to have the agreement declared invalid, you have the burden of proving that there was a problem in its formation. An attorney will review the validity of the agreement at its creation. It can be very expensive to challenge the validity of a prenup or postnup during the divorce process, and many agreements contain language that you will be required to pay your spouse's legal fees if you are unsuccessful. If it is held valid, the agreement will likely make the divorce process easier and help you determine how your case will be handled and what outcome is to be expected.

Post-Divorce Financial Obligations

The continued financial obligations after your divorce are final per your judgment. Divorce rarely ends the relationship with your ex-spouse in total, especially if you have children. The potential for change exists, both favorable and unfavorable. Your recovery and survival depend on your financial security and preparedness.

7 Splitting Up Your Property: The Balancing Act

The process of dividing up marital property and negotiating your fair share is both a science and an art. You have to:

- ❑ Identify the property
- ❑ Characterize it (marital or separate)
- ❑ Value it
- ❑ Divide it

In Chapter 3, I discussed property ownership, transmutation of property (a change from marital to separate property or vice versa), and how property is divided in a divorce. In Chapter 4, I described the financial phases of divorce and identified a checklist of financial assets and liabilities. In this chapter, you will learn how to value property and decide what you want and need so you can disentangle and separate your financial life from your spouse.

You and your spouse will make strategic financial decisions when you negotiate a property settlement; if not, you may face a court battle where the judge will decide for both of you. As a general rule, the courts can divide only property that exists at the time of divorce, with very few exceptions.

It is essential that you realize property division is a one-shot deal in divorce. Therefore, you must take your time to understand each and every asset and liability.

⚠ **Caution:** Not all assets are treated the same tax-wise. Some may also have hidden costs or additional costs if they are to be maintained, sold, or liquidated.

ⓘ **Tip:** It is almost always smart to pair up an asset to the party who also is the debtor on that particular asset. For example, if you are driving a Volkswagen Jetta and your name is on the lease, you should keep the car and avoid confusion as to who will service that particular debt (see Chapter 14 for more information about debts and credit).

What Do You Want to Have and Hold?

You have the opportunity to plan for your financial future. You need to know what to ask for so you can reformulate financial goals. Once you know, you can make a game plan to get what you want. It is important to consider what assets you cherish most and also be prepared to let some go.

What Is the Property You Have to Value?

- Savings, financial investments, and businesses (Chapter 8)
- Cash value of life insurance and annuities (Chapter 8)
- Retirement accounts (Chapter 9)
- Contingent interests—deferred compensation (Chapter 10)
- Real property (Chapter 11)
- Debts and credit (Chapter 14)

How Is Property Valued?

When analyzing property division, you will value the marital property as of a certain date, which is known as the cutoff date. Often it is the date of commencement of your action because the court considers the marriage was ended when your action commenced. However, you need to ask your divorce attorney what the "official date" is in your state unless you and your spouse can agree on a specified date (refer to Chapter 2).

All property can be valued, but no single method is universally applicable and accepted for all assets. Just as assets are diverse, there are many valuation approaches, such as the following:

- **Appraised value**—An evaluation of a property's value based on a professional's opinion at a given point in time. This value is arrived at by using one of three methods: (a) cost approach, (b) income approach, or (c) market comparison. Appraisers do not represent either party's interest in a property when determining value.
- **Fair market value**—The amount at which the asset can be bought or sold in a current transaction between a willing buyer and a willing seller engaging in an arm's-length transaction. This value is always changing according to market conditions.
- **Replacement value**—The amount you would have to pay to replace a lost or destroyed asset at present. The IRS provides instruction for determining the replacement value of an item.
- **Present value**—Present value, also known as discounted value, is the time value of money and is based on the assumption that a dollar today is worth more than a dollar tomorrow. It is the current worth of a sum of money or stream of cash flows expected in the future discounted by a specified rate of return. Present value is used to calculate today's value of a future pension and annuities.

Where Do You Begin?

First, address any items that require appraisals because it takes some time for a professional to perform a formal appraisal of the property and write a report detailing its value. You'll need appraisals for your house, real estate, artwork, collectibles, antiques, jewelry, vintage cars, and wine. If either party owns an interest in a business, that will need to be appraised. Certain pension benefits will need appraisals also.

You can obtain estimates of the fair market value of:

- Your automobile by consulting with Kelly Blue Book or NADA Guide and then subtracting any loan balances from their indicated values;
- Your furniture, electronics, boat, furniture, tools, and equipment by comparing prices from online merchandisers, newspapers, or bargain news; and
- Your financial accounts and investments by referring to the statement as of the "valuation date" for each account and finding the balance in the account as of that date.

For business interests, hire a valuation expert to appraise the business using a combination of methodologies: the income approach, book value approach, capitalization approach, and/or market approach.

For pensions and annuities, you should hire a professional to calculate their worth as of the "valuation date." An actuary specializes in these calculations to determine the present value of the amount of money you would have to give your spouse to buy out his or her interest in it. If you don't want to give your spouse a portion of the pension benefits, then you can pay your spouse the present value of the benefits she or he would have received later.

How Do You Divide Property?

You may have the opportunity to prioritize what is in your best interest and to "cherry pick" assets to achieve your fair share. You may be able to pick and choose certain assets or debts; to ask for cash in lieu of an existing asset; to pay off debts before the divorce is final; or, to postpone the sale of an asset until a future date. At other times, property is divided in kind and proportionately; for example, transferring to each spouse one half of the money market fund by equally dividing the cash in the fund. Certain assets are contingent, such as inheritances, and these can be divided on an "if, as, and when" basis.

You can agree to divide property based on value. Remember different assets may have different valuation dates. Value can be determined by

- The dollar value
- The number of shares/units
- A percentage

You also can allocate assets by type:

- Real property
- Financial assets
- Retirement assets
- Contingent assets
- Business interests
- Debts

Before you decide to take possession of an asset as part of the property distribution, you need to know how each type of asset will benefit you, based on your preferences, age, needs, and risk tolerance.

Things You Need to Know

Do you understand the distinctive nature of each asset before you agree to anything? Is the asset liquid or not? Does it have a high- or low-cost basis? What is the real net after-tax value of the asset? Is it a tax advantageous retirement account or not? Does the asset produce income or is it a money pit—can you afford to keep the asset after you divorce?

Do you know the consequences of taking on debt? Is the debt amortized, or does it have a balloon payment due? Does the debt need to be refinanced, and if so, how much more will it cost? Is the debt at a fixed or adjustable rate? Is it a secured debt or unsecured? In Chapter 12, I discuss debt in greater detail.

Finally, do you know that some assets may have a dual nature? Some assets can be considered both income and assets, such as deferred compensation, family businesses, and pensions. This dual nature often leads to controversy about how it should be treated, as well as to claims of "double dipping or double counting."

"Double dipping" is a term to describe the alleged unfairness that results when property is awarded as an asset to you but is also treated as a source of income for purposes of calculating your spousal support. Like many things, you may have to negotiate how to appropriately classify property relying on the facts of the particular asset or on how the court will resolve the dispute.

What Are Liquid and Illiquid Assets?

There are two kinds of assets: liquid and illiquid. The benefits of having liquid assets are that they can be easily converted into cash, and they can be valued on any date. While the divorce case is pending, you may prize having the flexibility of liquid assets to meet short-term expenses. It is prudent to set aside and maintain some liquid assets, usually three to six months' worth of living expenses, as your rainy day emergency fund.

There is nothing inherently wrong with having an illiquid asset. It just calls for you to be willing to accept a long-term investment horizon. The return on the investment should be high enough to compensate you for taking on added risk.

Liquid:

An asset is said to be liquid if it is easy to sell or convert into cash without any loss in its value. Examples of liquid assets include:

- Cash
- Deposit account funds (checking and savings)
- CDs
- Stocks
- Mutual funds
- Bonds

Illiquid:

An asset or security that cannot be sold quickly due to a shortage of interested buyers or a lack of an established trading market is an illiquid asset. These assets cannot be easily converted into cash without potential for losing a significant percentage of their value. Examples of nonliquid assets include:

- Real estate property
- Jewelry
- Commodities (gold, oil, pork bellies)
- Artwork
- Electronics

What Is the Cost Basis of the Asset?

In divorce, you assume the cost basis of any property transferred to you from your spouse according to the terms of your divorce. You do not pay any taxes on any property received as part of your divorce. You may be liable to pay taxes only if you sell it after you receive it. You always should require the adjusted cost basis of all property you receive for your tax records in the future.

- The cost basis of property as defined by the IRS is the original purchase price you paid in cash, debt obligations, other property, or services to buy the property. Your basis is usually its actual cost to you.
- Cost basis can change over time: Capital improvements on a home, depreciation, reinvested dividends and capital gains, stock splits, return of capital, etc., can all increase your original cost basis. This is called the "adjusted cost basis."
- The cost basis is the value used to determine the capital gain or loss (your profit or loss), which is the difference between the asset's cost basis and the current value of the asset when sold.

NOTE: A capital gain or loss has a tax impact to you, and this is known as the "tax basis." If you sell or liquidate your asset after divorce, you will have a tax event.

ⓘ **Tip:** You may want assets with high-cost basis if you are in high-income tax bracket.

What Is the Real Net After-Tax Value of the Asset?

In divorce, the net after-tax value of an asset is the real value of the asset. Two distinct marital assets may appear to have the same market value; however, when taxes are taken into consideration, each asset can have a very different net after-tax value.

Net of tax is an accounting term for the value of an asset adjusted for taxes. Net of tax is commonly calculated by taking the gross figure (market value) and subtracting the taxes paid or owed.

ⓘ **Tip:** Cash is king; it requires no adjustments for after-tax value.

The IRS taxes assets and income differently. The tax rate can vary enormously and is different depending on the characterization of the type of asset or income. You need to know the after-tax value of all property and its impact on property division.

- Short-term capital gains—If you sell an asset you have held for one year or less, any profit you make is considered a short-term capital gain. Short-term capital gains do not benefit from any special rate. They are taxed at the same rate as your ordinary income.
- Long-term capital gains—If you sell an asset you have held for more than one year, you make a long-term capital gain. You benefit from a reduced rate on your profits of 0 percent, 15 percent, or 20 percent, depending on your total income.
- Capital losses—If you sell your asset for a loss rather than for a profit, you can use these losses to reduce your taxes. The IRS allows you to match up your gains and losses for any given year to determine your "net" capital gain or loss. If you end up with a loss, you can use up to $3,000 per year to reduce your taxable income.
- Gains in your retirement accounts—Since you do not generate capital gains or losses in your retirement accounts, you do not have any tax impact. Only when you withdraw from your retirement account will you be taxed at the same rate as your ordinary income on all contributions and earnings in the account.

ⓘ **Tip:** You benefit from tax-deferred growth in a retirement account but lose out on long-term capital gains rates.

Before comparing the values of assets to each other, be sure you understand any underlying tax liabilities, sales charges, surrender charges, or other fees associated with the asset. You will also need to determine if it makes sense to assign these costs to the asset. For example, if a house will not be sold, should selling costs be applied in divorce?

Is Your Asset a Retirement or Nonretirement Asset?

Retirement assets typically constitute the largest assets of the marriage. Retirement assets can be one of two types: employer-sponsored plans or individual accounts. The most common advantage of a retirement asset is they offer tax-deferred growth as long as you keep your savings in these accounts. This benefit means you do not pay any taxes on dividends, interest, or capital gains on investments held in retirement accounts. When you make withdrawals, you pay tax at ordinary income rates.

Other advantages of retirement assets may include the opportunity for employers to match fund employee contributions; a guarantee of a fixed, pre-established monthly benefit during retirement; inflation-adjusted payouts; a lump-sum payout; and portfolio management. Dividing retirement assets requires different paperwork for different kinds of accounts and plans. In Chapter 9, the benefits, rights, advantages, and types of retirement assets are described in greater detail.

 **NOTE:** Negotiating for a share of your spouse's retirement benefits can be one of the more contentious financial issues.

How Do You Compare the Value of a Retirement Account to Other Types of Assets?

In the table below, several common types of assets and their corresponding tax treatment are listed.

Asset Type	Tax Deferred/ Taxable Growth	Tax on Sale or Distribution	Liquidity
Retirement Accounts	Tax deferred	Ordinary income	10% penalty on early distribution
Deferred Annuities	Tax deferred	Ordinary income	10% penalty on early distribution
Money Market	Tax on interest—Ordinary income	None	Liquid
CD	Tax on interest–Ordinary income	None	Penalty on early withdrawal
Stocks	Tax on dividends and capital gains when sold	Capital gain/ Ordinary income[1]	Liquid—commission may apply
Real Estate	Tax only on sale	Capital gain/ Ordinary income[2]	Nonliquid—selling costs apply

(continued)

Mutual funds	Tax on dividends and capital gains	Capital gain/ Ordinary income[3]	Liquid—possible surrender charge

[1] The holding period of a capital asset determines the tax rate (i.e., over 12 months = long-term capital gain and 12 months or less is short-term gain taxed as ordinary income). Stock dividends produce ordinary income, but it is taxed at the long-term capital gains rate of 15 percent or 20 percent under current law. Taxpayers in the 10-percent and 15-percent brackets pay no tax on long term capital gains or dividends.

[2] An exclusion of capital gain up to $500,000 may be available for qualified real estate sales.

[3] Mutual funds distribute taxable gains and dividends to the shareholders at the end of each year regardless of any sale of the account.

What Will Your Asset Cost You: Are You Being Realistic?

You should know as best as possible how much any asset will cost you to keep it, how much it will cost you in future years, how much value you can realize from it, and how much of your time is required to manage it. Costs associated with any asset negatively impact your immediate cash flow and, in the worst case, can force you to sell it or go into default if you cannot afford immediate and ongoing expenses.

Sometimes an asset will cost you more money than what you pegged its value to be when you divided the marital estate. Some assets may change in value because you just do not understand the nature of the asset, the risk of your investment, tax consequences, economic forces, or how it is valued. Sometimes assets become illiquid, nonmarketable, or valueless.

If your divorce case is drawn out and highly contentious, assets, such as a family business, may lose value because of a party is distracted by the divorce, a party has disincentive to invest in the business, financial resources are depleted, and/or there is uncertainty in the market for the business.

> ⓘ **Tip:** It is important to perform your due diligence on every asset included in marital estate.

Can You Be Forced to Sell an Asset?

You may petition the court for permission to liquidate assets during a divorce. Upon the finding of good cause, the court may order the liquidation of the asset to avoid unreasonable market or investment risks. The court itself can order the sale of an asset apart from your petition to the court. This action frequently happens when you and your spouse cannot agree on how to divide marital property or when there are insufficient funds to satisfy marital support obligations.

⚠ **Caution:** Any potential tax liability arising from the sale of an asset may or may not be considered by your state's courts as a factor in the property division. Many states refuse to consider tax liability unless the triggering event is mandated by the divorce decree or is otherwise incident to the divorce (immediate and specific). Other states consider tax liability if it is reasonably predictable, is a factor affecting the fairness of the property distribution, or retains jurisdiction over the matter until the liability is incurred.

Accounting for Your Share of Marital Property: Making Sure You Get All That You Are Due

You are responsible for the logistics of tracking, executing, completing, and accounting for your share of marital property post-divorce. You need to follow the terms of your divorce agreement and comply with all court orders.

You may want assistance from a divorce financial planner or legal professional to:

- Open new bank and brokerage accounts
- Open a major credit card in your name
- Transfer ownership of contracts (e.g., life insurance or annuity)
- Engage an attorney to prepare a QDRO to secure and transfer your interest in a qualified retirement plan (401K or pension)
- Quitclaim a deed or property title to your ex-spouse
- Become knowledgeable of vesting schedules for exercising your rights over nontransferable assets (stock options or stock rights)
- Close out joint credit cards and other joint debts
- Open/transfer liabilities into your individual name
- Terminate trusts
- Designate beneficiaries on your financial assets
- Apply for and secure required life insurance
- Notify service providers to change a title to the responsible party
- Adjust automatic debit or deposits for bill paying
- Set up automatic debit or deposit sweeps for support obligations
- Update estate planning documents

You can accomplish several of the above tasks before your divorce is final; others must be handled after your divorce is final. Your objective is to make all transfers and changes in legal title or possession as seamless as possible within a reasonable period following the date of divorce.

Remember, your divorce decree, whether it is an agreement between the spouses or an order fashioned by the court, is an enforceable order under state law. Any order, judgment, or decree issued by the family court is legally binding. You and your spouse can be compelled by the court to comply with its terms. If your ex-spouse does not comply, you can hire an attorney to file for enforcement. If a party is in contempt of the court's orders, sanctions may be applied. Your attorney will inform you of your options for recourse to enforce the terms of your divorce decree.

Be prepared if you have to go back to court. You will be required to describe your ex-spouse's violations of the property agreement in exact detail. Motions to enforce property settlements may be expensive and the cost-benefit of filing a legal action should be weighed.

In summary, your divorce may take longer than you expect, cost more than you projected, and take turns you never imagined. You may be tempted to just get it over with. Or, alternatively, you may expend enormous emotional energy and legal fees fighting for sentimental tokens lacking genuine worth. There is a light at the end of the tunnel, but you must be patient and diligent. You deserve a fair and equitable outcome with enforceable terms—and without hidden costs, hidden taxes, or foolish mistakes. The division of marital property is just one piece of the whole equation of divorce; however, it is a one-time determination that will impact your life for a significant period of time.

8 Financial Investments: What Are They?

How Are Your Assets Invested?

In Chapter 6, I discussed relevant factors for negotiating the division of property by focusing on the nature of assets, tax implications, and potential hidden costs. In this chapter, I describe in detail the variety of financial investments you may have to share and divide.

I provide practical tips for how to manage and split these financial investments both during divorce and afterward. Your goal is to be a well-informed decision-maker and reach a deal for your fair share of the marital assets.

Investment, as the dictionary defines it, is something that is purchased with money that is expected to produce income or profit. Investments are classified into three main groups:

- ❑ Cash equivalents
  - Cash, checking and savings accounts, money market accounts, cash held in brokerage accounts, CDs, security deposits, retainer balances, and escrow accounts
- ❑ Lending (a receivable from lending your money to someone else)
  - Personal loans and promissory notes
- ❑ Ownership (a share or interest in a business corporation or fund)
  - Stocks, bonds, mutual funds, real property, cash value of life insurance, annuities, nonpublicly traded investments, personal and household items, and family-owned/or closely held businesses

Assets That Are Cash and Cash Equivalents

- **Cash, checking and savings accounts, CDs, and money market funds:** Cash equivalent investments provide a return in the form of interest payments. They are typically lower risk than other investment options, such as individual stocks or stock funds, but they also offer a lower return.
  - A savings account is a deposit account held at a bank or other financial institution that provides principal security and a modest interest rate.

- A CD is a savings certificate where you choose a specific amount of time to invest your money, and at the end of that period, you receive your money back along with interest.
- Money market funds are mutual funds that hold a portfolio of high-quality, short-term investments. They pay a variable yield based on the performance of low-risk debt investments and seek to preserve principal. They do not guarantee principal value.
- Security deposits are any cash deposit you give as security for purchasing something or services, such as for an apartment rental, a car or boat lease, a time share, a vacation home, or even a country club membership. Security deposits may also include a retainer you may give to any allied divorce professional, including your divorce attorney.

Practical Tips for Dividing Cash Equivalents

Dividing and transferring these cash-equivalent assets is straightforward.

1. At some point, you will close all joint accounts. Before then, you should know that as a joint account holder, you have full power to withdraw all funds from the joint account. In practice, however, this is rarely a good idea if not completely disclosed to or approved in advance by your spouse. You do not want to be perceived as "cleaning out the bank accounts" during divorce. Some states prohibit a spouse from withdrawing funds from joint accounts while a divorce action is pending.
2. You can withdraw half the money in each account and deposit it into a new individual account in your name, unless your state prohibits withdrawals during pendency of an action. By opening this new account, you establish your financial identity, and you can put your money where it isn't accessible to anyone but you.
3. If you are concerned about money sitting in joint accounts, look to see how the account is titled; i.e., John "and" Mary Doe or John "or" Mary Doe. The differentiation is important between "and" and "or." Most banks will only freeze all outgoing activity (withdrawals, automatic debit payments, wires, transfers, etc.) in the accounts labeled "and"; the bank will make sure they do not allow any transactions without authorization from both you *and* your spouse. Although not 100-percent foolproof because banks make errors, this is a good tactic to prevent your money from being wired out to a foreign country if your spouse lives overseas.
4. Another option is to close all joint accounts and deposit your money into one frozen account, such as an "escrow account," which an officer of the bank is assigned to monitor or which your divorce attorney holds in your name. Your spouse must consent and the bank officer or attorney must give written authorization before any transaction may be conducted involving the account.

Assets That Are Lending Investments (a receivable from lending your money to someone else)

Lending is where you are owed money by someone else. You can make loans to another person or a business. There is always a risk of nonpayment, and collection efforts can be very expensive.

The best way to protect yourself against default or late payments is to secure your loan with a contract. It can be in the form of a personal loan agreement, an installment note, or a promissory note. You have legal remedies you can use to collect the debts you are owed, including small claims court, debt collectors, debt settlement agreements, and attorneys.

You must include all the details of debts owed to you or your spouse by friends, family, customers, business colleagues, or third parties. Make a list of the amount of the loan, to whom it was made (including addresses), the date of the loan, and any interest rate attached to each loan.

Practical Tips for Dividing Lending Investments

1. You need to assess how probable it is to collect on this debt.
2. Determine if there are there sufficient other assets to offset the amount of the debt when dividing marital estate.
3. Consider if it is important for you to keep this debt to avoid negatively impacting your personal relationships with friends or family.

Assets That Are Ownership Investments (a share or interest in a business corporation or fund)

As the term implies, you invest in something, and in exchange for your investment, you own a piece of the entity. There are many different kinds of securities and investments that you can own, and each type has its particular risk and reward.

Ownership investments are the most volatile and profitable class of investment. Ownership investments will fluctuate with market conditions, potentially giving you a higher rate of return than what you might receive from cash equivalents or from lending your money.

The following are examples of ownership investments that are publicly traded financial accounts:

- **Bonds** are a type of debt. You can think of a bond itself as a sort of IOU because when you buy a bond, you're lending money to a government, city, town, or corporation. In return, you receive specified interest payments and the value of the bond, known as the principal, when it matures or comes due.

Being a bondholder is often considered safer than being a shareholder because if a company fails (liquidates its assets), it must pay its bondholders before it pays its shareholders. Bonds are traded throughout the day; if you hold the bond until its maturity, you will receive par value (100 percent face value of the bond).

- **Stocks** are shares of ownership in a company. When you buy a stock, you are purchasing a share of a company and are a shareholder. You have a claim to a part of the corporation's assets and earnings, which are reflected in the value of the stock. A stock can be issued by a publicly traded company or a privately held company.

  The stock will increase or decrease in value depending on how well the company performs, the overall market conditions, and many other factors. Publicly traded stocks are traded throughout the day, so prices fluctuate continually. Privately held stocks change hands in private, unpublished transactions. There are critical differences between public and private stocks, and both carry vastly different risks.
- **Mutual funds** are a type of investment security that enables investors to pool their money together into one professionally managed investment. Mutual funds are "baskets of securities," and they can invest in dozens or hundreds of stocks, bonds, cash, and other assets. These underlying security types, called *holdings,* combine to form one mutual fund, also known as a *portfolio.*

  Mutual funds are attractive to investors because they are widely diversified and professionally managed. As an investor, you have a share ownership in the entire mutual fund, not in the underlying individual securities. Mutual funds trade only once a day, and the price for the shares of the mutual fund is determined after the close of the markets.
- **Exchange-traded funds (ETFs)** comprise a single investment that holds a basket of securities (such as stocks and bonds), trades like a stock (versus a mutual fund), and tracks an index. You have a share ownership in the entire ETF fund, not in the underlying individual securities. You can buy or sell ETF shares (like a stock) anytime throughout the trading day, and prices will fluctuate depending on the market.

Practical Tips for Dividing Publicly Traded Investments

1. Contact your broker, advisor, or financial officer immediately to give notice of your impending divorce.
2. Request that no cash, stocks, or other holdings be moved or transferred without the knowledge and written approval of both you and your spouse.

   Be sure to ask for their written confirmation of your request via email or fax because any transactions can happen in a split second. If they cannot put in place these restrictions on individual accounts, then at a minimum, you should make them aware of the future legal action to divorce. If you suspect any unusual activity in the personal accounts, you and your divorce attorney can obtain historical statements to understand any activity better and trace money flows. If you are concerned about actively managing the account, you might want to specify instructions for what the broker should or should not do to engage in normal transactions.

3. Ask about charges and fees for dividing accounts and securities positions, which can be quite significant.
   a. Brokerage accounts:
      i. Transactions fees: If you want cash from an account, have the securities liquidated before dividing the account. By doing this, transactions fees are shared proportionally between you and your spouse. There will be tax consequences and these will apply to the account owner before any transfers occur up until the date of divorce.
      ii. Ask if there are any fees for transferring securities or cash to your new account (either held with the same broker or to another institution).
      iii. Margin loan: Ask if there are any margin loans outstanding. How much is the value of your share of the account reduced by this loan? How much interest will be charged to your share of the account? Will your spouse assume full amount of margin loan? Do you want or have to pay down any security margin loan?
      iv. Additional borrowing: Do you want to make sure your spouse cannot initiate or increase a margin loan with the broker to withdraw cash, profits, or stocks?
      v. Ask if there are any overdraft lines attached to the account. How will any outstanding balance be allocated between you and your spouse?
   b. Mutual funds:
      i. Do you own a load mutual fund? This fund has a sales charge or commission. You could pay the load up front (front-end load) when purchased, when the shares are sold (back-end), or pay for as long as you own the fund (a level load). The "load" is what compensates whoever sold you this mutual fund.
      ii. Redemption fees: You may incur financial charges for dropping below a fund's minimal balance level and triggering a redemption fee. The general mutual fund company practice is to use a 90-day holding period—although some extend as much as a year—for a redemption fee to discourage in and out trading by investors. Any fund shares sold prior to 90 days after an initial purchase in the fund would be, for example, subject to a 1-percent charge. Be sure you are aware if you want cash instead of the mutual fund.
4. Other strategic considerations for how individual and joint accounts are handled during divorce include:
   i. Managing investments: Do you want to permit ongoing active management of your investments by your spouse if she or he has been doing so continuously?
   ii. What would you like to have in place if there is volatility in the markets?
   iii. Are there any kinds of limits you want to put on the type of investment decisions or transactions?

5. Your new account:
   i. Do you have an individual account open with the same institution?
   ii. Do you need to open an individual account elsewhere?
   iii. Are you ready to receive your share from dividing the accounts?
6. Transfer instructions:
   i. Do you and your spouse agree on the transfer instructions for your bank and broker?
   ii. Are you clearly identifying what asset should be transferred?
   iii. Who initiates and monitors the transfers and deposits?

Other Types of Ownership Investments

Real Property

Real property includes the marital home, vacation home, raw land, investment property, buildings, and rental properties purchased during the marriage as well as any mortgages. In Chapter 11, I specifically discuss the marital home and all related financial and tax issues for how to handle the decision of whether to keep, sell, or transfer it in divorce.

Your primary residence (i.e., your marital home) should be appraised by an expert as to its fair market value so that you can determine the equity value in your home. The marital home you live in fills your need for shelter and security. It also represents prosperity, and although it may appreciate over time, one typically does not purchase a house with an expectation of profit.

Houses, apartments or other dwellings and real property that you buy to rent out, repair, resell, or develop are investments. There are many strategies for investing in real estate: "flipping" properties for profit, purchasing property with the intent to hold onto it for many years, etc. When you invest in real estate, you are taking your money out of your liquid financial assets (stocks, bonds, CDs, and cash) and investing it in a very illiquid asset.

> ⓘ **Tip:** People will invest in real estate to make a profit, cash flow, or both. Assess your goals and make sure you always have some reserve cash.

Practical Tips for Dividing Real Property Investments

1. Determining which spouse gets the marital residence is a major issue (see Chapter 10). If children are involved, usually a judge will grant the home to the primary custodial parent for consistency sake of the children's routines and school. This preference is not always the case but is fairly typical.
2. If your house is determined to be joint marital property, you cannot force your spouse to leave without obtaining an order of exclusive possession from the court.
3. You should consider if the value of equity in real estate should be adjusted for potential taxes and sales commissions related to any sale (imminent or anticipated).

4. You and your spouse have to agree on how upkeep and repairs to the property will be paid for during the divorce.
5. Disposition of investment property (income-generating real estate) is a complicated issue. The way you and your spouse own it (hold the deed), variations in state law, and changes in tax law can all affect the valuation of this property.
   a. While your divorce is pending, all rental income should be deposited to a dedicated property management account and not used by either you or your spouse. Monies should be withdrawn only to pay property expenses upon notice to both you and your spouse. However, this is often a simplistic strategy and, realistically, most of the time one spouse has complete control and income is applied to pay expenses.
   b. Valuing rental property extends beyond the equity and includes the cash flow, potential for appreciation in value, and tax-sheltered depreciation benefits of property ownership. An accountant can assign a value to the property based on its overall benefits for you to utilize in divorce.
   c. If you own marital rental property that has no equity, you should consult with your divorce attorney and tax advisor to determine the best course of action.
   d. Courts in all states have the power to divide any leases, even if it is in your name alone. If you don't want your lease, the best option is for you to negotiate directly with the landlord or find out the cost of breaking it and communicate it to your divorce attorney. If a landlord refuses to remove your ex-spouse's name from a lease, you can offer a "hold harmless" clause in your divorce agreement to alleviate your spouse's worry and to protect them in the event of damage to the property.

Cash Surrender Value of Life Insurance

This applies to "whole life," "universal life," and "variable life" insurance policies. It does not apply to "term" insurance. You can find out what kind of insurance you have by examining the most recent premium statement or the policy. If you don't have either, call the insurance company or broker and ask if any policies have a cash value.

Cash-value life insurance is a type of life insurance policy that pays out upon the policyholder's death and also accumulates value during the policyholder's lifetime. With cash-value policies, policyholders can use the cash value in a variety of ways, such as:

- A tax-sheltered investment or savings (cash value grows on a tax-deferred basis);
- A means to pay policy premiums later in life (and also perhaps you add to your death benefit); and
- A benefit you can pass on to your heirs.

If you are the owner of the policy, you may be able to borrow from cash value at lower interest rates than a traditional bank loan. You are not obligated to pay it back since you are borrowing from yourself. However, any money you do borrow, plus interest, will be deducted from the death benefit when you die.

You may have the option to withdraw all or some of your cash value. Check first to know the impact of any cash withdrawal you make. You could chip away at your death benefit or even wipe it out altogether depending on your policy and the size of your cash value. Some policies reduce the death benefit dollar for dollar with each withdrawal; others may reduce the death benefit by an amount greater than the amount you withdraw. If you fully cash out and surrender your policy, you will receive accrued cash value less any surrender fees or charges.

ⓘ **Tip:** In divorce, you have to be aware of any loans or withdrawals taken out against the cash value to be sure you know what the actual current death benefit is.

Practical Tips for Dividing Cash-Value Life Insurance

1. Ask your divorce attorney how to assess a value to the insurance policy—is it based on any separate premarital contributions, the current cash value, total premiums paid, or other factors?
2. Consider the real "value" of your policy:
   a. A whole life policy pays dividends, and this rate may be more attractive than a typical bond portfolio.
   b. If you liquidate this policy, can you replace it? Are you or your spouse still insurable based on your current age and health status?
3. Before liquidating a policy to satisfy equitable distribution, consider a 1035 exchange, which allows the insured to "roll" the cash value of a life insurance policy into an annuity without any immediate tax consequence. This rollover may be an attractive alternative investment.
4. Do not name minor children as beneficiaries on the life insurance policy. This error is far too common. Any death benefits paid out with this designation will be placed in an UGMA account for a minor child. If a custodian is not listed on the account form, a court will appoint one—and it doesn't have to be the surviving parent. More troublesome is that the child will have unrestricted access to the account when they attain majority age.
5. Decide who should own the life insurance policy. Should it be you, your ex-spouse, someone else, or a trust? Most divorce agreements do not take into account any estate planning considerations for removing the life insurance proceeds from the estate of the deceased to save taxes. Tax savings can be accomplished with an irrevocable life insurance trust, which will own the policy. If the concern is not estate taxes but control, you could allow the non-moneyed spouse to be both the owner and beneficiary, where the moneyed spouse pays the premiums.
6. If you are not the policy owner, you must require proof of the existence and good standing of the life insurance at least annually; get permission from your ex-spouse to allow the provider to communicate with you at your request.

7. Courts routinely require a payor of spousal support, child support, or college expenses to hold life insurance for as long as the obligation to pay support continues. This requirement must be considered before liquidating any life insurance policy.

Annuities

You or your spouse may own an annuity outright or as an element of your retirement plan. Annuities play an integral role in portfolio diversification and can provide income for those approaching retirement. In retirement, an annuity guarantees risk-free retirement income.

However, in divorce, annuities can also be the black sheep of the marital pie. First, let's define what an annuity is. Annuities were designed to be a reliable means of securing a steady cash flow for an individual during retirement years and to reduce fears of outliving one's assets. An annuity is a legal contract that binds an insurance company to provide guaranteed periodic payments to the annuitant for a particular period or lifetime.

Annuities come in all shapes and sizes. Each annuity contract varies among provider companies, and each has its set of rules. Each annuity contract specifies the structure (variable or fixed rate), any penalties for early withdrawal, surrender period, spousal provisions such as a survivor clause, death benefit, etc. Some are in retirement plans, and some are not; some have living and death benefits, others do not. Some are deferred or immediate, and some are nonqualified or qualified.

The complexity of the nature of annuities makes this asset very complicated to divide or value for purposes of equitable distribution in divorce. Unfortunately, annuities are not like other marital assets, which can be divided readily between both spouses. Divorce attorneys may not understand the impact of dividing annuities.

⚠ **Caution:** There can be significant risks with changing an original annuity contract, and there can be disastrous tax consequences if the annuity is not divided properly pursuant to a divorce. You could suffer lasting damage.

A starting point is to know if you own a *qualified or nonqualified annuity*. A nonqualified annuity is funded with after-tax dollars, which means there is no tax deduction for deposits into the contract. You have already paid taxes on the money you put in. When you take money out, each withdrawal will have two parts—some will be part of your original deposit (the principal), and the balance will be earnings (appreciation). Only the earnings will be taxed on withdrawal.

A nonqualified annuity is not governed by federal Employee Retirement Income Security Act (ERISA) laws; thus, splitting it does not require a QDRO. A QDRO is a judicial order in the United States that is entered as part of a property division in a divorce or legal separation and that splits a retirement plan or pension plan of the employee spouse and awards it to their ex-spouse.

A qualified annuity is like an IRA. You deposit money into the contract, and it is tax deductible; withdrawals are 100-percent taxable. Qualified annuities are also used in connection with tax-advantaged qualified retirement plans, such as defined benefit pension plans and 401K and 403b plans (e.g., tax sheltered annuities for teachers). If held in a qualified retirement plan, a QDRO will be required for dividing it in divorce.

When you divide any annuity, you can receive, at most, the benefits of the existing contract, nothing more. You need to read the annuity contract to know if you can get a lump sum, cash-out, or rollover to an IRA. Moreover, there may be drawbacks to dividing annuities in divorce. You should know if limitations are placed on dividing or transferring all or any part of the annuity.

Methods for Dividing an Annuity

An annuity is a complex financial asset that can be irreparably harmed by uninformed parties seeking to divide, transfer, or cash out in divorce. Insurance and investment companies do not make it easy for you to execute terms of your divorce agreement if instructions are unspecific or unclear and contrary to their own policies.

There are four options for dividing an annuity:

1. Take a withdrawal of all or part of the annuity with a direct distribution to you.
2. Accept an amount awarded to you, whether a specific dollar amount or percentage of total contract value, via a direct transfer to your IRA.
3. Have the insurance company take a "withdrawal" from an original contract and then issue two new contracts to you and your ex-spouse; the new contracts will set forth *pro rata* benefits and new account values. This method is preferred by the vast majority of insurance companies because processing new contracts is much easier and less of an administrative burden for the insurance companies.
4. Do not split the annuity but transfer ownership of the contract to one of you, in which case, a whole new contract will go into effect.

With any of these options, the annuitant must authorize the insurance company to split or transfer the annuity, and a QDRO may be required. Before you negotiate how to divide it, you should *always* confirm first with the annuity provider if they will allow an annuity to be split, transferred to a new owner, or pay a lump sum cash-out.

> ⓘ **Tip:** If you split an annuity, then any share of the annuity you receive will not be taxable at the time of transfer in the context of divorce.

Practical Tips for Dividing an Annuity

1. Act early and do your homework to understand your annuity better (call the company and get detailed policy information in writing).
2. Try to offset the annuity with other assets of equivalent value in the property division (you will need proper actuarial valuation).

3. Try not to split the annuity.
4. Explore sharing the income stream from the annuity in the future (if used for income).
5. Know when a QDRO is required to avoid tax disasters upon distribution.
6. If you have to split the annuity, ask what will happen with your new contract and if any adjustments will be made by the insurance company, such as:
   - Interest rate guarantees may be less than the original (favoring the insurance companies).
   - Some companies may treat a withdrawal as a taxable event in the absence of proper and precise instructions in the divorce decree.
   - If a living benefit rider is attached to the policy, a withdrawal will probably reduce both ex-spouses' future guaranteed income. Living benefits are a sort of guaranteed payout while the annuitant is still alive; it is based on the potential to invest more aggressively for growth while maintaining an income-guaranteed payout regardless of prospective investment returns. It is akin to a floor with only an upside. The usual trade-off is the relatively expensive income guaranty comes at the expense of losing or having limited access to principal.
   - If you exceed the lifetime guaranteed minimum withdrawal benefit, it is called an excess withdrawal. A withdrawal of half of the annuity value will be considered an excess withdrawal and will result in a reduction of future guaranteed income.
   - Some contracts also call for an excess withdrawal to reset the living benefit base to the new account value, thereby wiping out any additional benefits earned on the contract to date.
   - Many living benefit designs stop growing the income base at the guaranteed growth rate upon the first withdrawal.
   - The death benefit will likely be reduced *pro rata* by the amount of the withdrawal.
   - Surrender charges may apply to the withdrawal.
   - A new surrender period can be triggered with a new contract (you may have to wait up to 10 years before withdrawing).
   - Separate riders may not be renewed or available in new contracts.

Nonpublicly Traded Investments

Nonpublicly traded investments are investments not offered for sale to the general public. Investors who buy them must meet suitability requirements for income and net worth. Private investments include hedge funds, venture capital, private equity limited partnerships, joint ventures, certain fixed income securities, non-traded real estate investment trusts, and private debt. These "alternative" or private investments gained favor when markets became more volatile and unpredictable; investors seek out different investment opportunities in uncorrelated markets. Most are unregulated by the Securities Exchange Commission.

Valuing these assets is much more complicated and convoluted than the average investment.

Nonpublicly traded investments are deemed to be high-risk investments. They charge high fees (performance, management, acquisition, carried interest, and asset management fees) because they are expected to deliver larger returns than publicly traded securities.

There is no secondary market for nontraded investments—making these investments completely illiquid. Your money can be tied up for a number of years before you are allowed to withdraw it (usually four to seven years on average). You have market risk as there is no guarantee that any of the underlying investments will grow at all, and the odds are that some will even fail or default. Lastly, you may be on call to contribute additional capital in the future or otherwise forfeit all you have invested to date.

In some circumstances, these assets are awarded incident to employment, and this can affect whether they are treated as an asset or as income (sometimes partially as both) and how they can be divided in divorce. The hurdle for an unsophisticated investor is very high for understanding how to invest in these kinds of investments properly.

Practical Tips for Dividing Nonpublicly Traded (Private Equity) Investments

1. Understand if you have a right to redeem your share in the investment. The investment may be open-ended or close-ended, which dictates when money can be withdrawn at certain times throughout the year. There may be a lock-up period when shares cannot be redeemed or sold. Each investment may have a distinct life cycle.
2. Engage a financial expert to obtain an independent objective valuation. Know how the assets are valued. The prices of the underlying mix of direct and indirect ownership shares cannot be readily obtained from quotes or active trading. You need appropriate tools, benchmarks, and specific dates to estimate the value of your share of the investment. For example, the amount listed for a private equity fund on a brokerage statement may be very different than the actual value of the underlying assets due to the conservative accounting policies followed by many funds. Valuations can be speculative.
3. Recognize the tax ramifications. Understand the distribution issues—is it income or a return of principal? Are distributions based on your existing investment or new contributions? What is the tax treatment of earnings and the distribution rights? Investors receive form K-1 on or near tax filing deadlines. As a result, there may be delays and additional costs for your income tax return preparation. There may be foreign taxes due as well if offshore vehicles exist in or outside the investment entity.
4. Assess any investor-specific perks. As an investor, have any fees been waived and have they been deemed additional contributions as new investments? Do you have to "have skin in the game" and always hold some money in it? Are there any clawbacks on your money in anticipation of future obligations or subsequent performance?

5. Understand the nontitled spouse's rights. If shares cannot be transferred, you may be able to participate in this investment in the future through your spouse. Issues to be agreed upon include how you will hold this asset post-divorce, whether you are comfortable with ongoing spousal interaction for making all decisions going forward, how you will control and monitor the asset (i.e., by one or both spouses), who will have access to the books and records of the investment, whether you will each indemnify the other for tax ramifications, and whether you can dictate when and if your share shall be sold or distributed.

Precious Objects

Gold, wine, oriental rugs, Da Vinci paintings, antique watches, and a signed Michael Jordan jersey can all be considered an ownership investment—provided that these are objects that are purchased for investment with the intention of reselling them for a profit. Other objects, such as commodities, precious metals, and collectibles, are also classified as investments. They may carry more uncertainty to value because they have a risk of physical depreciation (damage) and require upkeep and storage costs that cut into future profits.

Vehicles

Vehicles are ownership investments and can be valued in automotive industry Blue Books or by visiting several reputable used car dealers. Leased vehicles may have little value. Contrary to common belief, vehicles and other property are not necessarily granted to the spouse who holds sole title.

Personal Property and Household Items

Dividing personal property and household items such as furniture, photos, sports gear, paintings, kitchenware, silverware, books, and linens, can be a difficult part of the divorce process. However, the vast majority of divorcing couples can sit down together to decide who gets what and not necessarily assign a dollar value to each object. It is best to negotiate directly with your spouse to handle these items because courts do not like getting into these kinds of disputes.

Pets

In the eyes of the law, pets are considered personal property. However, this is becoming much more of a contentious issue in divorce where couples demand determinations of custody and visitation, even support, on behalf of their "fur child." In your state, there may or may not be any statute that specifically treats a pet as personal property or covers how animals are treated when a couple divorces. However, courts recognize this tension between custody and property law when it comes to pets. Couples may fashion agreements covering care and custody of pets, and if a judge finds the agreement fair, he or she will make it a part of the final divorce decree and it will have the force of law.

Practical Tips for Dividing Personal Household Items

1. Make a list and take pictures of your personal assets.
2. Agree on what needs to be appraised.
3. Decide on the logical owner.
4. Account for depreciation or usage—purchase value is difficult to agree to for old furniture or vehicles.
5. Use a mediator or flip a coin to decide who gets what by going down the list. Start with the biggest value items with each of you taking turns.
6. Hold a sale or auction if you cannot agree and divide the proceeds.
7. Moderate your emotions over these items—separate sentiment from economic value. For sentimental items such wedding gifts, photos, and your child's artwork, make copies and split the cost or keep whatever your family gifted to you.

The Family-Owned or Closely-Held Business

Divorce can become very complicated when there is a business that is family owned or closely held by one spouse. A business provides income for the family and is also considered property. The money put into starting and running a business is a financial investment. Funds contributed to, and generated from, the family business may be premarital, marital, or separate in character.

A family business may be one of the biggest marital assets. The value of the business, both now and in the future, must be considered.

You may not have any idea what the business is worth. If the business is small and there is no dispute as to its worth, you and your spouse can agree to a value to be used when dividing marital assets. If the business has a high monetary value or high cash flow, you should hire a business valuation professional.

It is often complicated because the business may be considered both a marital asset (for property division) and a source of income (to determine spousal support payments). One of the most prevalent problems in divorce involving a business or professional practice valuation is "double dipping," which refers to a situation in which one spouse receives double payment for a single asset, once in property division and again in the support award. Courts generally do not allow "double dipping," but others reject the premise and implications for spousal support and equitable distribution being interrelated. The fundamental approach to business valuation is critical to understand.

Business valuation is a process and a set of procedures used to determine the price someone is willing to pay or receive to affect the sale of business. There are three generally accepted valuation methods to give you a dollar value for your business:

- The market approach estimates the business value by comparing your business to one that has recently sold.

- The income approach estimates the business value by converting future economic benefits, such as profits or cash flow, into today's dollar value.
- The asset approach is based on the values of assets and liabilities of the business, including both tangible and intangible assets (such as goodwill).

Often, there are already certain business succession arrangements in place in contemplation of divorce. For well-established family businesses, these may include contractual agreements, trusts, or buy-sell rights that are all carefully designed strategies to protect and minimize the impact of divorce on the business. Courts are not bound to value a business by what any of these agreements may declare.

Unfortunately, many times in divorce, a business valuation becomes a battle of independent experts. It is important to assess the cost–benefit of a business valuation because you will incur expert fees, attorney fees, and court time and fees, as well as your effort to learn and understand the expert's valuation analysis.

ⓘ **Tip:** For a variety of reasons, it is unadvisable for the nonbusiness owner spouse to remain employed or a shareholder in the business with your ex-spouse after divorce.

Practical Tips for Dividing a Family-Owned Business in Divorce

There are three basic options for dividing the business in divorce:

- Co-ownership: Both you and your spouse continue to own and run the business after divorce. If you remain amicable, it may be possible to work together, but this is not common.

⚠ **Caution:** The courts generally "disfavor" ex-spouses continuing to be involved in a family business because it requires ongoing contact and communication between the parties.

- Sell the business and distribute the profits: Most small businesses that are owned jointly by two spouses can be divided without dispute. You use the proceeds to invest in your own business venture, and you terminate ties to one another.
- Buy out the other spouse's interest: You receive the business while your spouse receives financial compensation. Payments from a co-owned business can be made over a specified period to ensure that both spouses gain from any financial success. Or, you could offset the value of the business with other assets allocated to your spouse. If you opt for the buy-out option, it is always a good idea that you have a credible expert value the business.

9 Retirement Assets: What Makes Them Special?

It can be heart-breaking to realize that all the money you saved for retirement and your golden years will be fractured because of divorce. Just like all your other assets accumulated in marriage, your retirement plans and individual retirement accounts may be community property or marital property that is subject to equitable division in a divorce.

For most people, retirement assets are a significant portion of your total assets. For this reason, you must know whether and how to divide a retirement account or interest in a retirement plan in a legal separation, divorce, or other domestic relations proceedings.

What Is a Retirement Plan?

There are two types of employer-sponsored retirement plans: qualified and nonqualified plans; the distinction is the tax treatment. Qualified money is "before-tax" money. Nonqualified is "after-tax" money. Most of us recognize qualified employer-sponsored retirement plans to be either (1) a defined contribution plan (such as a 401K) or (2) a defined benefit plan (a traditional fixed "pension" such as a government employee might receive).

What Are Retirement Accounts?

Usually, this means individual retirement accounts, such as a traditional individual account (IRA), a ROTH IRA, SEP IRA, Simple IRA, or a health savings account (HSA). Individual retirement accounts may or may not be funded with pre-tax money.

Types of Retirement Plans

Qualified Employer Sponsored Retirement Plans

1. *Defined contribution plans'* value fluctuates depending on employee and employer matching contributions, investment gains or losses, loans, and withdrawals. These plans include:

- 401K, 403b, and 457 plans: Employees contribute a portion of salary on a pre-tax basis that may be matched in full or part by the employer. There are limits on salary deferrals. Some employers also offer designated ROTH plan accounts.
- Profit-sharing plans: Employers contribute to the employees' account if the company is profitable based on a fixed or discretionary formula. This formula gives employers and small businesses flexibility and discretion to supplement their employee's accounts.
- Thrift plans: These are similar to 401K plans but are for employees of the federal government, including members of the Armed Forces. Employees contribute a portion of salary on a pre-tax basis that may be matched in full or part by the employer.
- Money purchase plans: These are similar to a 401K plan, but employers are required to contribute a fixed percentage of an employee's salary to his or her account every year.
- Employee stock ownership plans (similar to a profit-sharing plan): Employees can receive regular shares or stock options without paying for them as a benefit for working at the company. These plans are usually formed to provide motivation to employees and stability. When employees leave the company, they receive stock that the company must buy back from them at its fair market value.
- Tax-sheltered annuities: These are similar to a 401K but are for employees of certain nonprofit and public education institutions (schools and universities). Investment options include annuity and variable annuity contracts with life insurance companies.

NOTE: A current account statement will show the value of any of these plans, less any loans outstanding.

2. *Defined benefit plans* are pensions that promise a specified monthly dollar benefit at retirement. The benefit is calculated through a plan formula based on factors such as years of service and salary. Federal insurance protects most traditional pensions and employee benefits.

⚠ **Caution:** These are future benefits to be paid in future years. If you want the value of these future benefits in today's dollars, you need to have a pension valuation expert or actuary calculate it. Do not assume today's value is what the employer provides on the employee's statement of benefits.

Nonqualified Employer-Sponsored Retirement Plans

A nonqualified plan is funded with after-tax money, and you get no up-front tax break. There is no tax deferral benefit. Nonqualified plans are tailored for employers to recruit, motivate, and reward, as well as meet the needs of key executives and other select employees. The contributions made to these plans are usually nondeductible to the employer and are taxable to the employee. However, they allow employees to defer taxation until retirement, presumably when they are in a lower tax bracket.

NOTE: Do not overlook these employee benefits as they can be valuable.

There are four major types of nonqualified retirement plans:

- Deferred compensation plans: The employee's compensation is set aside to be paid in the future (refer to Chapter 10).
- Executive bonus plans (sometimes called IRS Section 612 plans): The employee's bonus is tied to certain benchmarks, and the employer pays the premiums on a permanent life insurance policy owned by the employee. Employees can make additional premium contributions, so cash value builds and provides supplemental income at retirement over and above death benefits.
- Group carve-out plans: The employer offers high-value employees a specialized term and universal life insurance plan that does not expire on retirement, builds cash value, is owned by the employee, and is portable.
- Split-dollar life insurance plans: These are life insurance policies that are shared and split between the company and employee, producing advantages for both. The policy can be shared and allocated in several ways, such as cash value, premiums, death benefits, ownership, and dividends.

Types of Retirement Accounts

Pre-Tax Money Accounts

You contribute pre-tax money, and it grows tax deferred. If you qualify for the IRS deduction, your contribution is deducted from your taxable income, dollar for dollar, in the year of your contribution. If you take money out before age 59 1/2, you may incur a 10-percent early withdrawal penalty. When you take out money for retirement, you pay ordinary income taxes based on your income tax bracket at the time of withdrawal. Contributions, withdrawals, and exceptions are subject to IRS limitations (refer to IRS Publication 590).

- Traditional IRA: Anyone can contribute pretax money up to a certain dollar limit each year, and your money grows tax free. There are limitations to contributions and deductibility if you are covered by a retirement plan at work or if your taxable income exceeds a limit if you file jointly with your spouse who has a retirement plan at work.
- Simple IRA: This is a plan that allows small employers (fewer than 100 employees) to set up IRAs and must match or make unmatched contributions for employees up to certain limits.

- SEP IRA: This kind of account is primarily used by self-employed or small business owners. As an employer, you can deduct up to 25 percent of your income or up to a dollar limit set annually by the IRS.
- Solo 401K: A sole proprietor can set up an individual 401K and make contributions as both the employee and employer, up to a total dollar limit set annually by the IRS.
- Health Savings Account HSA: Those with high-deductible health insurance plans can save money tax-free in an HSA. You can contribute up to a dollar limit annually as an individual or family. You can withdraw money and not pay taxes on the withdrawal, from the HSA to pay for allowable medical expenses, and if you don't spend it, it rolls over to the next year. If you don't need it to pay for medical expenses, you can invest it as you would other retirement savings.

These are individual accounts you open on your own at any financial institution (bank, life insurance company, brokerage, or mutual fund company) that provide tax advantages for retirement savings. You do not pay taxes until you withdraw money.

NOTE: The value of any of these individual retirement accounts is what appears on your current statement.

After-Tax Money Retirement Accounts

Recent changes in tax rules have made it more attractive to contribute or increase after-tax contributions to retirement savings. Contributions are not tax deductible in your savings year but grow tax-free. Tax-free withdrawals help reduce your taxable income when reaching retirement. Contributions, withdrawals, and exceptions are subject to IRS limitations (refer to IRS Publication 590).

- A ROTH IRA is an individual retirement account that is funded with after-tax money up to a certain dollar limit each year, and your money grows tax-free. You can convert traditional IRA funds to a ROTH IRA by paying income tax on any account balance being converted.
- A solo ROTH 401K can be set up by a sole proprietor who can make contributions as both the employee and employer up to a total dollar limit set annually by the IRS.
- An annuity is a long-term insurance product that that provides a combination of protection and tax deferral that pays out income in retirement.

Dividing Qualified Retirement Plans

All retirement plans must conform to rules and comply with federal regulations. The type of retirement plan—a qualified, nonqualified, or individual retirement account—determines which rules apply to how they will be divided in a divorce.

 **NOTE:** A separate legal term applies to each kind of asset division.

Valuing and dividing qualified employer retirement plans is not simple. Retirement plans are complicated and have long-term consequences. Some retirement plans may require an expert who can value them in present value dollars if a divorcing spouse prefers to offset (or trade) the value of the retirement plan with other marital assets. You must pay close attention to successfully dividing retirement assets and avoiding common errors.

ⓘ **Tip:** A QDRO is the legal order for allocating interests in a qualified retirement plan. You will need an attorney who specializes in dividing qualified retirement plans. Many divorce attorneys don't wish to test the strength of their malpractice coverage by dabbling in them.

Features of retirement plans vary enormously. Even when two plans with the same employer look similar, they may have different benefits and terms. For example, one plan may allow for a lump sum payout, while another may not. One may have annual adjustments for inflation, while another has fixed payments. Under the law, you are a beneficiary with the right to receive such information.

It is your responsibility to carefully read the policy plans to understand the key advantages and financial factors of each. Only then can you compare assets and be sure you exchange assets of equal value or, if not equal, at least you know the value of what you are exchanging.

Retirement assets are not automatically divided at the time of divorce. You must explicitly ask for a share of these assets and follow specific procedures so the court awards your share to you. You must not wait until later when your ex-spouse retires.

If you have one or more accounts (401K and a pension) to transfer, your settlement agreement must identify and refer to each asset you want to divide. Transfers incident to your divorce are not taxed.

The movement of funds may be executed as either a direct transfer or a direct rollover by the retirement plan custodian. Instructions should be clear to the judge and in your divorce agreement referring to the division of retirement funds. If the transfer of funds is inadequately prepared and executed, you are at risk and may owe both tax and early withdrawal penalties on the entire amount you receive.

What You Need to Get Your Share of Your Ex-Spouse's Benefits: QDRO

Dividing 401K, 403b, and 457 Plans and Pensions

All qualified retirement plans require a QDRO, which "creates or recognizes the existence of an alternate payee's (the receiving spouse's) right to, or assigns to an alternate payee the right to, receive all or a portion of the benefits payable with respect to a participant's benefits payable under the participant's plan."[2] A QDRO provides a mechanism to rollover monies to a new retirement account or for a pension to be paid to an alternate payee. A QDRO is necessary to avoid tax consequences and penalties for withdrawing retirement funds.

A state authority, generally a court, must issue the judgment, order, or decree, or include it as part of the divorce decree, to formally approve the property settlement agreement before it can be a domestic relations order.

QDROs resemble transfers incident to divorce in that they are tax-free transactions as long as they have been reported correctly to the courts and the retirement plan custodians. Any transfer done incorrectly will incur taxes and penalties. You can roll QDRO assets into one or more of:

- ❑ Your own qualified retirement plan,
- ❑ A traditional IRA, or
- ❑ A ROTH IRA (if permissible).

Timing is critical. Be sure you address all issues related to dividing retirement assets concurrently with the drafting of a QDRO. Begin this process early because it takes time to obtain necessary information from employer plans. You want to negotiate your interests based on complete information.

Some nonqualified retirement plans cannot be divided by QDRO. This does not mean the retirement asset should be ignored when the property division is being negotiated. Before you reach a final resolution and draft your divorce agreement, do your homework! If this information is not available before arriving at a settlement, it is always best to include language that covers such a contingency and offers an alternative way to handle the division of the asset.

You also must determine if there is any outstanding loan against the plan. If there is no loan against the plan, it is important that the settlement includes language that explicitly acknowledges the lack of any loan to protect the nonemployee spouse. If there is a loan against the plan, the parties must determine how the loan was used. If it was used for marital purposes, you both might agree to share the debt. If, however, the loan was used for one party's sole benefit, the loan may be excluded from calculations of the nonemployee's portion. Language should prohibit any further loans from being withdrawn while the QDRO is prepared and processed. Last, it should be noted that loans may not be transferable to a nonemployee spouse.

A QDRO is not a neutral document. It depends on who drafts the document. Certain provisions can be more favorable to one spouse than the other. You must review the content of the QDRO to ensure it reflects your understanding of your share of benefits before it is certified as a legal order. Your oversight eliminates the person drafting the QDRO from guessing or making choices in the drafting that benefit one spouse over the other. QDROs typically take about 60 to 90 days to implement, meaning the time from the date the administrator of the qualified

2 ERISA § 206(d)(3)(B)(i); IRC § 414(p)(1)(A)

retirement plan receives the QDRO to the date the nonemployee spouse receives the retirement benefit. A QDRO cannot become a court order until the date of judgment, at the earliest.

A QDRO must include detailed and accurate information regarding how and when to divide retirement assets, including employer institution, account numbers, percentage or dollar amount to be transferred, and names of (sending/receiving) financial custodians for each retirement asset. It is necessary to incorporate all provisions of both state and federal laws that pertain to the division of the qualified retirement asset.

Ideally, you include provisions regarding retirement benefits in your divorce agreement and have the court certify the QDRO at the same time the decree of divorce is entered. You and your ex-spouse must determine how you each will share any earnings or losses between the date of division and the date the funds are finally divided. Between these dates, values fluctuate, and you want to be sure you understand this to avoid litigation after the divorce.

⚠ **Caution:** Timing is also crucial. If your funds are transferred before your divorce is final, you are at risk and will be subject to taxes and penalties if younger than 59-1/2.

Getting Cash Out of Retirement Assets Without Penalty

Participants in retirement plans who take money out of a plan or IRA early will usually incur charges, ordinary income taxes, and early withdrawal penalties (if before retirement age). Annuities may impose surrender charges on top of penalties and taxes. In simple terms, you need to decide if you need money so badly that you must effectively cash out your interest in retirement savings.

However, if you need cash and have to get it from retirement assets, you have a unique opportunity only when you divorce to avoid early withdrawal penalties with proper planning. This choice can be especially helpful if you want to pay expenses, pay down debt, have emergency funds, or have cash for a down payment on a major purchase, such as a new house.

IRS Rule 72 (t)

Under IRS Rule 72 (t), if you are the alternate payee (receiving the distribution), you can pull cash out of a retirement account and avoid the 10-percent penalty for early withdrawal if you are under 59-1/2. The withdrawal of cash from the retirement plan must be written into your divorce agreement and explicitly specified in any QDRO. The withdrawals, however, are still taxed at your ordinary income rate.

EXAMPLE: You withdraw $50,000 in cash from your ex-spouse's 401K plan pursuant to divorce via a QDRO, which specifies that cash is to be paid to you. You will NOT pay a penalty of 10 percent × $50,000 = $5,000, but you

WILL pay income taxes (federal and state) on the $50,000. Assume federal tax of 25 percent plus state tax of 6.95 percent = 31.95 percent × $50,000 = $15,975 in income taxes due to government. You will end up with $50,000 less $15,975 = $34,025 net.

⚠ **Caution:** After your divorce, if you make withdrawals from your retirement accounts before age 59-1/2, you will be subject to a penalty of 10 percent and ordinary income taxes.

Dividing Pensions

A pension is a qualified retirement plan, also called a defined benefit plan, that pays a monthly benefit to the employee spouse after retirement. The benefit is usually calculated using a formula based on years of service and highest final average salary. This benefit is paid when the employee reaches his or her normal retirement age for a payout term often elected before retirement. The employee spouse (the plan participant) and the nonemployee spouse (the alternate payee) should both agree to the election to preserve their share.

A QDRO is required to divide a pension. Most defined benefit plans will not pay out a lump sum; however, you should read the plan documents carefully to see if this is a possibility. As the alternate payee (nonplan participant), you must abide by all of the terms of the plan. The earliest you can begin to receive your share of your ex-spouse's pension is his or her "earliest retirement age." In some cases, your commencement of benefits is only available when your ex-spouse retires.

Most plans use the separate interest approach to dividing benefits. Using this type of QDRO, your share as alternate payee is actuarially adjusted and payable over your lifetime. This calculation means that your future monthly payout of the pension, even if equally divided, will be adjusted in an amount based on your lifetime expectancy. Your benefits are protected even if your ex-spouse dies after benefits have commenced.

If you are the employee and plan participant, using this approach you will have the right to designate any new spouse as beneficiary to receive survivor benefits relative to the remainder portion of your pension.

Alternatively, QDROs can be drafted for a shared interest approach. By using a shared approach, if your ex-spouse dies after benefits begin, you as alternate payee could receive the entire pension amount (his or her share plus yours), or, depending upon the pension plan, the alternate payee's payment could end.

Finally, under most plans, the death of the employee before the commencement of benefits would cause the pension to be forfeited, and the only benefit payable might be a qualified preretirement survivor annuity (if this is available).

How Is Your Share of the Pension Calculated?

Most courts say that only the "marital portion of the qualified pension" can be divided at divorce. This statement means only the pension benefits accumulated during the marriage count as marital property. If you and your spouse were married all of the time she or he worked under the pension plan, then the entire pension would normally be marital property. But if you were married for only part of your spouse's career under the pension plan, then only that part is marital property.

⚠ **Caution:** Some states do not necessarily differentiate between the part of a pension earned before and the part of the pension earned after the marriage.

Professionals use a number of different ways of figuring the marital property portion of the pension. One of the simpler methods often used by courts and divorce attorneys negotiating property settlements is called the *time rule.*

The time rule says the marital property portion of the pension is equal to a certain fraction of your spouse's pension benefit. The top number in the fraction is the number of years your spouse worked under the plan during your marriage. The bottom of the fraction is the total number of years your spouse worked under the plan for the employer. Your share is multiplied by this fraction. A share may be expressed as a dollar amount or as a percentage.

EXAMPLE: Dollar amount (where monthly benefit is known)

Wife's share: 50 percent
Husband's monthly pension benefit: $200
Married: 16 years
Worked under plan: 20 years
50 percent × (16/20) × $200 = **$80** (Wife's share of the future monthly benefit)

EXAMPLE: Percentage amount (where monthly benefit may not be known)

50 percent × (16/20) = 50 percent × 80 percent = **40 percent** of the future monthly benefit

Dividing IRA Accounts

IRAs are divided using a process known as "incident to divorce." A transfer may be made to your spouse if it is pursuant to a decree of divorce or a written instrument incident to divorce (such as a separation agreement). A Letter of Instruction and a copy of the Final Judgment or Settlement Agreement is often sufficient to transfer funds from an IRA in divorce. You do not need a QDRO to divide IRAs.

If your divorce judgment specifically orders your ex-spouse to make a transfer from their IRA to your IRA, you will not pay any taxes or penalties on the separation transaction. The movement of funds is classified either as a direct transfer (trustee to trustee) or a direct rollover by your ex-spouse's IRA custodian to you.

ⓘ **Tip:** Either you or your spouse can initiate the IRA transfer. Either you "pull" it as a request from your IRA account institution to his, or he "pushes" it to you from his IRA institution.

However, if your divorce decree fails to label your division correctly as such, your ex-spouse will owe both taxes and early withdrawal penalties on the entire amount that you receive. You will lose out on the tax-advantage nature of the funds and face the challenge of recouping the loss of this financial benefit from your ex-spouse.

It is almost always ill-advised to take a direct distribution from a retirement plan or IRA. However, if you do, you only have 60 days to roll it over to your IRA or retirement plan before you pay taxes and penalties. With an indirect rollover, the sending financial institution may withhold 20 percent for taxes. When you then roll the funds over to your IRA, you will need to deposit an amount equal to the taxes withheld; if you don't, the amount may be treated as an early distribution.

⚠ **Caution:** You must provide clear sending and receiving instructions to IRA custodians as well as satisfy your state laws.

ⓘ **Tip:** You do not need a QDRO to divide an IRA because IRAs are not subject to ERISA.

⚠ **Caution:** Many divorce attorneys and courts confuse the distinction in dividing IRAs and qualified plans by labeling both types of divisions as QDROs. This mistake can complicate and impede the transfer of these assets.

Dividing Nonqualified Retirement Plans

Nonqualified retirement plans can almost never be divided or assigned to anyone other than the employee. These plans will usually not accept a QDRO. These plans routinely contain provisions that specifically prohibit them from making payments directly to a former spouse regardless of what any court order instructs.

Do Not Dismiss Nonqualified Plans

Do not neglect to ask about or overlook nonqualified plans because:

- These benefits are often substantial components of the marital estate.
- Certain trigger events may affect these benefits; for example, your ex-spouse's plan may include certain dates or events that trigger immediate vesting or payout of these plans, and they can be divided and shared with you.

NOTE: You may be "tied" to your ex-spouse post-divorce for a long period of time in your effort to secure your share of these benefits, which are most likely nontransferable.

In conclusion, retirement assets can be defined contribution plans, defined benefit plans, pensions, individual retirement accounts, or some form of hybrid nonqualified retirement plans. These plans are all vastly different and have different implications for dividing them.

Knowing the type of plan and benefit that can be divided will help you ascertain if you desire it, if it can be paid out as a lump sum or as a future stream of cash, or if it is forfeitable (at risk). If QDROs are required, determine if you can minimize the number of qualified plans to divide to reduce the costs and inconvenience of transferring money from each and every account.

Know what is not transferable and how you will deal with offsetting its value, or, if you choose to assume a payout risk for nontransferable assets in the future on an "if, as, and when basis."

Practical Tips for Your QDRO

1. Include in your divorce agreement the type of retirement plan you are dividing (qualified or nonqualified benefit plan, defined contribution or defined benefit plan). Include the full and correct name of your account and the plan.
2. Describe how you will be receiving your benefit (lump sum at time of divorce or in the future, payments now or in the future beginning on a set date.
3. Find out FIRST if you can rightly divide the plan—mistakes are made when you do not know if a plan can be divided. If it is nonqualified, find out if it can be divided; if not, include specific language for how the participant will share benefits with you. If it is a nonqualified plan, most do not offer survivor benefits, and this is critical to identify and address during negotiations. You might want to negotiate a credit against other assets.
4. Set a definite date for dividing the accounts. It helps to pick a date as close as possible to the date of divorce—for practical purposes, it is easiest to pick the first day or last day of the month because it is easier to get an account statement and account value as of that date.
5. Address investment gains/losses and interest/dividends only for defined contributions plans and individual accounts. Values fluctuate over time, and this affects the balance to be divided. You must indicate if you want a fixed dollar amount (plus gains/losses) or a fluctuating amount (percent of total). This approach is nonapplicable for defined benefit plans.
6. Do not neglect survivor benefits regarding defined benefit plans. This oversight is one of the most litigated areas in QDROs.
7. Do not attempt to equalize dissimilar types of retirement assets. It is nearly impossible to accomplish the task since equalizing values as of a particular date may or may not fluctuate for all plans until distribution. Do not attempt to equalize defined contribution plans and defined benefit plans. Do not try to equalize traditional IRAs and ROTH IRAs. It might be better to offset any differences in values from other assets.

8. Identify from which account you will make the distribution to equalize the retirement values.
9. Do not overlook any loan balances—make sure you know if there is a loan against any account and if a loan exists, track any recurring payments made to the account during the pendency of the divorce and subsequent period. Loan balances must be recognized to avoid confusion about the value determination when the QDRO is implemented.
10. Always state who the QDRO attorney is, the date by which they have to be engaged, and how they will be paid.
11. Have a process in place for you to stay in contact with the plan administrator—years from now when you are entitled to your share of benefits; they will need to know how to pay you and where to reach you. Make sure you let them know how to contact you and keep you aware of the status of the retirement benefits.

What Happens to Your Share If Your Ex-Spouse Becomes Ineligible to Receive the Pension?

If your former spouse stops receiving his or her pension for whatever reason, you may be unable to receive the benefits you expected. This contingency might happen if your ex-spouse waives his or her pension to receive another, greater benefit from a different plan or retirement system or, after being retired for several years, he or she decides to return to work for the previous employer who stops paying the pension in the meantime.

If you are negotiating a property settlement that includes a pension benefit, be sure to include a provision in which your ex-spouse agrees not to take any action that would reduce or eliminate your pension benefit and that if she or he does, you will be compensated for your loss.

Garnishing Pensions for Support

If your former spouse stops paying court-ordered child support or spousal support, his or her pension plan might be demanded to pay you what is owed. This order is done by a legal procedure often called a "garnishment" or "attachment." Federal law expressly permits certain retirement benefits to be garnished when child support or spousal support payments are overdue. Typically, you need your attorney to ask a state domestic relations court to issue a garnishment order.

Special Attention to Military Pensions

Get a specialist to help you if you are attempting to divide or garnish a military pension division. A military pension is divisible just like any other pension and is treated as marital or separate property in every state. A state court must have jurisdiction over the military member to be allowed to divide member's retired pay. Finding the right court can be a challenge for military families who move frequently.

It is a common misperception to believe you can only divide military retired pay if the marriage lasted at least 10 years. A state court has the discretion to award a share of the military pension to a former spouse of a military member regardless of the length of the marriage. However, if a former spouse wants to receive a *direct payment* from the Department of Defense, the former spouse must have been married to the military member for at least 10 years, with at least 10 years of the marriage overlapping a period of military service creditable to retired pay. This is called the 10:10 overlap rule, and it can be confusing. The 10:10 overlap is not necessary for child support or alimony garnishment.

If the former spouse is receiving spousal support or child support in addition to the division of the military retired pay, the former spouse cannot receive by direct payment any more than 50 percent to 65 percent of the military retired pay. Disability pay is not subject to division as property, but it is subject to garnishment for alimony or child support.

10 What Is a Contingent Interest in the Marital Estate?

Defining a Contingent Interest

A contingent interest is an asset or liability that refers to a future interest that is uncertain and largely depends upon the happening of a future event only if specific conditions occur. By definition, the final calculation of the value of a contingent asset or liability cannot be determined with certainty until the actual occurrence of a future event.

In divorce, the recognition of contingent assets and liabilities represents one of the more difficult and unique issues to resolve. Contingent interests can be problematic when you do not have a value until long after the date of divorce. Circumstances call for different remedies, including the apportionment of value on an "if, as, and when basis."

- Contingent assets include:
  - Accrued sick and vacation pay
  - Accrued bonuses
  - Contractual rights to receive a contingent fee related to employment
  - Stock options, restricted stock, phantom stock, and stock appreciation rights (all contingent upon equity compensation plans and/or on remaining employed with a company)
  - Prospective inheritances (what you expect to inherit or what you expect your spouse to inherit)
  - Expectancy of gifts
  - Interests in trusts
  - Impending lawsuits (your side is plaintiff)
  - Life estates in the future
  - Future commissions or fees
- Contingent liabilities include:
  - Unpaid taxes and tax deficiencies
  - Repossession of marital property
  - Debts managed by another party
  - Medical bills
  - Civil lawsuits (your side is defendant)
  - Environmental costs
  - Earn-out payments

How Is a Contingent Interest Treated in Divorce?

In general, community property states will evenly divide contingent assets and liabilities. In equitable distribution states, attention is focused on what the asset or liability represents.

ⓘ **Tip:** If you are involved in a lawsuit and a divorce, be sure you know what the potential award represents. The nature of the award may determine how it will be allocated in divorce.

Contingent assets are potential financial awards that can be marital or nonmarital property. For example, if the contingent interest is a lawsuit and the damages are for lost wages or past earning capacity during the marriage, the proceeds will be considered a marital asset. If the award does not specify what the damages represent and it is made to both of you, probably the entire award will be marital property.

However, in divorce, some marital awards arising from lawsuits are not subject to division. Compensation for future losses or pain and suffering are treated as nonmarital assets in a divorce and belong to one spouse only. If each of you is awarded amounts separately in the judgment, the separate amounts will be considered nonmarital assets.

Contingent liabilities are potential debts where a party's responsibility has yet to be determined. At the time you and your spouse are divorced, you may have pending situations where the outcome will depend upon future events, leaving you unable to determine for sure the amount you will owe or even whether you will owe anything at all.

Contingent liabilities create problems when deciding how to divide marital property and debts because they can alter a party's financial position months or years after the divorce case is closed. In some states, even a separate debt—one incurred before marriage begins or after it ends—can affect how a court divides marital property and debts.

The amount of contingent liability for debts also influences a party's ability to pay or the need to receive spousal or child support. Other assets may be more identifiable and tangible for valuation purposes, such as various kinds of deferred compensation.

ⓘ **Tip:** It is important to resolve as many contingent liabilities as possible before finalizing your divorce.

What about Contingent Assets Related to Deferred Compensation?

In many professions, *contingent compensation* is a significant part of the total compensation for an individual. Contingent or deferred compensation simply means that the employee's receipt of compensation is delayed until a future date.

Typically, there are two general types of deferred compensation plans:

- Elective deferral plans (where the employee elects to defer) and
- Supplemental benefit plans (where the employer makes a binding agreement to pay supplemental compensation).

Forms of deferred compensation include bonuses, stock options, restricted stock, restricted stock units, stock performance units, stock appreciation rights, and phantom stock. These assets come with a variety of performance, vesting, transferability, tax, and assignment rights all related to current and future employment by the employee spouse.

⚠ **Caution:** Most deferred compensation plans do not show up on tax returns, W-2 forms, or other financial documentation until the awards vest, are exercised, or are paid. This lack of visibility means you need to perform full discovery with the employer.

Components of Deferred Compensation

- Bonuses: Cash or a cash equivalent is given in addition to an employee's regular compensation.
- Stock options: These are stock options that have been granted to specific employees of a company and give the employee the right, but not the obligation, to buy or sell the stock at an agreed-upon price within a certain vesting period or on a specific date. Stock options are usually nontransferable in divorce.
- Restricted stock: This is stock that has been granted to an executive employee that is nontransferable and subject to forfeiture under certain conditions, such as termination of employment or failure to meet either corporate or individual performance benchmarks. The restricted stock becomes available to the recipient under a graded vesting schedule that lasts several years. Recipients receive dividends and have voting rights on the stock received. When the restricted stock is fully vested, it becomes taxable, and the entire amount of vested stock must be includable as ordinary income in the year of vesting.

ⓘ **Tip:** Shareholders of restricted stock are allowed to report the fair market value of their shares as ordinary income on the date they are granted instead of when they become vested if they so desire under IRS Section 83(b) election. Why is this important? The employee spouse is increasing his or her taxable income based on the current value of this asset (which is not exercisable) and taking the bet that the stock price will later increase. In divorce, income will be overstated, taxes are higher, and stock may be more valuable later as an asset.

- Restricted stock units (RSUs): These are similar to restricted stock, except RSUs represent an unsecured promise by the employer to grant a set number of shares of stock to the employee upon the completion of the vesting schedule. Some plans may allow for cash instead of stock. The employee may or may not receive dividend equivalents. No IRS Section 83(b) election is permitted because the recipient has not received any actual shares until the year of vesting. Typically, these are nontransferable in divorce.

- Stock performance shares: Shares of a company's stock are given to employees only if certain company-wide performance criteria are achieved, such as earnings per share targets, product sales, and product development. The goal of performance shares is to tie managers to the interests of the shareholders. These grants offer companies seeking to align performance with compensation incentives a greater variety than just stock options and restricted stock. They are usually part of long-term incentive plans and are nontransferable. They are taxed at the time of vesting, unless the plan allows the employee to defer until the payment date.
- Stock appreciation rights (SARs): An SAR is a right given to an employee to receive a bonus in cash or shares of stock equal to the appreciation in the company's stock over a specified period. SARs gain in value if the company's stock price rises. They are similar to stock options and vest over time at a set price with an expiration date. The employee is not given any actual stock. SARs do not reflect dividends and stock splits. They are nontransferable and taxed when exercised.
- Phantom stock: Rather than getting physical stock in the company, an employee receives "pretend" stock as a bonus. Even though it is not real, the phantom stock follows the price movement for the company's actual stock, paying out any resulting profits when vested. It can be based on full value of the company's stock or the appreciation only (similar to SARs). Phantom stock may reflect dividends and stock splits. These plans are used primarily by closely held corporations and sometimes are called "golden handcuffs" to discourage employees from leaving the company. They are nontransferable and not tax qualified. They are taxed when exercised.

How Is Deferred Compensation Divided in Divorce?

Marital or Separate

Dividing deferred compensation is one of the most problematic and contentious areas of negotiating the marital distribution of assets. The challenge lies in determining the circumstances under which an employer gives awards to its employees. Companies have many creative ways to provide their employees with stock or incentive-based compensation.

The analysis of labeling assets as marital or separate therefore calls for determining whether they were granted for past work or future work. Usually, if these assets were granted during a marriage and vest before the divorce date, it is straightforward and they are considered marital property.

It becomes more complicated when these assets do not vest until a date beyond the divorce or when they are awarded for future performance. For example, an employee can receive a grant as a reward for past performance even after the date of separation, but it should be recognized as a performance bonus for work performed during the marriage.

⚠ **Caution:** There is rarely a clear delineation between grants based on past work and grants based on future work.

This ambiguity means you need to do some intensive fact-checking, including getting access to the employee handbook, human resources employment letter, and all documents that can highlight the employer's motives for granting these awards. Once these factors are considered, your state will classify the award as marital or separate property and, if marital, how it will be valued and the manner in which you (the nonemployee spouse) will be compensated.

Vested or Unvested

Not only do you need to worry about if these assets are marital or separate, but you also need to concern yourself with if they are vested or unvested. Some states will only allocate vested awards if deemed marital property; others will allocate both vested and unvested if deemed marital. Some use a "time rule" running from the date of grant, akin to a time coverture formula calculation for pension valuation.

Value

Once these assets are determined to be marital property, a value has to be attached to them. Several methods exist for valuing deferred benefits, and each method has its strengths and weaknesses. States vary on which method is generally acceptable. The methods for valuing stock options are the intrinsic value method; the Black-Scholes model; the coverture fraction approach; and, lastly, the "wait and see" approach. Other incentives and stock-based plans are usually pegged to hypothetical shares of stock.

Risks

There are significant issues with accessibility, liquidity, and forfeiture concerning these assets. Many times, employers control the exercise of these assets with blackout dates, retention requirements, company profitability, and uncertainty over the company's future existence.

If an employee leaves the company before the vesting date of deferred assets, the employee spouse typically forfeits whatever has not vested. Exceptions occur, depending on the terms of the employment agreement or whether under the plan, the reason for the employee's termination (e.g., retirement or disability) accelerates the vesting or lets it continue.

Some plans such as restricted stock have "cliff vesting" by which all shares vest on an "all-or-nothing" basis depending on the length of employment and performance goals. Typically, you forfeit the entire grant if you leave before vesting. It is vital for you to know the details of vesting schedules and policy for every deferred compensation plan.

How to Distribute in Divorce

Finally, you have to determine how to distribute these assets in a divorce. A court may present an array of remedies to determine the marital estate. The easiest way to divide contingent marital interests is for the employee spouse to offset the value of these assets and pay from other assets.

If there are insufficient other assets, or if you want these contingent assets, then there is the deferred distribution approach. You share the proceeds of the awards at the time payments are made on an "if, as, and when" basis. As with any future payout arrangement, be sure you are protected for taking the risk with clear language in your divorce decree that prescribes exactly how and when you will get your share.

On occasion, unvested (and sometimes vested) stock options included in the marital estate will not be divided in the future as an asset; rather, they will be included in the income stream for support calculations. They have a dual nature; they have the characteristics of an asset but also are a central means of incentives for compensation.

NOTE: The vast majority of companies do not allow for the contingent asset to be held in the name of the nonemployee spouse in an account with the employer's plan or the benefits to be transferred to nonemployee spouse. Companies offer these awards as incentives to their employees to stay longer with the employer. If an employee could transfer this award to someone else, the company would lose the desired benefit.

Being nontransferable, you must remain connected to your ex-spouse in the future for as long as these awards take to vest.

Strategies to Protect Your Fair Share

You should negotiate to protect your fair share of these benefits and include specific language in your divorce agreement that addresses any of the following circumstances:

1. Receiving your awards or benefits even after spousal support term ends if the awards have not been paid because of any restriction, the vesting schedule, or an inability to value.
2. Receiving your awards if they are converted into different financial instruments in the future by your ex-spouse's current employer or with any other business entity due to a merger, sale, or other transaction involving your ex-spouse's employer.

3. Receiving timely notice if your ex-spouse's awards are repurchased by the employer if employment terminates through retirement, termination, death, or disability.
4. Being made whole if your ex-spouse forfeits any unvested benefits upon voluntary termination of employment or termination for cause.

Taxes on Deferred Compensation

You have a choice—as does your ex-spouse—when you exercise your right to either cash out or to purchase the underlying stock. And as with anything that has value, you will incur income taxes once the value is realized.

The tax implications differ depending on the kind of asset. The tax burden cannot be transferred to the nonemployee spouse, so you have to anticipate the tax burden in advance. Taxes on profits from exercising your right can be significant and should factor into the evaluation of what these assets are worth to you. If you receive the award as an asset on an "if, as, and when" basis, usually there is some witholding of taxes (at the employee's tax rate) on the distribution of the sale proceeds to the employee. The net proceeds are divided on an after-tax basis at the employee's tax rate. If it is divided as part of income, then the recipient of spousal support will potentially owe taxes depending on the language of the agreement. It is advisable that you have a tax professional analyze your potential tax liability during negotiations.

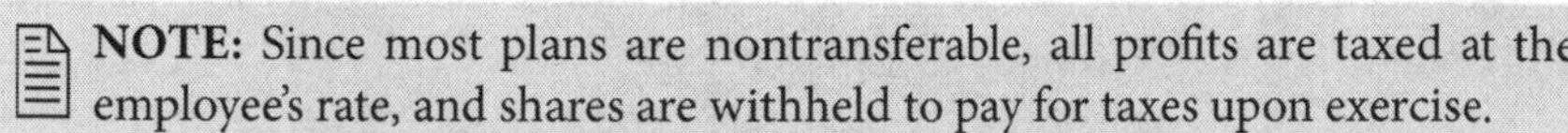

NOTE: Since most plans are nontransferable, all profits are taxed at the employee's rate, and shares are withheld to pay for taxes upon exercise.

ⓘ **Tip:** If your ex-spouse is in a much higher tax bracket than you, you may be able to negotiate for a "true-up" calculation to equalize the net after-tax proceeds you each receive from the exercise of the deferred compensation.

Trusts in Divorce

Trusts serve a variety of purposes. A trust is a legal vehicle for holding property for the benefit of another. A trust is created by a settlor, who transfers property to a trustee. Trusts are frequently used as a means for gifting assets or protecting them, often to avoid certain estate taxes. In some instances, trusts can protect assets from unintended beneficiaries (such as a soon-to-be ex-spouse) during a divorce.

In a divorce, a trust can own significant assets. How it will be treated for purposes of property division depends on what kind of trust it is, as well as who, how, and when it was funded. Trusts are complicated and by necessity involve an examination by experts.

There are two kinds of trusts: revocable and irrevocable. A revocable trust can be terminated (revoked) at any time the creator wishes. When it is terminated, the creator receives all undistributed principal and accumulated income. An irrevocable trust is one that cannot be controlled or revoked by the creator.

Property held in trust is defined as the corpus (principal) and as income if generated by that principal. Income can either be distributed (out of the trust) or undistributed. In divorce, the first question to ask is whether or not a spouse's interest in a trust constitutes property. Not all interests held in a trust are property, and if not, it cannot be divided in a divorce.

Revocable Trusts

If You Are the Beneficiary

If you are a beneficiary of a revocable trust in divorce, the established general rule is that your interests do not constitute property. Interests under a revocable trust exist only at the whim of the creator. It can be revoked at any time. It offers no presently enforceable right to receive anything and only holds the promise of a benefit in the future.

If the creator owns the trust's assets, then these assets cannot be owned by the beneficiary. It is a useful way to keep the potential ex-spouse of a beneficiary from entitlement to trust assets or income in states that allow the division of gift or inheritance property in a divorce.

NOTE: If your mother-in-law creates a revocable trust naming your spouse as primary beneficiary, your spouse has no legal rights because the creator retains complete control over assets. Since your spouse's rights are speculative, these interests are not divisible property.

If You Are the Creator

If you are the creator of a revocable trust, then the property remains under your control, and the issues are how to divide the property held in trust and how to amend or terminate the trust if both spouses are involved.

Irrevocable Trusts

When a trust is irrevocable, it creates legal rights for the beneficiaries. The creator has no power to withdraw or change the trust once it is established. Any property deposited into the trust becomes the property of the trust and is no longer within the possession or control of the creator.

If You Are the Beneficiary

If you are the beneficiary of an irrevocable trust, your inheritance may be unrealized at the time of your divorce. Usually it is considered your separate asset, not marital property in a divorce, and is therefore not divisible in a divorce. Some exceptions exist.

If You Are the Creator

If you are the creator of an irrevocable trust, courts cannot divide the assets because they are owned by a third party, the trust itself. If you place the assets into the trust before your marriage, the assets are separate property and would not have been divided in a divorce. You, however, can't ever get these assets back.

If you place assets in trust during your marriage, you no longer own them, and typically they are not divisible in divorce because they are no longer part of your marital estate. However, there is one exception to this rule called the relevant state fraudulent conveyance statute.

Fraudulent conveyance exists if the assets were transferred into the trust with the actual intent to defraud creditors or steal marital property. Grounds for attacking the conveyance are duress, undue influence, fraud, mistake, or being unconscionable.

For high-net-worth individuals and families, there is another protection strategy called a Domestic Asset Protection Trust (DAPT). A DAPT shields assets from creditors but allows the trust creator to also be a discretionary beneficiary (the best of both worlds). You do not hold legal title to assets, but you do hold power to appoint trustees and have control assets. DAPTs can be formed in only 15 states, with Nevada offering the best protection in a divorce.

Income Interest in Irrevocable Trusts

Courts will look to income interests in the irrevocable trust as property. Income received from a trust is used in some states for calculating spousal support and child support. An income interest is the right to receive periodic distributions of income from the trust. An income interest can be mandatory—one which requires the trustee to distribute income—or discretionary—one which merely permits the trustee to distribute income.

A mandatory, unconditional income interest constitutes property. Discretionary and conditional income interests do not constitute property, primarily because the trustees cannot be forced contractually to distribute income to the beneficiary. Where income interest is divisible as property, it is included in the marital estate and your spouse may be awarded a portion of that income after the needs of both parties and any children are considered.

> ⓘ **Tip:** A failure to plan for what will happen to an irrevocable trust in the event of divorce could result in the ex-spouse receiving significant funding from the trust despite the dissolution of the relationship between the parties.

Trusts and Commingling

In a state that recognizes separate property, you have the opportunity to prove your trust funds belong solely to you. You will have to trace all contributions and provide documentation that shows the source of separate funds. You can defend your separate assets only if you have not commingled, or mixed, marital assets with separate trust property assets. If you have muddied the waters, the court may order you to give a portion of that money to your spouse.

11 Real Property and Your House: Sell It, Keep It, or Transfer It?

Real estate includes your home, vacation home, timeshare, condo, coop apartment, commercial real estate, raw land, mineral rights, water rights, real estate developments, real estate partnerships, and investment properties, as well as any contracts for purchasing real estate. Of all types of real property, the priority is your primary, or marital, residence.

The primary residence is frequently the largest marital asset in a divorce. The decision to stay or not to stay in it is not just financial, but often highly emotional. A house can be perceived as the center of one's life, aside from children, and it is very often the most visible vestige of the dream of marriage that is now broken. As with any important decision, you need a proper perspective about keeping or letting go of the house.

Some couples can deal peaceably and reasonably with one another when it comes to making a decision about the marital home. When the marital estate is sufficiently large, it is common that one party stays in the home, while the other party retains some other assets of similar value as an offset. When available, this simple off-set method allows the party who retains the house to keep it or sell it as they may choose.

If there are not sufficient assets to off-set the value of the marital home, you both may agree it is nevertheless important for one spouse to stay in the home because it provides stability for that spouse and/or continuity in children's lives. Sometimes, it represents significant sentimental value to the party who desires to keep it.

You may both agree that it is simply not practical to sell the marital home because it is underwater or unsaleable (barring a short sale or foreclosure) and redeeming the mortgage or making improvements necessary for a sale would require a substantial and unrecoverable financial outlay. Parties may also find, particularly where the mortgage has been substantially paid down or paid off, that retaining the marital residence represents a less expensive alternative than renting a comparable house.

Finally, there may be no definite reason for either spouse to stay in the house and it is practical to sell it immediately. Perhaps neither of you wants to remain in the same environment as when you lived there married. Or perhaps the house is a major focal point of dispute between the parties, and keeping or selling it is a subject of endless argument. Selling the marital residence may be the only acceptable resolution to an emotional deadlock.

There are four options for how to deal with a house in a divorce. Each option has its advantages and disadvantages. If you cannot agree on what to do, a court will make the decision for you. In court, a judge has the discretion to enter orders that will impact each party's right to the marital residence. Frequently, the court awards the marital home to one spouse as part of property division or orders it to be sold. It can be stated that whatever you and your spouse can agree upon represents a better alternative to having the court force a solution upon you and your family.

Your Four Financial Options

Option 1: Sell the House and Divide the Proceeds with Your Spouse

Advantages

Sometimes you do not have the financial capability to keep the house because of your limited assets and income. An immediate sale is a clear-cut strategy for dividing limited marital assets equitably or equally. The terms of the sale are important, and it is best if you and your spouse can cooperate to make it happen. If you cannot agree upon the terms, you might consider jointly selecting a trusted real estate professional to help you make these decisions and help manage the process efficiently. As a couple, you can exclude up to $500,000 of profit from capital gains taxes if you jointly file your income taxes. If you file separately, you and your spouse each can exclude up to $250,000 of profit from capital gains taxes. If the house is held for less than two years, a prorated portion of the exclusion is allowed under divorce hardship rules. Another advantage to selling the house is that you will be released from the old mortgage when it is sold, thereby making it easier for you to obtain a mortgage for your new home.

Disadvantages

You both lose the home. In addition to the fix-up costs associated with the sale, you may be required to share in paying for all related expenses, including repairs, until it is sold. It can take time to sell a house, and if it is worth less than the mortgage balance (underwater), you might be forced to consider a short sale, deed in lieu of foreclosure, renting it out, foreclosure, or holding on to it longer. Each of these alternatives involves a complicated transaction that requires a lot of forethought. It is best to review these alternatives with a professional.

Option 2: Sell Your Share of Equity in the House to Your Spouse and Transfer It to Her or Him

Advantages

By selling your interest to your spouse, you receive your share of the equity in the form of cash, or some other asset, and accomplish a clean break from the house and its related liabilities. You no longer bear any responsibility for the house. Selling your interest is easiest when you were never on the mortgage. If you are on the mortgage, your divorce decree should require your ex-spouse to obtain a release of your liability from the bank. If the bank is unwilling to release you, your ex-spouse can release you by refinancing the mortgage in his or her name. If she or he cannot do so within a reasonable period, it is customary that the agreement require the ex-spouse to sell the house. You will not have to pay taxes on any monies received in exchange for your interest in the house since your receipt of funds is considered a tax-free transfer between spouses incident to divorce under Internal Revenue Code § 1041. Section 1041 permits tax-free transfers between spouses as long as it is "related to the ending of the marriage." A transfer that occurs within one year of divorce is presumed to relate to the divorce. A transfer that occurs more than six years after the divorce is presumed to not relate to the divorce.

Disadvantages

In addition to incurring the costs of relocation, you may not receive enough to purchase a new home. It may seem unfair to you that one parent continues to live in the family home, particularly if children are involved. You may be uncomfortable if your ex-spouse brings in a new partner to live in the home. If your ex-spouse cannot refinance the joint mortgage and is not obligated to sell or cannot sell the home, then you remain liable for the mortgage. This liability may include any shortfall in the event of a foreclosure or short sale. Being on the mortgage could impact your credit rating and credit availability to purchase your new residence.

Option 3: Buy Out Your Spouse's Share, and You Decide If You Keep the House or Sell It in the Future

Advantages

You continue to own the home. You have sufficient other assets that you can finance the buyout of your equity value by transferring other assets to your spouse. You have minimal disruption and no significant change in lifestyle immediately following divorce. No sales or capital gains taxes are incurred until you decide to sell in the future. The house may appreciate in value as an investment.

Disadvantages

You bear the full responsibility for owning, maintaining, repairing, and living in the home. You have to finance the buyout of your spouse by either offsetting the value with other assets or by leveraging the equity in the house (with a new mortgage or line of credit). You own a significant asset that is illiquid. When the house is later sold, you will bear all of the costs of the sale and may have to pay capital gains taxes if the profit exceeds $250,000. You also bear the risk that the house could depreciate in value.

Option 4: You Both Continue to Own the House Up to a Certain Period, After Which You Sell and Divide the Proceeds

Advantages

If you both own the house, you could have a variety of living arrangements. The most common is for one spouse to vacate and one spouse to continue to live in the home. You and your spouse agree in advance to a presumptive time that is best to sell the house (i.e., child graduates from high school, wage-earning spouse attains age 65, etc.).

Some parties have engaged in a temporary parenting practice called "nesting," where each parent takes turns living in the home with the children based on a parenting schedule to minimize disruption to their routines. In many such cases, an alternative residence (i.e., a small apartment) is rented at joint expense to accommodate the parent who is not in residence with the children. Nesting arrangements warrant a significant deviation from typical spousal support and child support orders. Neither spouse is forcing the other to make a final house decision or to be solely responsible for the house and expenses.

It is particularly advisable to set an end date to this arrangement. Since the nature of this arrangement requires a high level of cooperation, it often ends at the discretion of one parent. And as with any end to a temporary arrangement and a deferred decision, it is best to address how the property will be sold, the distribution of the proceeds, and the responsibility for any deficiency.

With joint ownership of any property comes joint decision-making, the sharing of expenses, and tax deductions. Your ex-spouse may pay part of the mortgage, real estate taxes, insurance, repairs, or maintenance costs through child support or spousal support. Capital gains taxes and costs of sale might be shared.

Disadvantages

You have to carefully negotiate all practical aspects of owning a home jointly after you divorce. You have to set personal boundaries, establish privacy, and have respect for one another concerning the arrangement. You must lay out details for when or what triggers the sale of house, who is in control of the decision related to such sale, and how will the sales proceeds be shared. Will the spouse who pays the mortgage receive a credit for the post-divorce reduction of principal that they paid from their separate share of assets or income?

Continued dealings between parties can lead to frustrations, misunderstandings, and conflict. There is a real danger if your ex-spouse might file for bankruptcy or is being sued by creditors. While you will have no control over judgments by creditors and no way of stopping them from attaching to the home or forcing its sale, there are procedures to protect your interest in property, such as a *lis pendens*, which you may wish to discuss with your attorney at the commencement of the divorce proceeding. A recording on the land records the judgment that distinguishes your share of the equity from your spouse's share.

Depending on how you hold title together as owners of the house after divorce, you may also need to protect your estate in the event you predecease your ex-spouse. If you do not want your ex-spouse to receive title to the real estate if you die, you must break any survivorship tenancy. Then, you each have the right to leave your share to whom you want to upon your death. If you want your ex-spouse to receive your interest in the real estate in the event you die before the house is sold, you should execute a deed holding title as joint tenants with rights of survivorship so the resident spouse can continue to stay as planned. You should also update your wills as soon as possible.

Factors in Making Any Decision about the House

You have three primary financial issues to deal with concerning your marital home. The first is determining what your home is worth. The second is determining whether you can you afford it. The third and last is if you can afford to buy out your spouse's interest if you desire to stay in the home. If so, what does it mean in terms of trading other assets for it, the debt you must acquire, or shouldering the multitude of logistical and practical considerations relating to home ownership?

Your first step is to value the house. Next, you need to create an accurate income and expense statement and cash flow projection. You need to be sure that the costs of your home fit within your budget so you can still meet your other financial needs (such as saving for retirement).

What Is Your House Worth? Fair Market Value and Equity Value

How do you figure out the fair market value of your house and what is the net equity value? There are two main ways to determine the fair market value of your home: a real estate market appraisal or a market analysis (comparable sales). Parties frequently overestimate the value of their home or dispute the fair market value of the house. It is advisable to get a real estate appraisal even if you and your spouse agree upon the fair market value of the house. Internet-based value estimators are generally not sufficiently reliable estimates of actual fair market value for divorce purposes or financial planning purposes. The same is true for tax valuations given by municipal assessors.

Fair Market Value

Fair market value is defined as the amount for which real property would be sold in a voluntary transaction between a willing buyer and a willing seller, neither of whom is under any obligation to buy or sell. It is the amount for which your house would sell on the open market if put up for sale. Real estate appraisers and brokers use "comparable" sales of similar property in the area to determine the listing price or current market value. The values are arrived at by adding or deducting amounts based upon differences in location, characteristics, quality, and size of the property. They may also estimate value based on replacement cost (i.e., what it would cost to purchase similar land and build a similar property) and adjust this number based on the current condition including wear and tear.

Equity

Equity is defined as the difference between the fair market value of the real estate owned and the amount still owed against it (e.g., any debts attached to the property, such as first and second mortgages, HELOCs, other lines of credit, liens, and/or tax liens). You may be able to adjust the value of the equity in the house further and reduce it according to a reasonable broker's fee and any anticipated selling taxes, transfer taxes, conveyance taxes, home staging costs, or repairs to arrive at a net equity value.

EXAMPLE:

Value of home:	$750,000 (fair market value)
Less mortgage:	($200,000)
Less HELOC:	($55,000)
Total marital equity:	$495,000

ⓘ **Tip:** If you are not going to sell your house immediately, you may have to negotiate for any costs associated with selling it in the future because they are not incurred now.

⚠ **Caution:** Make sure you have a recent appraisal value of your home. An expert opinion as to value is considered stale after six months and should not be relied upon.

Pegging an Equity Value If You Are Not Selling Now

How does one get money out of the "house" if it is not being sold at time of divorce? Valuing equity is not necessarily easy. You should include clear language in your divorce agreement about how you and your ex-spouse will close the "deal" on dividing equity in the house. You can use any of these methods: (a) protecting the equity value until expiry of term (no further encumbrances); (b) offering the right of first refusal (either spouse has the right of first refusal to buy out the other at fair market value); (c) paying off your ex-spouse from your own resources; or (d) putting the house up for sale pursuant to your legal order.

The ultimate payoff of equity should be addressed as either a lump sum amount or as installment payments in the divorce decree. The challenge is to *set the value of the equity* in the divorce decree so you have closure on how this value will be calculated in the future.

Fixing the Equity Value as of the Date of Divorce for a Future Payout

You can agree to fix the value of house equity at the time of your divorce. At the expiry of an agreed-upon period, you pay your ex-spouse their share of this amount established as of the date of the divorce. For example, you and your ex-spouse both agree you will stay in the house for three years and that you will assume all responsibility for the house until it is sold. You set the equity value based on the fair market value as of the date of your divorce, and when it is sold (e.g., three years in the future), you pay your ex-spouse their share of the equity value pegged as of the date of divorce. You bear all the risk of expenses and risk of depreciation in value, and, conversely, you entirely benefit from any appreciation in value. Your spouse has no risk should the property depreciate in value and loses all opportunity for price appreciation.

Fixing Equity Value at a Future Date for a Future Payout

Alternatively, the equity can be set as a percentage of the future fair market value (at the expiry of the term) to be allocated at a future date between spouses. For example, you and your ex-spouse both agree you will stay in the house for three years and that you will both share in major repairs, extraordinary maintenance, and agreed-upon improvements until the future sale. You and your ex-spouse agree to share 50 percent of the equity value based on the future actual sale proceeds. You both share risk of depreciation or appreciation in value.

How Do You Know If You Can You Afford to Keep the House?

Now that you know the value of your house, the second question you must address is whether you can afford it. To answer this question, you must calculate what your total monthly shelter expenses are. You need to list the amount you pay for each item relating to your housing and estimate what you pay annually (and then divide it by 12 for a monthly figure).

A small mortgage monthly payment can be deceiving and keep you from facing many of the other costs of owning a home. The price of owning and maintaining a home always exceeds your monthly mortgage payment, and if you decide to keep the house, all these expenses will be your sole responsibility.

A Sample of Monthly Housing Expenses

- Mortgage or rent
- HELOC or second mortgage payment
- Property taxes
- Association fees and charges
- Condo maintenance fees
- Utilities:
  - Electricity
  - Gas
  - Propane
  - Fuel/oil
  - Telephone
  - Internet/cable TV/satellite TV
  - Water
  - Trash

- Homeowners insurance
- Umbrella liability
- Furniture, furnishings, and housewares
- Household supplies
- Housecleaning
- Appliances including maintenance
- Repairs
- Painting/wallpapering
- Gardening/landscaping/lawn care
- Snow removal
- Exterminator
- Gutters/windows
- Pool maintenance and repairs

The Debt-to-Income Ratio

How do you know if your housing costs are too much for your budget? The most important factor that lenders use is your debt-to-income ratio, which determines how much of your income is needed to pay your debt obligations, such as your mortgage, your credit card payments, and your student loans.

> ⓘ **Tip:** A rule of thumb used by creditors and mortgagors is that the ratio of housing expenses to total expenses should be 30 percent to 36 percent. You must have sufficient support and income sources to cover total housing-related expenses. Total mortgage + taxes + utilities/total budget = a maximum of 36 percent.

Lenders typically want no more than 28 percent of your gross monthly income (before tax) to go toward your mortgage payment, property taxes, and homeowner's insurance. Once you add in all your other debts, this ratio shouldn't exceed 36 percent of your gross income.

The mortgage rule of thumb is sometimes called the rule of 28/36.

EXAMPLE: Your gross monthly income is $5,000 before taxes are deducted. Take this total and multiply it by .28 and then by .36.

$5,000 × .28 = $1,400

$5,000 × .36 = $1,800

THIS RESULT MEANS THAT YOUR MORTGAGE, TAXES, AND INSURANCE PAYMENTS CAN'T EXCEED $1,400 PER MONTH AND YOUR TOTAL MONTHLY DEBT PAYMENTS SHOULD BE NO MORE THAN $1,800, WITH MORTGAGE PAYMENT INCLUDED.

⚠ **Caution:** Under what circumstances would you not be able to afford the house and how likely are these events? Plan for contingencies to protect against late payments, default, or worse.

Does It Make Sense for You to Keep the House?

It may not make *financial sense* for you in the long term to keep it even if you can afford the house. Keeping the house, if you can, does provide for stability and familiarity in a time of transition. You may not know exactly where you want to go after divorce. Making a long-term decision to move may not be feasible or wise if you feel unsettled.

To help you decide whether to keep it or sell it, here are some questions to ask yourself:

1. What are the likely alternative housing costs: house, condo, rent versus buy? There are some helpful websites for calculating the rent-versus-buy decision.
2. Is the house a desirable investment, and will it be so in the future? Is it a good idea at this time to have so much money tied up in the house?
3. Will the house drain you financially? How much of an economic benefit will this house be? Typically, it makes more economic sense to buy rather than to rent because of tax-deductible expenses and future appreciation of the asset. However, real estate is not as marketable as publicly traded securities. Further, real estate has not appreciated as rapidly as more publicly traded securities over the long term.
4. Would you be better off taking other assets in exchange for the family home? Why not take the opportunity to get a fresh start?
5. Are you ready to assume the full "burden" of home ownership and maintenance? What logistics do you face if you want to keep the house?
6. Does it make sense to keep the house in the short term to enable a co-parenting "nesting arrangement" to minimize disruption to household routine? (See the section on the pros and cons of jointly owning a home.)

The Logistics of Keeping the House: What You Need to Know Now

If you keep the house, certain legal documents may need to be updated, such as the mortgage loan, title, property tax records, and homeowner's insurance. These updates all cost money. For example, what are the costs associated with refinancing a mortgage or reapplying for insurance? Should these costs be shared with your soon-to-be ex-spouse?

In situations where you do not sell the house and you have a mortgage, you need a strategy to either remove, refinance, or assume the mortgage in your name alone. Be aware that when you divide your property, a quitclaim deed only affects how the property is titled and has no impact on the loan obligation.

> ⓘ **Tip:** A word to the wise: Do not take on debt in your name unless you also have the asset in your name. You may lose control over the asset and be stuck with all of the liability on the debt.

Mortgage Strategies

If there is a mortgage (or more debts) on your house, you have three strategies for dealing with it if you are keeping the house:

1. Refinance the mortgage.
2. Assume the mortgage.
3. Pay off the mortgage.

One Spouse Keeps the House and Refinances the Mortgage

This common strategy is if you want to keep the house. In this situation, you buy out your ex-spouse's equity share and refinance the mortgage in your name alone. If you retain the house, it is important to have your ex-spouse sign a quit claim deed, which relinquishes their ownership and rights to the property.

ⓘ **Tip:** Shop around early during the divorce process to obtain refinance quotes for mortgages. Make sure you apply for an amount sufficient to cover all expenses associated with the refinance as well as the buyout amount.

⚠ **Caution:** Lenders may require evidence of support payments for at least six months, which means you may not be able to refinance until after six months to one year.

One Spouse Keeps the Home and Assumes the Mortgage

A divorce mortgage assumption can be a good option if your bank approves it, but you should realize not all mortgages are assumable. If your mortgage lender allows you to assume the loan, you complete an assumption agreement and a release of liability. The lender will need documentation that you can pay the mortgage based solely on your income (or on support payments after a period). If approved, the lender executes a release of liability to your ex-spouse.

One Spouse Pays Off the Mortgage

You may be tempted to pay off the mortgage and live debt free. But should you? It depends on many variables and wholly depends on your personal financial situation. Good reasons to pay off the mortgage include the following:

- You have low risk tolerance,
- You have reason to believe your support payments or income may not be consistent,
- You plan to live in the home for a long time,
- You are conservative or approaching retirement years, and
- You have no other need for cash.

By paying off the mortgage early, you'll save on additional interest expenses that would have been incurred in your regular payments. This savings can be significant.

However, you may lose the mortgage interest tax deduction if you itemize, which can be an invaluable financial planning tool. You also lose the opportunity to invest your funds elsewhere if you use those funds to pay down the mortgage. The lower your interest rate on your mortgage, the less you stand to benefit from using funds for pay down when you could have otherwise invested at a higher rate of return (i.e., maxed out investing in your retirement savings). Your mortgage may be cheap money, and if you have high-cost debt, like high-interest credit cards or student loans, it doesn't make sense to use your capital to pay down a low-cost debt like a mortgage.

Frequently Overlooked Costs Relating to Taking Ownership of a House

1. Have a home inspection done before signing divorce papers if you wish to keep the marital home. It is better to know if expensive repairs will be needed to make it livable or saleable. This may also be helpful if the house is appraised, as most appraisers presume that there are no obvious defects or repairs required.
2. Perform a title search to make sure you know who owns the house and if there are liens against it.
3. Are there any transfer taxes to be paid when you change title to the home?
4. Are there any other fees or costs associated with having to have your ex-spouse quitclaim the deed to you?
5. What if you want to keep the house but sell it the near future? You should estimate now how much it will cost you to sell and consider alternatives (e.g., should you sell it now while still jointly owned, or continue to hold title jointly until future sale?)
   a. Staging costs
   b. Appraisal fees
   c. Refinancing costs
   d. Realtor fees
   e. Attorney fees (retitling, quitclaims, and closing costs)
   f. Rezoning costs and building permits
   g. Insurance costs
   h. Assessment fees and special assessment taxes
   i. Unpaid taxes
   j. School, town, and sewer taxes
   k. Conveyance taxes
6. Understand what your individual capital gains tax liability is should you decide to sell the house in the future. Be sure to retain documentation to establish the tax cost basis of your home, the closing statement from purchase, and receipts for all capital improvements.

How Do We Jointly Hold Title to the House Post-Divorce?

Suppose you both decide to own the house jointly after you divorce. How should you own the house after divorce? Each type of ownership and debt obligation describes your legal rights and affects how property is transferred to someone else or what happens if you die.

Tenancy in common allows an owner the greatest flexibility to transfer the property as he or she wants. Each co-tenant in a tenancy in common has an interest in the property and is free to transfer this interest during life or through a will. The co-tenants can have different ownership interests; for example, three owners could own 5 percent, 35 percent, and 60 percent of the property, respectively, as tenants in common. Each tenant can sever their relationship with the other tenants by conveying their interest to another party. This third party then becomes a tenant in common with the other owners. You could end up being an owner with a third party if your ex-spouse dies and leaves her or his share to an heir (including a widow). The designation of a specific percentage of interest has significance for capital gains taxes.

Joint tenants, on the other hand, must have equal ownership interests in the property. So, two owners would each have a one-half interest in the property. If one of the joint tenants dies, his or her interest immediately ceases to exist, and the remaining joint tenant owns the entire property. The advantage to joint tenancy is that it avoids having an owner's interest probated upon his death. If your spouse dies, you will then own 100 percent of the house regardless of what is in your ex-spouse's will.

A disadvantage to both joint tenancy and tenancy in common, however, is that creditors can attach the tenant's property to satisfy a debt. So, for example, if a co-tenant defaults on debts, her or his creditors can sue in a "partition proceeding" to have the property interests divided and the property sold, even over the other owners' objections.

Is It Smart to Continue to Jointly Own Your Residence after Divorce?

At the outset, ask yourself if you and your ex-spouse can agree how to deal with both the routine as well as significant repairs and maintenance:

- How will expenses be shared?
- Do you both have to agree to the type and amount of cost?
- If your ex-spouse does not agree to the expense, will you be able to recoup any expenses you choose to pay for from future sale proceeds of the house? What if the house is not put up for sale?
- Does either one of you get extra credit for increased equity from paying down the principal on the mortgage?

- Do you get extra credit from future sales proceeds for your time and effort put into maintenance until the sale?

If you feel comfortable with the above considerations, then move on to examining the pros and cons of joint ownership after divorce.

The Pros and Cons of Continuing to Jointly Own Property Post-Divorce

The Pros

- If one spouse cannot buy the other out, the advantage is to stay in the house with the children until you are ready to sell or have enough cash to buy out the other spouse.
- Ease of co-parenting in a familiar space or a "nesting arrangement," which is uniquely child-centered.

  Parents take turns moving in and out of the primary home so that the children remain in one home rather than having to adapt to the parents' needs and living in two separate dwellings. The parents can either live in their separate places when not with the children or share and rotate with the other parent.

  It is a novel, child centered arrangement that can be either semi-permanent or temporary to allow the children a smoother transition to life as a divorced family.

  It is not a recommended option for long-term parenting.

  Obviously, nesting will work for some but not all parents. It will only work if both parents live nearby and have demonstrated that they can cooperate amicably both outside and in the family home when it is their turn for parenting the kids.
- Both parties are jointly liable for the mortgage and property taxes (you each share the burden of protecting this asset).
- In case of hardship, checking accounts can be prefunded from marital or separate assets to pay shelter-related expenses. Adjustments to the ultimate distribution of equity in the home can be made for unequal sharing of expenses during the period of joint ownership.
- If you hold legal title for jointly owning the house, you may be eligible to claim your share of itemized tax deductions and deem house-related payments as "spousal support" for tax purposes.

The Cons

- You both show the entire amount of both mortgages on your credit report—limiting your credit availability to get additional credit.
- Any defaults may negatively impact your credit rating.
- You remain involved with your ex-spouse.
- You may lack privacy with your ex-spouse.

- Without an emotional disentanglement, a long-term commitment to this situation may be unpleasant.
- Either one of you may have a change of heart to move on sooner than anticipated or to bring a new spouse into the house.
- At some point the proposed arrangement ends and the house will be sold or one spouse will buy out the other. Unless this transaction is contemplated by your divorce agreement, you risk losing an important tax benefit of Internal Revenue Code Section 1041, which says transfers between spouses as a result of divorce are not taxable. Section 1041 applies only to spouses as long as transfers take place within one year of the divorce becoming final or as long as "it is related to the ending of your marriage (up to 6 years from date of divorce).[3]" You must write this provision into your divorce agreement to benefit from this tax-free transfer between spouses.
- Consider what happens if you die while you and your ex-spouse are still are co-owners as tenants in common. If you want your former spouse to keep the house for any period of time, make sure each of you designates the other as beneficiary of their share of the house—you can do this by holding title as joint tenants with rights of survivorship or by including it in your updated will.
- You may need life insurance on each other in the event of death to cover any expenses or obligations of former spouse to keep the house or, if you are tenants in common, to buy it from the deceased's estate.
- Another risk is if your former spouse becomes disabled, bankrupt, or is sued by creditors. Your former spouse's share of equity could be seized, possibly resulting in a forced sale and no protection for you.

What about Spousal Support Paid to You as Mortgage and Property Taxes?

You continue to live in the house as the sole occupant (or with children) and your ex-spouse offers to pay all or some of the mortgage and property taxes on your behalf as "spousal support." There are special rules to follow, and any payments made between you and your ex-spouse must meet the IRS definition of spousal support and be called as such in the provisions of your divorce decree or legal separation.

Payments to third parties that are intended to be spousal support should be specified as such under the terms of your divorce. Similarly, payments to third parties that are not intended to be spousal support should be specified as such under the terms of your divorce.

The IRS is specific about how each of you can treat spousal support payments made in the form of mortgage and property taxes. IRS Publication 504 describes

3 Internal Revenue Code Section 1041: (c) Incident to divorce: "For purposes of subsection (a)(2), a transfer of property is incident to the divorce if such transfer—(1) occurs within 1 year after the date on which the marriage ceases, or (2) is related to the cessation of the marriage."

any entitlements to deductions based on how the house is owned, who is living in it, and who is paying spousal support.

House 100% Owned by the Spouse Receiving Spousal Support

Provided that the other requirements of IRC § 71[4] are met, you must report as spousal support 100 percent of all payments made to third parties by your ex-spouse in the form of mortgage payments, home insurance payments, and real estate taxes on the home you own. Your ex-spouse may deduct these payments from their taxable income. You are entitled to deduct a portion of the mortgage loan interest and real estate taxes, even though your ex-spouse in fact paid these expenses on your behalf.

House 100% Owned by the Spouse Paying Spousal Support

Mortgage payments, real estate taxes, and insurance premiums paid by your ex-spouse for a home *they own* are not taxable or deductible as spousal support. The IRS states that payments for use of property and payments to keep up the payor's property do not qualify as spousal support.

The underlying obligations are already the payor's responsibility—even if you are living in the house rent-free. Your ex-spouse cannot deduct the payments as spousal support, and you, as a recipient, don't have to report payments as income. If you are granted use of your ex-spouse's residence pursuant to a divorce order, your ex-spouse may still be able to deduct interest and real estate taxes if the house is a "qualified residence" even if not living there.

House Owned by Both Spouses

If you and your ex-spouse both own the home or are both liable on the mortgage, your ex-spouse, who is payor of spousal support, is entitled to claim one-half of the mortgage payments, real estate taxes, and property insurance as spousal support. You must report one-half of these payments as spousal support.

Both you and your ex-spouse may each claim one-half of the real estate taxes paid, as well as mortgage interest paid as itemized deductions, provided the home is a "qualified residence." The exception is when you and your ex-spouse own the house as "tenants by entirety" or in "joint tenancy"—then none of the real estate taxes your ex-spouse pays may be deducted as spousal support, and only the party who actually pays the real estate taxes can claim the itemized deduction.

4 Parties cannot be members of the same household at the time payment is made, parties cannot file a joint-income tax return in the year payment is made, and payments must terminate upon the death of the recipient (IRS § 71 (b) (2)).

Summary of the IRS Treatment of Expenses for a Jointly-Owned Home (IRS Publication 504)

IF you must pay all of the . . .	AND your home is . . .	THEN you can deduct and your former spouse must include as alimony . . .	AND you can claim as an itemized deduction . . .
Mortgage payments (principal and interest)	Jointly owned,	Half of the total payments	Half of the interest as interest expense (if the home is a qualified home).[1]
Real estate taxes and home insurance	Held as tenants in common,	Half of the total payments	Half of the real estate taxes[2] and none of the home insurance.
	Held as joint tenancy or tenants by entirety,	None of the payments	All of the real estate taxes and none of the home insurance.

[1] Your spouse (or former spouse) can deduct the other half of the interest if the home is a qualified home.

[2] Your spouse (or former spouse) can deduct the other half of the real estate taxes.

What Are the Tax Benefits of Owning a Home?

There are tax benefits to home ownership that you should not overlook. These tax benefits reduce your gross monthly housing costs by your tax savings. You need to analyze not only your gross monthly expenses, but also the actual net cost of owning your home on an annual basis. However, while you may receive tax breaks for ownership, it is more important to feel confident that you can meet your gross monthly shelter expenses within your budget.

Tax breaks are available for any home—mobile home, single family residence, townhouse, condominium, or coop apartment. And, most homeowners also enjoy tax breaks even when they sell the residence.

However, to take full advantage of your home, you need to itemize your expenses on Form 1040 and Schedule A, where you detail all tax-deductible expenses.

Your Biggest Tax Breaks Are

- Your mortgage interest payment on your primary residence and a second residence.
- Your property taxes (including any taxes assessed for street, sidewalk, utility, curb, sewer, and other property improvements—call your tax assessor to confirm).
- Interest on up to $100,000 HELOC or home equity loan.

- Points you paid when you purchased your house.
- Points you paid to get a better rate on your home loan, HELOC, or home equity loan. Be careful to check if you can deduct the points all in one year or if you need to amortize the deduction.
- Premiums paid for mortgage insurance premiums.
- Home improvements made for medical care.

What if you are the owner of multiple properties? Mortgage interest on a second home is also fully deductible. In fact, additional property doesn't strictly have to be a house. It could be a boat or RV as long as it has cooking, sleeping, and bathroom facilities. You can even rent out your second property for part of the year and still take full advantage of the mortgage interest deduction as long as you also spend time there (at least 14 days or more than 10 percent of the number of days rented out).

For high-income earners, be aware that according to the IRS, the maximum mortgage amount you can claim interest on is $1 million on first and second homes. The amount is reduced to $500,000 for married taxpayers filing separately. Also, if you have adjusted gross income (AGI) of over $166,800, your mortgage interest starts to get phased out. For every $100 of income over $166,800, you lose $3 of itemized deductions, multiplied by 33.3 percent for up to a maximum loss of 80 percent of your itemized deductions.

How Much in Taxes Do You Save?

The actual amount of money you save on your annual income tax bill depends on a variety of factors:

- Your filing status (single, head of household, married filing jointly, or married filing separately)
- Your standard deduction amount
- Other itemized deductions
- Your taxable income

Your home-related itemized deductions plus your other itemized deductions must add up to more than the standard deduction or they won't save you any money. Some high-income taxpayers may not be able to deduct expenses because of high-income phase-outs and alternative minimum tax (AMT) rules.

AMT rules provide for a separate method of determining a "floor" for a taxpayer's liability to ensure that taxpayers with income as well as significant deductions, exemptions, losses, or credits are still required to pay a minimum amount of federal income tax. AMT rules have their own definition of taxable income, exemptions, and tax rates. At certain income levels where AMT applies, certain deductions are reduced or eliminated. If AMT issues exist, check if itemized deductions are negotiable (i.e., mortgage interest and property taxes)—they may be worth more to you than to your ex-spouse.

Tax Implications If You Sell Your Home

Tax implications relating to the sale of the marital home are important to know. Homeowners are entitled to a generous tax break on any profits—called the home sale exclusion—when they sell their primary residence depending on specific IRS criteria. Depending on how long you owned and lived in your home and how much profit you make on the sale, you face the possibility of having to pay capital gains taxes when the house is eventually sold. Whoever is granted title to the house will ultimately be responsible for this capital gains tax.

The general rule is if you owned and lived in the place for two of the five years before the sale and you have not sold another home in the last two years, then up to $250,000 of profit is tax-free to you as an individual. If you are married and file a joint return, the tax-free amount doubles to $500,000 if *either* spouse meets the ownership requirement, *both* spouses meet the use requirement, and *neither* spouse has sold another house in the last two years.

However, if you are granted the use of the former marital home under a divorce or separation instrument, the nonoccupying former spouse does not need to satisfy the occupancy agreement. Divorced taxpayers may "tack on" the ownership and use of their residence by their former spouse if both agree to sell it in the future to split the proceeds and it is written in the divorce agreement. Each is entitled to exclude $250,000 of profits from the sale, but they must continue to own it jointly. There is no time limitation as long as it remains jointly owned. Either party may lose this exclusion as it relates to the sale of the jointly owned marital home if they use that exemption to defray the gain on the sale of a different home within two years of the sale of the jointly owned home.

Calculating Your Actual Gain (or Loss) on Sale

Most people assume their gain is the profit on sale of the home or the same as equity in the home. This assumption is incorrect. The IRS calculates your gain differently. Your gain is your home's selling price, minus deductible closing costs, selling costs, and your cost basis in your home (which equals the original purchase price, plus purchase expenses and the cost of capital improvements, minus any depreciation and any casualty losses or insurance payments).

EXAMPLE:

Sales price of home (fair market value):	$750,000
Less selling commission (6 percent):	($45,000)
Less capital improvements:	($33,450)
Less settlement fees and closing costs:	($2,000)
Add back claimed depreciation for home office:	$12,000
Less purchase price:	($379,500)
Profit on sale:	$302,050
Individual exclusion on profit:	($250,000)

Profit subject to capital gains taxes:	$52,050
Less assumed 20 percent rate for tax:	($10,410)
Net profit on sale*:	$41,640

* *Less a potential net investment income tax of 3.8 percent based on your modified AGI and if taxable house profit exceeds the pre-existing statutory exclusion of $250,000 for an individual and $500,000 for married filing jointly. The extra tax of 3.8 percent is applied only to nonearned income. (Net investment income does not generally include wages, unemployment compensation, Social Security benefits, alimony, and most self-employment income.)*

Capital Improvements That Increase the Cost Basis of Your Home

Additions
Bedroom
Bathroom
Deck
Garage
Porch
Patio

Lawn & Grounds
Landscaping
Driveway
Walkway
Fence
Retaining wall
Swimming pool

Exterior
Storm windows/doors
New roof
New siding
Satellite dish

Insulation
Attic
Walls
Floors, pipes, and ductwork

Systems
Heating system
Central air conditioning
Furnace ductwork
Central humidifier
Central vacuum
Air/water filtration systems
Wiring
Security system
Lawn sprinkler system

Plumbing
Septic system
Water heater
Soft water system
Filtration system

Interior
Built-in appliances
Kitchen modernization
Flooring
Wall-to-wall carpeting
Fireplace

What Is the Reduced Exclusion for a Second Home Also Used as a Primary Home (Vacation and Rental)?

As of January 2009, new rules apply. If you sell a home that you sometimes used as a vacation or rental property and sometimes as your primary residence, you're eligible for only a portion of the capital gains exclusion that corresponds to the amount of time you really lived there as your primary residence. And, if you never lived there as your primary residence, you are disqualified from using the exclusion.

Usage Test

$$\text{Capital Gains Exclusion} = \text{Profit from the sale of the home} \times \frac{\text{Number of days the home was "primary"}}{\text{Number of days the home was owned}}$$

Commonly Asked Questions

1. Is it considered abandoned property if my spouse walked out on me?

   No, your spouse remains owner of marital assets.
2. What can I take out from the house if I move out?

   Whether you can remove items from the house depends on the rules of the court where you are divorcing. In most instances, you can only remove items that are agreed upon, and in many jurisdictions, such agreements need to be in writing and signed by the parties. If a property division is in dispute and you take items, you can be penalized. The court may decide that the value of the items will either be subtracted from your final property share or that you have to give back the items to your spouse. It is best to avoid conflict over taking these items or getting into trouble.
3. Who gets the house?

   Which party gets to remain in the house post-divorce depends on the circumstances and is frequently determined by practicality rather than emotions. For instance, if you have young children, usually it is the parent who provides the majority of the childcare who keeps the marital home for a period of time that is reasonably necessary.

   If there are no children and one person purchased the house with separate funds, then they will keep it and the other partner will be expected to vacate the home. If there are no children involved, and no practical reason to prefer one party's retention of the house over the other, then it might be practical to sell it immediately.

   Courts vary considerably on how they distribute the marital home. During the pendency of the divorce, issues often arise over whether one party should leave. Neither party typically has a legal right to ask the other to leave, but one partner can always request it. It is not legal to lock the other party out of the house. Nor is it lawful to pressure a spouse to vacate by use of physical or economic intimidation. If you and your spouse cannot agree, the court will decide based on the rules in its state and which kind of property system your state has.

   In extreme cases involving domestic violence, where there is genuine and imminent fear for one's safety, all states have emergency procedures whereby someone can immediately seek a restraining order, including an order of immediate custody of the minor children and expulsion from the home. These measures should be used only when truly necessary for extraordinary relief.

Use of such extraordinary relief without sufficient justification will reflect poorly on a party who is perceived as making unfounded claims. If the judge believes you have done this, you can seriously jeopardize your claims to marital property and child custody.

4. Can we still own the house jointly after divorce?

   Yes, many couples divorce and retain joint ownership of property. Some do it indefinitely. Others do it until it can sell. Beware of the tax implications and be sure any logistics for mutual ownership are absolutely worked out. The pros and cons of joint ownership are described earlier in this chapter.

5. Is a portion of the house considered separate property if I used separate monies for the down payment?

   The answer is complicated, not just because of your state's divorce laws, but also because of the circumstances and factors relating to the division of marital and separate property in your state. You need to ask your divorce attorney.

6. What happens if our house is worth less than the mortgage balance (underwater)?

   The problem is that there is nothing to divide—no value and only responsibility for paying expenses and any resulting liability. You might need to investigate mortgage bailout, a short sale, renting it out, negotiating with the mortgagor, or bankruptcy. You need to work with a financial consultant and your divorce attorney.

12 Child Support

Child support is a parent's legal obligation to contribute to the financial care and costs of raising his or her child. Child support orders are issued by the family court, which bases the amount of the support on the prescribed state guidelines. These guidelines vary from state to state. State legislatures enact various bills that address child support and family law.

When a parent does not pay court-ordered child support, the state also has laws that allow them to use enforcement techniques to collect. Additionally, Congress has mandated immediate income withholding as part of all child support orders unless parents agree to an alternative arrangement. Child support enforcement is usually a major focus in all of the states.

Child support is a support award that is "income driven" based on two general methods:

1. Income shares: Income is prorated between parents; the noncustodial parent has the child support obligation as prorated (the majority of states), or
2. A percentage of parents' income: A state-approved percentage is applied to income.

State guidelines establish the amount of support that must be paid based on the parent's income, ability to pay, and the number of children. Child support is an amount to cover basic necessities of food, shelter, clothing, and often medical insurance coverage. Child support is an ongoing, periodic payment from the noncustodial parent to the custodial parent.

Every state requires a court to order a noncustodial parent to pay child support after divorce. In cases of joint custody, even on an equal basis, one parent will inevitably owe some amount of child support. Unless parents have exactly equal income and share equal custody, which is highly unlikely, someone pays child support. Sometimes the court may order a parent to pay child support to a third party who cares for the child and has custody.

It helps to think of the legal right to child support as being possessed by a child for his or her proper care and upbringing. Courts tend to be guided by the doctrine "best interests of the child." They consider a number of factors related to the child and the parent's circumstances, with the child's ultimate safety and well-being the paramount concern. The court can deviate from mandated guidelines if there are significant reasons to do so. In many states, the law specifies some or all of the factors to be considered for deviation, including the impact of custody arrangements (time sharing).

In all states, child support is ordered until a child attains the "age of majority," a date when the child turns 18, 19, 21, or 23, as established under your state's law. Each state's termination laws also determine that child support ends on the day the child becomes emancipated (marries, dies, enters military service, is adopted, or is deported). A child support order also ends if the person paying the support dies.

What Are Children's Expenses?

Mandated child support may be sufficient to meet your child's basic needs and have a standard of living that is the same as both parents. Child support payments do not need to be kept separate from other household money, and the payor does not get to determine what expenses the child support covers. A parent has discretion in determining how to use child support but cannot misuse it to the neglect of a child since it is their fundamental right.

Most states also recognize that even the maximum child support may not address the "extras" required to cover a broad array of child-related expenses. Mandated child support may be supplemented with additional parental financial contributions for "child-related add-on" expenses on a case-by-case basis.

If the court orders a parent to contribute to other expenses beyond basic child support, the court will factor in the lifestyle and standard of living that the children had experienced while the marriage was intact. The court also looks to the essential financial and support needs of a child and reflects those requirements in a child support order. Modification of any court order is always available to either parent.

Typical child-related add-on expenses include:

- Extracurricular expenses
- Work-necessitated childcare, childcare related to looking for work, or if the parent is in school
- Health insurance
- Uncovered/unreimbursed medical expenses
- Educational fees (school fees, supplies, and related costs)
- Transportation
- Entertainment
- College expenses

Special Circumstances for Deviation from Child Support Guidelines

- High income over guideline tables (maximum income in guidelines differ state to state)
- Special medical factors
- Stipulation (an agreement between you and your ex-spouse)
- Custody arrangements (time spent with each parent)

What Income Is Used to Calculate Child Support?

Each state's child support guidelines contain a definition of "gross income." Child support guidelines tend to define it as expansively as possible. You must ask your divorce attorney what is included in your state's specific definition of gross income for child support purposes. It usually includes money received from any source, including but not limited to:

- Salaries and wages (including bonuses, overtime, tips, commissions, profit sharing, deferred compensation, and severance/sign-on packages)
- Perks (nonmoney items) including a free or subsidized company car, lunches, housing, financial services, reimbursed expenses, etc. These perks reduce a spouse's personal living expenses and increase the amount of funds available to the parent to pay child support.
- Income from second jobs
- Income from investments (dividends, interest, and capital gains)
- Income from contractual agreements (consulting, advising, etc.)
- Income from self-employment (including rent, royalties, and business draws)
- Pension income
- Social Security income
- Trust or estate income
- Annuities
- Veteran's benefits
- Income of a new spouse (to the extent it reduces the expenses of the parent)
- Alimony received from a person other than the other spouse
- Gifts and prizes
- Benefits earned in place of earned income (worker's compensation benefits, disability insurance benefits, unemployment benefits, strike pay)

⚠ **Caution:** The amount of income someone earns can be in dispute in many child support cases. The challenging issues tend to arise mostly with:

- Self-employed individuals
- A parent with a significant amount of investment income
- A parent who is paid on commission
- A parent who is paid in cash
- A parent whose income fluctuates
- A parent paid in nontraditional ways, such as equity interests, options, or in-kind services.

Sources of Unrealized Income for Child Support

States also take many different approaches for how to handle unrealized income—income that exists on paper but has not yet been received. There are various sources of unrealized income:

- IRAs: Interest that is earned on an IRA may be considered "income."
- Unrealized gains from unexercised stock options: However, very few states have held that the capital gains an employee could realize from exercising stock options could be considered "income."

- Retained earnings of a corporation, partnership, or sole proprietorship: States are divided on whether the retained earnings can be considered income for purposes of child support.
- Income from a trust: If income is put back into a trust and is not accessible to a parent, this phantom income is usually not considered income.
- Capital gains from stock transactions: Capital gains may be considered income in some states.

Practical Issues Concerning Income Available for Support

There are practical issues concerning what income is available for support and how to use it in support calculations. For example:

- Ability to earn: A judge can examine a parent's capacity to earn as well as what the parent is actually earning. The judge may order higher child support if there is a discrepancy.
- Return on assets: A court can prescribe a reasonable rate of return on assets and may need evidence in the form of expert testimony to determine this amount.
- Retirement: Retirement assets may be tapped to pay child support or child support arrearages. A judge orders an amount that should be paid and has a QDRO executed. The noncustodial parent is responsible for any taxes owed on the distribution because child support is nontaxable to the recipient; hence, the distribution must be grossed up for any taxes (such as withholding of 20 percent) deducted by the plan.
- The double dip: Double dipping is when you allocate an asset in the division of marital property, and you also count income arising from that asset for support calculations. Marital assets that generate income include pensions, rental real estate, and businesses.

  Courts tend to consider either of the two extremes: (1) A cow can provide milk or meat, but not both; or, (2) double dipping for child support is permissible because children derive no share of the marital property when divided, so they do not benefit twice from an income-producing asset. Ask your divorce attorney.

Payment of Child Support

Payment of child support is tax-free money to the receiving parent and not deductible from income by the paying parent. If you pay or receive child support, you do not report it on your income tax return. Because child support payments are based on income, the support amount may change as circumstances of the parents change.

Child Support Order in Divorce

A child support in divorce can be negotiated in three different ways:

1. You and your ex-spouse agree to an amount in negotiations and formalize it in your divorce agreement.
2. You and your ex-spouse resolve your differences through the use of out-of-court alternative dispute resolution proceedings.
3. The court determines the amount of the child support order for you.

The result is a written document that finalizes an amount and all specific details relevant to child-related expenses for any deviation criteria or add-ons. As long as a judge is satisfied that the child support agreement is fair and the terms do not contradict the state guidelines, the agreement usually receives court approval.

Nonpayment of Child Support

Both parents have a legal responsibility to care for a child financially. This obligation must be taken seriously. Child support payments cannot be discharged in bankruptcy. A parent cannot unilaterally decide to modify or stop paying child support without going to court to amend the child support order. There is an unyielding national policy in place to ensure that children receive support from their parents and strict child support enforcement laws to get a delinquent, non-custodial parent to pay.

The Child Support Enforcement Act of 1984 (part of the Social Security Act [SSA]) provides all states with the power to collect child support and to set up a payment arrangement. This Act put the federal, state, and local governments in the business of child support establishment and enforcement. The court can order the payor to follow instructions or jail time can be imposed. The court can also order other consequences as a remedy:

- Withholding federal tax refunds and using these funds to pay child support
- Garnishing wages
- Seizing property
- Suspending an occupational license (license to practice medicine, to teach, etc.)
- Suspending a business license
- Revoking a delinquent payor's driver's license
- Denying the payor the issuance of a passport

An individual is subject to federal prosecution if she or he willfully fails to pay child support that has been ordered by a court for a child who lives in another state, if the payment is past due for longer than one year, or if the amount due exceeds $5,000.

If Your Ex-Spouse Moves Out of State and Fails to Pay

The Uniform Interstate Family Support Act sets out procedures for you to be able to enforce child support upon your ex-spouse or child's parent in another state. Under this Act, a state must cooperate with other states in establishing paternity, locating absent parents, and securing compliance with an order issued by the state. Several enforcement tools exist to penalize deadbeat parents. It is a federal crime for a parent to refuse to pay child support to a parent living in another state.

How Long Do You Have to Pay Child Support?

Child support can be terminated for many reasons but it usually centers on the child's age of majority or emancipation. Emancipation of a minor refers to a court process through which a minor can take responsibility for his or her welfare, can make legal decisions on their behalf, and no longer requires financial support from parents. When used in the context of divorce, it typically means when a child has been freed from the control of his or her parents and becomes economically independent.

Factors of Emancipation

- The child attains the age of majority (varies in each state from age 18 to 23) or graduates from high school
- The death of either the child or the person paying child support
- The child's marriage
- The child's deportation
- The adoption of the child
- The child's enlistment in the Armed Forces
- The child does not finish school and goes to work full time
- A change in legal custody

States regulate emancipation by statute. These statutes specify the conditions required or the procedures for seeking emancipation. Statutes vary widely from state to state. No fixed age of emancipation exists, yet a minor is presumed to become emancipated upon reaching the age of majority. In most states, age 18 is the age of majority and the legal age at which an individual is no longer a minor and has the right and responsibility to make certain legal choices that adults make.

Some state laws give courts the power to award college support beyond the age of majority, also called postsecondary or postminority support. College support may be in addition to child support, a part of child support, or a separate payment after regular child support ends.

Other states have no statutes holding parents responsible for college support; however, a parent can always make provisions if they agree to include it in their agreement.

The Exception to Child Support Guidelines for the Child with Special Needs

Most states also have legislation or court decisions extending the parents' obligation to adult children or nonminor children who are incapacitated or disabled. An exception to child support ending at the age of majority occurs when the child is disabled. In cases where a child is disabled mentally or physically and therefore unable to support himself or herself upon reaching the age of majority, most states have adopted a rule that parents have a duty to still provide support.

Some courts look at disability in terms of economic hardship, and a parent is usually allowed to receive support—even beyond the age of majority—to adequately care for a disabled child. States differ as to whether support for an adult disabled child is determined by the state's child support guidelines or by the needs of the child as balanced by the parents' ability to support. You can find more specific information about divorce and special needs children in Chapter 15.

If Your Circumstances Change: Modifying Child Support

Life events can dictate when support payments become unfeasible, such as a loss of job, disability, change in mental status, or change in marital status/household. If you are having difficulty paying child support, you must file a formal motion with the court requesting modification of child support reflecting your financial situation.

All decisions relating to a child are modifiable. Flexibility is essential because it is impossible to know and plan for every possible change in a growing child's needs and interests and his or her parent's needs, responsibilities, and priorities over time.

As parents, you must consider how the two of you will deal with their different interests and expenses, now and in the future. If you communicate well and hold similar values for raising your children, you will be able to project and agree on a method for problem-solving in the future.

If you and your spouse cannot agree on most financial items, specifically how the children will be raised, it is best to lay out a clear and unambiguous methodology for identifying, quantifying, limiting, and sharing children's expenses in your divorce agreement. You also might want to include language for mandatory recourse to mediation or arbitration for resolving child-related issues post-divorce.

Practical Tips for Modifying Child Support

1. File to modify a child support obligation as soon as your circumstances change or when you think they will take immediate action. Keep making payments as best as you are able. The current orders will remain in effect until you file for modification.
2. Inform yourself about what constitutes a substantial change in financial circumstances that is sufficient to merit a reduction in child support.

3. Keep track of your change in financial circumstances and be ready to provide evidence of your reduced capacity to meet your obligation. If you are seeking relief, it must be serious because you lost your job or earn less money. Even then, you must demonstrate your efforts to earn comparable income or job hunt.
4. Try to negotiate with your ex-spouse and formalize your agreement. In many cases, you can try mediation or collaborative to resolve and reach an agreement. Formalize your new agreement with the court.

If you are having difficulty collecting child support, you should follow procedures of your state's child support enforcement agency and provide detail on the amount owed and the length of time past due amounts have been accruing. The delinquent noncustodial parent will then be sent a notice from the enforcement agency.

In conclusion, courts will factor in the essential financial and support needs of a child when issuing a child support order.

> ⓘ **Tip:** It is not advisable to transfer marital property during divorce into the names of the children as a means for diverting funds from your spouse. Premeditated transfers or atypical spending on behalf of children will be examined and could be a costly mistake for the perpetrator.

Proving Child Support Goes to the Children

Courts do not require parents to prove the child support payments they receive go toward specific activities, except in cases where a child's basic needs are not being met. The assumption is that parents with physical custody of a child are paying the necessary expenses to raise a child, and therefore courts will not monitor the spending habits of a custodial parent.

What Are the Different Forms of Child Custody?

In divorce, the term "child custody" is used to describe parental rights and obligations regarding the care of a child. Child custody is broken down into two elements: legal custody and physical custody. It is important that you both understand what these terms are and how you as a parent are bound by your custody arrangement with your child.

Legal Custody

This involves major legal decision-making responsibilities affecting the welfare of your child. These decisions include religious education and upbringing, choice of schools, parent/teacher meetings, tutoring, cultural education and upbringing, extracurricular activities, routine and emergency healthcare, school and medical records, etc. In many states, courts routinely award joint legal custody, which means that the decision-making is shared by both parents. Legal custody has nothing to do with physical custody.

Physical Custody

This refers to where the child lives on a regular basis and defines residency. If you cannot agree on physical custody, the court will determine physical custody based on several factors that vary state by state. In most states, the courts use the gold standard of the "best interests of the child" and often consider who has been the child's primary caregiver during the marriage (often dubbed the Maternal Preference).

Various Child Custody Combinations

Sole custody: One parent has both physical and legal custody of the child. The other may have visitation rights but does not have custodial rights and cannot make any decisions affecting the child.

Joint legal custody: Both parents have legal decision-making authority that impacts a child. In the event of a dispute, the courts can intervene. Courts have a preference for joint legal custody.

Joint physical custody: Parents share joint physical custody, and the child splits time between living with both parents. It doesn't always involve a 50/50 time split, but it's usually more than any typical visitation schedule. It is not customary for a court to order 50/50 physical custody.

Joint legal and sole physical custody: Both parents have legal decision-making authority that impacts a child, but one parent is the primary custodial parent and has physical custody.

Practical Tips for Child Custody

1. Judges are very open to any custody arrangement that two caring and rational parents can agree to.
2. Joint physical or legal custody can become a battleground for parents who cannot agree on anything. The court could order joint custody but appoint one parent as a tiebreaker. Otherwise, if you leave your ex-spouse out of the decision-making process, you may be found in contempt of court.
3. It is practical to have sole custody if one parent lives far away, is abusive or neglectful, isn't involved at all in the child's day-to-day life, and doesn't spend any time with the child.
4. Sole physical custody provides a parent with the presumed right to relocate with the child. To prevent a move, the noncustodial parent must go to court and show how the move would be harmful to the child.
5. Joint custody can encourage both parents to remain actively involved in their child's life and for a child to have two real homes (not just have a place to "visit").
6. Joint custody is a legal order whereby the custody of a child is awarded to both parents and neither parent is a noncustodial parent. In other words, the child has two custodial parents.
7. With joint custody, both parents have to agree how you each will file for income taxes; e.g., if you meet qualifications for filing as head of household, if you can claim dependency exemptions and deductions and child tax credits, etc. You can switch back and forth each year, you can allocate the child to whoever benefits most income tax-wise, and you can split a number of children between the two of you to maximize your tax filing status.

Tax Benefits of Claiming a Child as a Dependent

The custodial parent is treated as the parent who provides more than half of the child's support and who the child spends the most time with. Generally, the custodial parent automatically gets the exemption for the child.

There are numerous standard tax benefits to claiming a child as a dependent. Either parent can claim a child as a dependent if the child meets the qualifying child test and the parents meet the IRS special rules for divorced parents (refer to IRS Publications 501 and 504). All statements for the qualifying child test must be true:

1. Are they a U.S. citizen?
2. Are you the only person claiming them as a dependent?
3. Are they filing a joint tax return? (They cannot be married and file a joint return with a spouse.)
4. Are they related to you?
5. Are they under age 19 or, if a full-time student, under age 24? (There is no age limit if they are disabled.)
6. Do they live with you for more than half the year? (Several exceptions apply.)
7. Do you financially support them (i.e., more than half their support)?

The child will be treated as a qualifying child of the *noncustodial parent* if all four of the following statements are true (IRS Publication 504):

1. The parents:
   a. Are divorced or legally separated under a decree of divorce
   b. Are separated under a written agreement
   c. Lived apart at all times during the last six months of the year, whether or not they are married
2. The child received over half of his or her support for the year from the parents
3. The child is in the custody of one or both parents for more than one-half of the year
4. The custodial parent signs a written declaration Form 8332 that he or she will not claim the child as a dependent for the year, and the noncustodial parent attaches this written declaration to his or her return. If the custodial parent releases the exemption, the custodial parent may not claim the child tax credit.

ⓘ **Tip:** Spell out all arrangements in your divorce decree and be as clear as possible.

If the *custodial parent* is allowed to claim the child as a dependent, they also can claim:

- The child tax credit;
- Head of household filing status;
- The credit for the child and dependent care expenses;
- The exclusion from income for dependent care benefits; and
- The earned income credit.

⚠ **Caution:** These tax benefits cannot be split with your ex-spouse, even by your agreement.

If the noncustodial parent can claim the child as a qualifying child, the noncustodial parent can *only* claim an exemption and child tax credit.

Tie-Breaker Rules for Filing Taxes

Only one parent can use the same qualifying child. If you and your ex-spouse cannot agree on who claims your child as a qualifying child and more than one person claims tax benefits using the same child, the IRS tie-breaker rule applies:

- The parent with whom the child lived the longest during the tax year;
- The parent with the highest AGI if the child lived with each parent for the same amount of time during the tax year; or
- If no taxpayer is the child's parent, the taxpayer with the highest AGI.

Children's Property

It is important to note that property owned by the children, such as UGMAs, UTMAs, bank accounts, brokerage accounts, children's IRAs, and education accounts, are no different from any other type of third-party property. These assets belong to the children, and the purpose of equitable distribution is to divide the property of the parties (parents), not of their children.

The Everlasting Ties That Bind You

Divorce may end your marriage, but it doesn't always end the financial ties with your ex-spouse. Child support and alimony (spousal maintenance) are legal obligations that bind the two of you. These payments differ in nature on methods of calculation, tax impact, and enforcement. You need to put together an agreement that leaves both of you in the best financial shape possible to protect the well-being of your children.

13 Spousal Support, Also Known as Alimony

It is a common misconception that most divorces involve spousal support. Only about 10 percent to 20 percent of all divorces or separations have any spousal support as part of their final divorce judgment. Spousal support, spousal maintenance, or alimony (depending on what it is called in your state) refers to a legal obligation of a person to provide financial support to his or her spouse during the marriage or after marital separation or divorce.

Historically, *the legal duty of support* arose from the marital relationship itself, when a wife merged her legal identity with that of her husband and could not own property or keep any earnings. If the marriage dissolved, a husband had a duty to protect and financially support his wife. Over time, and with the enactment of property laws, this concept of duty to support has been eliminated and replaced by an *entitlement* system based on numerous statutory factors and case law.

The basis for awarding spousal support is not to punish a guilty spouse, but to continue a duty to support the other. Spousal support is gender neutral and is available to either spouse. Spousal support is considered where one or both parties are not able to support themselves. In such cases, the family income is divided to assist a dependent spouse with meeting their financial needs.

The key to spousal support is understanding the term "standard of living" during the marriage. How one lived while married and how much it cost to live that way are usually reliable measures of the needs of a spouse.

The concept is a benchmark in divorce, where, to the extent possible, you and your ex-spouse will *maintain* or *share equally in a decline* of the standard of living. More often than not, parties are not able to reestablish something close to their marital lifestyle after divorce because there isn't enough money to make it possible. Most judges will look for a way to make the divorcing parties share the financial pain equally.

There are also many statutory factors that come into play in the determination of spousal support. Spousal support usually is the last piece of the financial puzzle to be finalized in divorce, following child support and division of assets. Since spousal support closely follows the gamesmanship surrounding these other financial issues, spousal support itself—the amount of the payment, tax treatment, modifiability, and the length of time it is paid—is unpredictable.

Analyzing spousal support awards, or the lack thereof, is complicated. Current policies and practices are inconsistently applied when courts must determine awards. Consequently, spousal support is one of the most contentious issues that tend to prolong divorce litigation. Support cases are among the most appealed; nearly 80 percent involve a request for modification of spousal support (post-divorce).

Increasingly, courts and state legislatures struggle to justify spousal support, even as they award it less frequently, in lesser amounts, and for shorter periods of time. States are taking a hard look at spousal support and are experimenting with the adoption of spousal support guidelines or a formula that offers judges a better framework for determining permanent awards.

The downside to using spousal support formulas is that if strictly adhered to, judges may lose discretion to create solutions to protect property and personal interests that are unique to each divorce. Proponents of the formulaic approach, who advocate for predictability and consistency, suggest that akin to child support guidelines, one solution would be to allow for factors that would justify a deviation in cases with unusual or compelling circumstances.

Types of Spousal Support

Given the variety of marital relationships, spouses in modern marriages are unlikely to find a single solution to be equitable. There are about six variations on spousal support, each applicable to a different family situation; not all types may exist in your state:

- Temporary—This support is ordered when necessary before divorce, whether the parties live together or separately. It is only in force until there is a final order.
- Rehabilitative or transitional—This support is given to the lesser-earning spouse for the time necessary to acquire paying work and become self-sufficient.
- Permanent or lifetime—This support is paid to the lesser-earning spouse until the death of the payor or recipient or upon remarriage of the recipient.
- Reimbursement or compensatory—This support is given as reimbursement for expenses incurred by a spouse during the marriage, such as for education.
- Durational—This support is paid for a specific period of time, measured by the length of the marriage or end of childcare responsibilities.
- Lump sum—This support is a precise, nonmodifiable amount paid at once or in installments.

⚠ **Caution:** Spousal support awards seem confusing and random. The courts must consider statutory factors, but these factors are not typically ranked regarding importance. For states that use formulas for spousal support, the goal is to have consistent calculations of how much and for how long rather than specify who is eligible to receive spousal support.

Statutory Factors for Determining Entitlement to Spousal Support

The Uniform Marriage and Divorce Act, on which many states' spousal support statutes are based, recommends that courts consider certain factors in making decisions about spousal support awards. These factors differ from state to state but most include many listed below:

- Length of the marriage
- Cause for divorce
- The contributions of each spouse to the marriage, both financial and nonfinancial
- The age, physical health, and emotional states of both spouses
- The number and age of the children, as well as parental responsibilities
- Desirability of the custodial parent to secure employment
- Station in life ("standard of living" during the marriage)
- The earning capability of each party, as well as their education, occupation, and employability
- Amount and sources of income
- Vocational skills and length of time the recipient would need for education or training to become self-sufficient
- Estate (division of marital property)
- Genuine needs of the parties
- The financial capacity of the payor spouse to support the recipient and still support himself or herself.

In determining whether spousal support should be awarded, as well as the duration and amount of the award, courts take into account the above factors. However, courts have broad discretion in how they weigh the importance of any given factor. Ultimately, spousal support awards are subjective and decided on a case-by-case basis.

Payment of Spousal Support

Spousal support is typically paid as a periodic payment. However, other alternative forms of payment exist. It is a payment to or for a former spouse under a divorce or separation instrument. It does not include voluntary payments that are not made under the divorce or separation instrument. Spousal support is nondischargeable in the event of bankruptcy.

Spousal support is usually a taxable event for both spouses and must meet certain criteria of the IRS tax for it to be tax deductible to the payor (dollar for dollar) and taxable to the recipient. Section 71(b) of the Internal Revenue Code (IRC) provides that the following must apply to establish spousal support:

The Five "D's" of Spousal Support (IRS Rules)

1. The recipient or third party must receive cash payments. (DOLLARS)
2. Payments must be required by a written order. (DOCUMENT)
3. The written order must designate the payment as "being alimony" and not some other form of payment. Payments may not be treated as child support. (DESIGNATE)
4. The payor and payee must not be members of the same household. The parties may not file a joint income tax return. (DISTANCE)
5. Payments must cease on the death of the recipient (DEATH)

Forms of Payment

There are two potential ways to pay or receive spousal support, a periodic payment or a lump-sum settlement. The most conventional way is a periodic payment for a particular duration.

Periodic Payments

A periodic payment is a series of payments of a certain amount (either in dollars or as a percentage of income) and duration.

- Advantages
  - You know you have a stream of income for a limited term.
  - You can plan with some certainty, knowing what you will receive each month.
  - You can modify the amount or duration based on a significant change in financial circumstances (unless precluded by the agreement).
  - You may be entitled to have payments withheld directly from payor's paycheck, or you could have payments directly deposited to your bank account to minimize any delays or interactions with your ex-spouse.
  - You can negotiate how to maximize tax credits and tax deductions.
  - You can contribute to individual retirement savings account based on spousal support received.
- Disadvantages
  - You may need to secure these payments with life insurance, wage garnishment, or some other means.
  - Nonpayment could occur for any of these reasons: (1) death of the payor, (2) loss of income/employment, (3) default, or (4) court-ordered modifications due to subsequent substantial change in your or your ex-spouse's financial circumstances.
  - If you agree to periodic payments:
    - You are connected to your ex-spouse over time long after the divorce is final.
    - You have the burden to modify the payments if your or her or his financial circumstances significantly change.

- You may have to file quarterly taxes.
- You will risk losing your spousal support if you cohabitate or remarry.

Lump-Sum Settlement

A lump-sum settlement is a one-time settlement, or an installment or structured settlement, as opposed to a series of payments over time. Lump-sum payments in cash will often result in significant tax traps for the unwary. The tax treatment may be subject to IRS scrutiny if a lump sum payment occurs one time or in conjunction with a series of periodic payments over time. Tax treatment of the lump-sum payment during divorce should determine how you calculate the amount and if it should be tax effected as well as discounted for time value of money (a discount). Post-judgment attempts by ex-spouses who agree to convert periodic alimony payments into a final lump-sum payment also run into challenges with the IRS. It is always important to consult with a divorce financial planner on this topic.

- Advantages
  - A lump-sum payment ends all obligations at one time. It is a clean break for both parties.
  - The lump sum is unusual in that it is payable even if certain events occur that would ordinarily cause the termination of spousal support, such as remarriage.
  - The present or future status of the recipient does not affect the spousal support lump sum. You can remarry, cohabitate, and earn income—all without fear of losing spousal support.
  - There is no need to maintain life insurance to secure spousal support.
  - There is no need to worry about if your payment will be received late or not at all.
  - You have immediate access to monies that can enhance your value of life and perhaps help you with the purchase of a new home.
  - Your ex-spouse pays a reduced amount today as opposed to periodic payments over time (discounted for the time value of money).
  - Your ex-spouse is free to earn as much as they can without fear you will benefit from her or his efforts post-divorce.
- Disadvantages
  - A lump-sum payment is rarer than periodic support awards for practical reasons.
  - Many payors do not have the ability or liquidity to make a lump sum payment (i.e., insufficient assets).
  - The potential for changed circumstances can outweigh factors favoring a lump-sum settlement, such as loss of income, disability, or the recipient's remarriage.
  - There are no "do-overs," and it is nonmodifiable.
  - You (recipient) may blow the lump sum with poor investments or spending.

- You may have difficulty budgeting with a lump-sum payment rather than a monthly payment.
- There may be tax implications if the lump sum is spread over three years as well as if it is improperly characterized in your agreement.

Waiver of Spousal Support

Spousal support can be waived by one or both spouses. The waiver needs to be in writing and signed by both spouses. By doing so, you may *forever* terminate your entitlement to an award of spousal support. Such waivers can be dangerous. If you simply fail to request spousal support at the time of your divorce, you may be forever barred from requesting spousal support in the future.

If you are unsure of whether you will need spousal support in the future, you can agree to provide a nominal amount of $1 per year of spousal support to keep your options open should your financial needs or circumstances change. The right to modify that nominal order of spousal support may become meaningful if at some point in time in the future you lose your job or become injured, incapacitated, or disabled.

It may also become meaningful if your spouse, who was unable to provide spousal support in the past, subsequently secures sufficient employment or has some other beneficial economic change in circumstance that increases their ability to contribute to your support.

Nullifying a Waiver of Spousal Support

If you already have a judgment of divorce and have waived your right to a spousal support award, there may still be a slim hope you can nullify your waiver. You may be able to have your judgment set aside if there was never a discussion in court regarding the effect of eliminating your right to receive spousal support in the future. You may also be able to have it set aside if your divorce decree does not clearly and unambiguously state that the spousal support award is nonmodifiable. You must ask your divorce attorney.

How Is Spousal Support Calculated?

There is no universal standard or formula for setting the amount and duration of spousal support. Negotiating and calculating spousal support can be a complicated process. Spousal support is separate from child support, and child support payments take priority over spousal support. However, a high spousal support payment may affect, and could result in, a reduction in child support.

The following is a four-step process for how to calculate spousal support payments:

1. Determine the requesting spouse's reasonable financial need (the difference between income and expenses is the amount of the deficiency or "need") and if additional income is required.

2. Determine the requesting spouse's ability to meet their own needs without contribution from the other spouse.
3. Determine which spouse has the capacity to pay support (e.g., his or her disposable income after taxes).
4. Know the marital circumstances and the amount of marital property and how it will be divided between the parties.
5. Identify how long the payments should last—look at the future earning capacity of either spouse, the ability to become financially self-sufficient, or a continuing or indefinite obligation that directly resulted from the marriage, such as a child with special needs.

The calculation of spousal support could be established using any of the approaches below. It is highly recommended you understand which one makes the most sense for you:

1. Determine the amount you need to break even. This amount is the spousal support necessary to get you to the point where your income (including your spousal support) covers all expenses plus all taxes. This number is called a "needs-based" amount.
2. Determine the amount that equates to a certain percentage of your ex-spouse's gross or net after-tax income.
3. Determine the amount that targets a proportionate mix of spousal support and child support (trade-off vis-à-vis total taxes paid to the government by both spouses) that enables you and your ex-spouse to maximize your total combined cash flow.
4. Determine the amount required if you switch child support payments entirely to spousal support (called *family support* or unallocated support). Because spousal support is tax deductible to the payor, there is often a tax benefit to trading off spousal support against child support. The advantage arises if the payor is in a higher tax bracket than the payee. The payee receives more cash flow up front that is taxable later.
5. See the amount you would receive if you get a lump-sum payment. The value of total spousal support obligation paid out over time can be quantified in today's dollars. Your ex-spouse can pay you a one-time lump-sum payment that is equivalent to the future stream of support payments, discounted for the time value of money (present value).

⚠ **Caution:** There may be tax consequences if you take a lump sum, and you could be taxed for the full amount in the year it is received. However, if it is labeled as "property settlement," you may not be taxed. You must ask your divorce attorney.

Some states have debated setting guidelines for a formulaic approach to calculating spousal support. The American Academy of Matrimonial Lawyers (AAML) proposes this approach:

Unless one of the deviation factors listed below applies, a spousal support award should be calculated by taking 30 percent of the payor's gross income minus 20 percent of the payee's gross income. The formula is not to be applied in any case where the combined gross income of the parties exceeds $1 million a year, and the calculated payment, in addition to the payee's income, may never exceed 40 percent of the combined gross income of the parties.[5]

How Long Do You Have to Pay Spousal Support?

The answer to how long you may receive spousal support depends on if you and your ex-spouse can agree to a time frame called the duration of spousal support. If you can't agree, laws vary from state to state. A few states still allow courts to order lifetime or permanent spousal support, but the trend is very much opposed to this scenario, and states are actively reforming spousal support laws.

General Guidelines about the Duration of Spousal Support

- Courts will look to prenuptial agreements, and you may end up with whatever term for spousal support is in your contract.
- Spousal support isn't preferred for short marriages or where you and your spouse earn the same amount of money.
- In states with rehabilitative spousal support, courts will try to determine how long it may take to "rehabilitate you" so you can become financially independent. Courts may also affix a date to end spousal support or set a review date.
- Spousal support could be temporary or be meant to reimburse one spouse for expenses for a fixed period.
- If there is no fixed date for spousal support payments to end in your divorce decree, they will continue indefinitely. This situation is called permanent or lifetime spousal support, and it is becoming rarer. Permanent support usually ends when your ex-spouse stops working at normal retirement age or when she or he eventually stops working. Lifetime support may continue during retirement years. For long-term marriages over 10 years, there is no hard or fast rule for how long spousal support should last. Many divorce attorneys use the rule of thumb for half the length of the marriage as a starting point.

The AAML proposes the following guidelines for determining the duration of spousal support based on the number of years married.

0–3 years: Multiply number of years by 0.3
3–10 years: Multiply number of years by 0.5
10–20 years: Multiply number of years by 0.75
Over 20 years: Permanent

5 Journal of the American Academy of Matrimonial Lawyers, Seq. 18, June 16, 2008, Appendix A: The AAML Commission Recommendations Adopted by the Board of Governors, March 9, 2007.

Tax Implications of Spousal Support

The IRC governs the federal tax treatment of spousal support, not any divorce agreements or court orders. There are several definitions of spousal support, and there are different domestic relations statutes in the Code.

It is important *not to assume* that just calling payments "spousal support" in your divorce decree makes them such under the Code to qualify for income tax purposes. The income tax deduction for payment of spousal support is subject to very specific rules (refer to the five "D's" described earlier in this chapter).

Spousal support is usually tax deductible to the payor and taxable to the recipient. If you receive spousal support, no taxes are withheld by your ex-spouse. This money is taxable to you as income in the year it is received. The added income for you means you should probably pay quarterly estimated taxes. You may need an accountant to calculate your projected quarterly tax payments or make other adjustments to your paycheck to increase your taxes withheld.

If you receive spousal support, you cannot file the shorter, simpler tax forms. You must now file the long form 1040 and report the full amount of spousal support on Line 11. If you are the payor of spousal support, you do not have to itemize deductions to deduct your spousal support payments from your income.

Taxpayers are free to choose the tax effect of spousal support. You and your ex-spouse can change or eliminate this tax treatment through an explicit agreement in your divorce decree. You and your spouse can designate in your agreement that payments are *not* deductible as spousal support by the payor and are excludable from recipient's income. By making this designation in a written agreement, you both may need to attach a copy of this agreement designating payments as not spousal support to your federal income tax returns *each year*.

Amounts paid under a divorce decree or a separation agreement must meet the alimony requirements outlined in IRS Publication 504 for federal tax purposes:

- *Separate returns:* You and your spouse or former spouse can not file a joint return with each other.
- *Cash payment:* The payment must be in cash (including checks or money orders).
- *Marriage relationship:* The payment must be received by (or on behalf of) your ex-spouse.
- *Contrary designation or election out of alimony:* The divorce or separate maintenance decree or written separation agreement cannot say the payment is not alimony.
- *Living together after divorce:* If legally separated under a decree of divorce or separate maintenance, you and your former spouse cannot be members of the same household when you make the payment.
- *Death of the recipient:* There is no liability to make the payment (in cash or property) after the death of the recipient spouse; payments can survive the death of the payor and continue through payments by the payor's estate.
- *Child support or property settlement*: The payment cannot be treated as child support or a property settlement.

Payments That Are Not Considered Alimony per the IRS

Not all payments under a divorce or separation instrument are alimony. Alimony *does not* include:

- Child support,
- Noncash transfers between spouses or on their behalf,
- Payments that are your spouse's part of community property income,
- Payments to keep up the payer's property, or
- Payments for the use of the payer's property.

Child support is never deductible. If your decree of divorce or separate maintenance provides for alimony and child support and you pay less than the total required, the payments apply first to child support. Any remaining amount is considered alimony.

Noncash property settlements, whether in a lump sum or installments, do not qualify as alimony.

Voluntary payments (that is, payments not required by a divorce decree or separation instrument) do not qualify as alimony.

How Can You Modify or Terminate Spousal Support?

It is not unusual for some component of spousal support to be nonmodifiable, but a court will rarely order nonmodifiable spousal support for *both* amount and duration. This type of spousal support is only created by mutual agreement of the parties.

Once a court grants or orders spousal support, the court has broad discretion in how they define circumstances for modifying it or a basis for terminating it. In considering whether to modify, suspend, or terminate a spousal support award, the court will once again look at the ability to pay vis-à-vis the needs of the recipient.

If in dividing up marital property, your spouse agrees or is ordered by the judge to make payments to you in one lump sum, this payment is not eligible for a reduction or elimination. In fact, this type of spousal support is one of the few types of support that would still be owed to your estate after you die.

Grounds for modifying or terminating spousal support differ in every state. A court may examine any of the following conditions:

- A date set by a judge in the divorce decree
- You cohabitate with someone romantically or live with a companion
- You remarry
- Your children are old enough to no longer need a full-time parent at home

- A judge determines that you have not made a sufficient effort to become at least partially self-supporting after a reasonable amount of time
- Your income changes from prior levels (goes up) and you are financially self-sufficient
- Some other significant event—such as retirement—occurs, convincing a judge to modify the amount paid
- Your former spouse will experience severe hardship due to the continuation of spousal support payments
- Your ex-spouse loses their job
- Your ex-spouse would be treated unfairly if required to pay
- One of you dies

Cohabitation

Cohabitation is ill-defined in legal statutes. It connotes when a couple is living together in a "marriage-like" manner. In some states, cohabitation alone does not automatically result in modification or termination of spousal support. In those instances, cohabitation must be paired with a substantial change in economic circumstances to affect spousal support. By cohabitating or living with another person (which, in some states, doesn't necessarily have to be a romantic relationship), it must have stability, durability, and a "supportive" interrelationship, as well as provide economic benefits.

Modification or termination of spousal support upon cohabitation is not automatic in some states. The payor spouse has the burden to prove evidence of cohabitation (financial, social, and/or sexual) and show how it triggers a change in financial circumstances. Since cohabitation is a factual determination, the paying spouse must petition the court to schedule a hearing and make an assessment. In other states, cohabitation effects an automatic termination of alimony. In those states, the payor has the burden of proving the recipient is living with another party. The burden then shifts to the recipient to prove the relationship is non-marriage-like; i.e., they are not engaged in a physical relationship. Most often the physical aspect is admitted, and the fight is around whether or not the parties are actually living together.

Evidence could look like:

- The establishment of a common household
- Shared bills and shared bank accounts
- Joint contribution to daily living expenses
- Recognition of the romantic relationship within the community

NOTE: In many cases, it is very difficult to prove a former spouse receives substantial support from a companion. In many cases, courts will reduce spousal support but not terminate it because of the provisional nature of cohabitation.

Once spousal support ends, it is absolutely over for both parties. If the receiving spouse wants to extend spousal support beyond the termination date stated in the divorce decree, they must request a modification before that date arrives. If the paying party can prove that spousal support has terminated under the terms of the prior court order (i.e., duration has expired or recipient has remarried or cohabits with another), then spousal support will be terminated and cannot be renewed again.

Spousal Support after Remarriage

If there is no provision in the divorce decree, most states often automatically end spousal support when the recipient spouse remarries. In rare cases, however, spousal support may continue after cohabitation or remarriage if you and your spouse agreed to it in your divorce order.

The court may also consider the continuance to pay spousal support after the recipient remarries alongside provisions of property division by the court. This analysis occurs if the agreement between the parties as to property division and spousal support would be undermined if spousal support ended prematurely, even if due to the recipient's remarriage.

If the payor spouse remarries, she or he still pays spousal support. However, the amount could be reduced if the new marriage produces a child and results in additional financial responsibility for the payor.

If you are obligated to pay spousal support, you can elect to appeal the judgment. You must petition the court and revisit your original document, provide a good explanation of how the financial condition of either you or your ex-spouse had substantially changed and why you want a change, and show all the evidence you may need to prove a change in circumstances. You must not unilaterally decide to stop or modify the amount you are ordered to pay. If you fail to pay, you could be penalized severely or even incarcerated. Your actions could result in a charge of indirect civil contempt of court, or even criminal contempt of court, depending on your state.

It is not a good idea to file for bankruptcy to avoid an obligation to pay spousal support. Domestic support obligations cannot usually be "discharged" (canceled or forgiven) in a bankruptcy proceeding.

⚠ **Caution:** Spousal support enforcement may be by wage garnishment and other enforcement mechanisms. You must sue your spouse for failure to pay spousal support.

The Alimony Recapture Rule

The alimony recapture rule under IRC Section § 71 only applies to the payor when spousal payments decrease substantially or end during the first three calendar years. This rule is intended to discourage divorcing spouses from improperly characterizing property settlement payments as spousal support and benefitting from the tax deductibility of spousal support payments. "Recapture" in this context means that the tax benefit was improperly taken at an earlier time and must be paid back.

Under IRC Section § 71, the IRS can force you into an audit and assess taxes for three years of what they call "front-loading" spousal support. The three-year period starts with the first calendar year you make a payment *qualifying as spousal support* under a decree of divorce or separate maintenance or a written separation agreement. Do not include any time in which payments were being made under temporary support orders. The second and third years are the next two calendar years, whether or not payments are made during those years. A dramatic reduction or end of spousal support after the third year of divorce will not trigger recapture.

Recapture triggers include:

- A change in your divorce or separation instrument
- A failure to make timely payments
- A reduction in your ability to provide support
- A reduction in your spouse's support needs

When to Apply the Recapture Rule

You are subject to the recapture rule in the third year if the amount of spousal support you pay in the first three years varies and decreases by more than $15,000.

Exceptions to Recapture

When you figure a decrease in spousal support, do not include the following amounts:

- Payments made under a temporary support order
- Payments required over a period of at least three calendar years that vary because they are a fixed part of your income from a business or property, or as a percentage of compensation from employment or self-employment
- Payments that decrease because of the death of either spouse or the remarriage of the spouse receiving the payments before the end of the third year

Calculating the Recapture

Two computations must be made to determine if recapture is necessary:

- A taxpayer is subject to recapture in the third post-separation year if the spousal support paid in that year decreases by more than $15,000 from the second post-separation year. The excess over $15,000 must be recaptured.
- A taxpayer is also subject to recapture in the third year if the payments made in the first post-separation year exceed the average of the payments in the second and third post-separation years by more than $15,000. Again, the excess over $15,000 is recaptured.

If both of these computations result in recapture, the amount recaptured under the first computation is subtracted from the second-year payments for purposes of making the second computation.

A simple and straightforward Recapture of Alimony worksheet for performing the necessary computations is provided in IRS Publication #504.

EXAMPLE:

Alimony Paid in Year 1: $60,000
Alimony Paid in Year 2: $40,000
Alimony Paid in Year 3: $20,000

1. Alimony paid in Year 2....................................$40,000
2. Alimony paid in Year 3....................................$20,000
3. Floor..$15,000
4. Add Lines 2 and 3...$35,000 ($20,000 + $15,000)
5. Subtract line 4 from Line 1...............................$5,000 ($40,000 – $35,000)
6. Alimony paid in Year 1....................................$60,000
7. Adjusted alimony paid in Year 2 (Line 1 less Line 5)..$35,000 ($40,000 – $5,000)
8. Alimony paid in Year 3....................................$20,000
9. Add Lines 7 and 8...$55,000 ($35,000 + $20,000)
10. Divide Line 9 by 2..$27,500
11. Floor..$15,000
12. Add Lines 10 and 11.......................................$42,500 ($27,500 + $15,000)
13. Subtract Line 12 from Line 6............................$17,500 ($60,000 – $42,500)
14. **Recaptured alimony**: Add Lines 5 and 13.....**$22,500** ($5,000 + $17,500)*

* *If alimony was deducted, this amount must be reported as gross income. If alimony was received, this amount is deductible.*

The Child Contingency Rule

To establish that spousal support remains deductible to the payor, the payments cannot run afoul of the IRS Child Contingency Regulations. Under IRS Code Section 71(c)(2). Reg. § 1.71-1T(c), when spousal support payments decrease, or end on or around the same time as a child-related event (called a child contingency—see below), a portion of spousal support payments leading up to that event may be reclassified by the IRS as child (not spousal) support. Spousal support payments cannot vary with the status of a child.

Further, any tax benefits received by the payor of spousal support, and any taxes paid by the recipient, are to be returned—the payor will owe the IRS and the recipient will receive a tax refund. With any one of the child-related contingencies, a portion of spousal support will be deemed as being nondeductible *child support from the start.*

The reason for this rule is to prevent people from deducting for tax purposes payments that effectively are child support (child support is not tax deductible).

Child Contingencies

The IRS provides examples of contingency events related to the child:

1. Marriage
2. Death
3. Reaching a specified age or income level
4. Leaving school
5. Becoming employed
6. Joining the military
7. Leaving home

The IRS may seek to reclassify your spousal support payments under the child contingency rule if you have a scheduled reduction in your spousal support payments in any of the above situations and apply one of the two situations below. However, you may be able to overcome this presumption, and it may be rebuttable, so ask your divorce attorney.

1. The Six-Month Rule: Payments are reduced not more than six months before or after the date the child reaches the age of majority in their state.
2. The Multiple Reduction Rule: If there is more than one child and the divorce agreement provides for more than one reduction in spousal support payments, and if the payments are to be reduced on two or more occasions that occur not more than *one year* before or after each child reaches a certain age, then it is presumed that the reduction is child support. The age at which the reduction occurs must be between 18 and 24, must be inclusive, and must be the same for each of the children.

Rebutting Presumptive Contingencies

The good news is that the IRS regulation stipulates in Publication 504 that "in all other situations, reductions in payments will not be treated as clearly associated with the happening of a contingency relating to a child of the payor" (IRS Code Section 71(c)(2) Child Contingency Regulations). You have the opportunity to rebut the IRS' presumption and introduce evidence to remove the effect of the child contingency ruling.

To rebut the presumed nature of the payments successfully, you must be able to show:

- That the reduction was independent of any child-related contingency;
- That spousal support payments are set for a period that is customary in the local jurisdiction; or,
- Regarding the first presumption, that the reduction is a complete cessation of spousal support during the sixth post-separation year.

One of the many tax-planning opportunities in divorce is to figure out how much support to allocate for child and spousal support. This exercise must be done with great care to structure it appropriately.

As you can see, despite seemingly straightforward IRS rules governing spousal support and child support, there are a multitude of variables that can have a direct impact on their taxability. The moral is, don't tie the reduction of spousal support to anything relating to the children!

What Happens If Your Spouse Dies?

Termination of Automatic Rights of a Spouse after Divorce

Depending on how your will is drafted, divorce may modify it. A divorce effectively cuts off your inheritance rights as a surviving ex-spouse in intestacy (when no will exists). Each state has its own laws regarding how property is treated after the court enters a judgment and decree of dissolution of marriage or annulment of marriage.

In general, states recognize that after divorce, most people do not want to leave their former spouse any assets in their will. If there are no updates to your will, any property that is supposed to go to your former spouse will instead pass on as if the former spouse failed to survive you. State statutes often provide for the automatic termination of individual property rights or interests after a divorce is entered.

However, a divorce does not automatically change any beneficiary designation on assets that will be distributed to the named beneficiary. If your ex-spouse forgot to update the designation of you as a beneficiary of any retirement plan, financial account, or life insurance policy, you would inherit these assets if your ex-spouse dies.

The plan administrator or provider is legally obligated to distribute funds upon your death to the designated beneficiaries on these accounts, even if you and your former spouse were divorced at the time of death. The fact is that post-divorce, you must take the additional steps to change or revoke beneficiary designations on these specific accounts, assets, and plans. Neither your will nor your divorce decree has the final say.

Financial Instruments with Beneficiary Designations

- Employer retirement plans
- IRAs
- Life Insurance Annuities
- HSAs
- Transfer-on-death (TOD) investment accounts
- Payable-on-death (POD) bank accounts
- Will
- Healthcare powers of attorney and living wills
- Powers of attorney
- Revocable trusts

- Survivor beneficiaries on pensions
- Advanced estate planning vehicles, such as irrevocable trusts

What Happens If Your Spouse Dies and You Are Not Yet Divorced?

Most states won't grant a pending divorce after the death of one spouse. The marriage has ended in death, and there usually is no need for a final divorce decree. You may, however, have a problem if most of the family assets were in the name of the decedent spouse who disinherited you, the surviving spouse. Some states permit disinherited spouses, and some states do not. Even in the states that do not, the decedent's spouse's ability to control assets during their life could result in the assets being removed from the marital estate.

Some states allow you to rewrite your will *after you file* for divorce; others do not. Some states allow you to bar your spouse from an elective share of the estate before their divorce is final. In those states that do not permit division of the marital estate upon the death of a party, there may be other contractual or equitable theories on which a surviving spouse can recover marital assets from the decedent's estate. You must ask your divorce attorney about laws in your state.

The Decedent's Nonprobate Assets

All states distinguish between probate and nonprobate assets when a person dies. Nonprobate assets pass directly to a named beneficiary by contract, and transfer of title happens without probate. For example, assets such as life insurance death benefits and retirement plan benefits usually have named beneficiaries. If the probate court has jurisdiction over deciding on the disposition of your marital estate, it has no control over these assets. They all go to the named beneficiaries regardless of your divorce plans.

⚠ **Caution:** In some states when you file for divorce, your spouse may be permitted to change the beneficiary designation. Other states have statutory restraints imposed during divorce that can prohibit either party from changing beneficiary designations or taking any actions without the written consent of the other party or order of the court.

The Decedent's Probate Estate or Intestacy

The balance of the deceased spouse's estate will probably pass through probate unless she or he created a trust. If she or he created a trust to distribute assets after death, the terms of the trust document would bypass probate and usually prevail.

Assuming that she or he did not create a trust, the divorce is dismissed, and probate proceedings begin. You will inherit your spouse's probate assets according to your state's probate laws, or you can contest the will to make a claim.

If your spouse dies without a will, then this results in intestacy. A surviving spouse has rights in an intestate estate, and you will inherit at least a portion of the estate (an elective share is usually one-third to one-half) according to your state's laws of intestate succession. A right of election protects a surviving spouse's right to inherit even if the deceased spouse attempted to give away his or her estate to the detriment of the surviving spouse (for example, if the deceased spouse held joint bank accounts or property with someone other than the spouse).

Late-Life Divorce and Unique Considerations

When you are over 50 years old and decide to divorce, you face unique age-related issues that can factor into your decision to divorce. You realize that you may have many more years ahead of you and may be sensitive to new tensions surrounding health issues, goals for retirement, losing parents and friends, and even pressures of financially dependent adult children.

One of the biggest challenges with late-life divorce is there is less time to recover financially. You are dividing the marital pie in half, and there are fewer years to replenish assets by earning money. Clearly, there are more concerns about what happens to the nest egg when it must cover the needs of two households.

Your decision to divorce calls for an examination of the following:

- ❑ What are your assets and debts? Most likely everything will be cut in half with a long-term marriage.
- ❑ How much more expensive are your insurances when you break them apart? You are older and may have more difficulty getting approved at a reasonable cost for health, life, auto, long-term care, and homeowners insurance.
- ❑ Child support and visitation may be out of the picture, but that doesn't mean adult children are not a consideration. Will you continue to support young adult children without any legal obligation to do so? If you assumed parent loans for your college-age kids, who will assume these debts?
- ❑ If you remarry, how will you blend families where there are children of different ages with different needs? Will you blend financial resources equally or equitably? Will you maintain separate finances for your own children?
- ❑ How will you pay for college versus save for your retirement?
- ❑ Getting a divorce has an impact on friendships and social circles; it is harder to make new friends or not to feel isolated or alone.
- ❑ When will you start receiving retirement benefits such as distributions (without penalties)? Do you have survivor benefits with your ex-spouse's retirement plan?
- ❑ Will you need to consider a reverse mortgage to stay in your home if you do not have sufficient cash flow or income?
- ❑ How long do you need to wait to apply for Social Security—either on your record or your ex-spouse's?

- ❑ Have you updated your estate documents and beneficiaries? What happens if your former spouse remarries, and how will blended families affect your children's inheritance?

The trend of gray divorce is growing rapidly. The divorce rate among people 50 and older is the fastest growing statistic and has doubled in the past 20 years. Perhaps the biggest reason for the increase in late-life divorces is the changing status of women, who initiate about 60 percent of divorces after age 40.

Many factors are primary contributors:

1. Longevity and how you spend time with someone
2. Greater confidence and self-respect—the ability to end a relationship that is not supportive or satisfying
3. Less social stigma surrounding divorce
4. Less tolerance or willingness to be a caregiver for someone with a serious illness
5. Financial stability and resources

According to a 2016 survey of AAML members,[6] the top three areas of dispute in gray divorce are spousal support (83 percent), retirement accounts and pensions (62 percent), and business interests (60 percent). The most common area of dispute is houses and other real estate (51 percent).

Since the time to recoup financial losses from divorce is finite, parties must focus on cash flow, taxes, and real estate. Building a professional team during the divorce process can illuminate opportunities to maximize outcome and preserve wealth.

As with any divorce, there is the prospect to develop new beginnings, no matter what age.

6 Survey conducted of AAML members and quoted by John Slowiaczek, then president-elect of the AAML, in Investment News August 19, 2016, "Gray divorce on the rise with longevity trend" by Mary Beth Franklin.

14 Debt, Credit, and Credit Worthiness: How to Protect Your Credit

What Is Credit?

Credit is defined as the ability of a customer to obtain goods and services before payment with the expectation that future payment will be made. Credit is a contractual agreement between a borrower and a lender. The borrower receives something of value now and agrees to repay the lender at some date in the future, generally with interest. Each person has the right to be considered equal to all other credit applicants. In divorce, the goal is to establish your individual credit and credit history to build your financial profile.

What Are the Different Types of Debt?

A *secured debt* is a loan where the borrower pledges some asset (e.g., a car or property) as collateral for the loan. The lender has the right to claim the borrower's collateral if they do not pay. It is debt that is guaranteed by an asset. A secured credit card is backed by a designated savings account used as collateral for access to the available amount of credit. Secured debt is typically less risky and has a lower interest rate than unsecured debt. Secured debt should always be paid first since it is much easier for a lender to foreclose on your home or car than it is to take your assets back with unsecured debt.

Unsecured debt is any debt or "signature" loan that relies on the borrower's word to repay. The borrower signs a contract or loan document and promises to pay back the money based on trust. Personal loans and unsecured credit cards are the most common types of unsecured debts. If you fail to repay, the lender can sue you and, if successful, place liens on your assets, garnish your wages, or take any other legal actions to get back their money. Unsecured debt typically carries higher interest rates.

Student loan debt is a unique kind of debt. In many cases, the government has provided security of payment on your debt and guarantees to the lenders the loan will be paid back. More stringent laws apply to student loans; for example, it is not dischargeable in bankruptcy. Student loan debt should also be paid before unsecured debt.

ⓘ **Tip:** Understanding the differences between secured debt and unsecured debt is essential to your financial well-being.

How Is Credit Reported?

Credit bureaus were established to act as clearing houses for your payment habits from the moment you create your first account. They provide creditors with your information so they can assess if you are—or are not—a good risk. The information collected by credit bureaus includes:

- The amount of credit extended
- The accounts receivable aging terms: (e.g., 30, 60, or 90 days and percentage of interest)
- Current account balance
- Amount that is overdue
- Promptness of payment

What Is a Credit Score?

Your credit score is a weighted measure of the mix of both secured and unsecured debt. A credit score rating is an assessment of an individual's creditworthiness. The current credit scoring model was first introduced in 1989 and was standardized by the Fair Isaac Corporation (FICO). It is called a FICO score. This evaluation is based on the individual's history of borrowing money and repaying debts. Not all lenders use the same credit scoring model.

A person's income and availability of assets factor into how much credit you can access and at what cost. Usually the larger your income, the more debt you can handle. Various formulas are used by institutions to calculate your debt-to-income ratio. The average goal is to keep debt to 20 percent or less. There are multiple online tools to help you do so. The *important concept is to borrow only as much as you need.*

If you are just starting out and building a credit history, your credit score will frequently change with your financial activity. There are three main credit rating bureaus that use the standardized FICO model: Experian, Equifax, and Transunion. They are private (publicly traded) companies and not government agencies. These credit rating companies use credit scores to gauge your creditworthiness.

Credit scores range from 350 to 850 points. The higher the score, the better. The majority of scores range between 600 and 700. Scores differ over time and from agency to agency. Lenders may use a different scoring process.

How Is a Credit Score Used?

Banks, leasing companies, credit unions, mortgage lenders, department stores, insurance companies, and various other institutions use credit reports and credit scores to determine whether to extend credit to you, how much to give you, and how much to charge for interest. Credit scores affect the cost of mortgages, loans, leases, home and auto insurances, rental/lease deposits, etc. Your credit score is essentially your financial reputation in numbers.

EXAMPLE:

720 – 800 Excellent
690 – 720 Good
650 – 690 Fair
350 – 650 Poor
000 – 349 No Credit

Several factors are given different weight to calculate your credit score. These factors are:

- Payment history—Assigned a weight of **35 percent** (Pay your bills on time!)
  - Your payment history is best described by the presence or lack of derogatory information, including bankruptcy, liens, judgments, settlements, charge-offs, repossessions, foreclosures, and late payments.
- Amounts you owe—Assigned a weight of **30 percent** (Keep your balances down! Avoid maxing out your limits!)
  - Your total borrowings are your debt burden. FICO uses several ratios, not just the maximum credit card debt–to–limit ratio. It's best to keep balances at less than 50 percent of available credit. Also, the number of accounts with balances, the amount owed across different types of debt, and the amounts paid down on installment loans are factored into this score.
- Length of credit history—Assigned a weight of **15 percent** (Keep a good track record!)
  - As a credit history ages, it has a positive impact on one's FICO score.
- New Credit—Assigned a weight of **10 percent** (Apply only when you need more credit!)
  - Recent searches for credit, such as numerous hard credit inquiries when you apply for credit, can hurt your FICO score. "Rate shopping" within a short period and any "soft inquiries" made by you or your employer do not have any impact.
- Types of credit—Assigned a weight of **10 percent** (Establish a variety of loans, such as mortgages, student loans, revolving credit, and installment loans.)

What Do You Need to Do to Check Your Credit?

You should check your credit history by requesting credit reports. You can obtain your credit reports for free from all three reporting agencies—Experian, Equifax, and TransUnion—at least once a year. There are some online resources; one authorized by federal law is annualcreditreport.com.

Be sure to correct any erroneous or inaccurate information. Everything in a credit report is considered accurate unless disputed. The Fair Credit Reporting Act protects you by requiring consumer reporting bureaus to report acceptable information in your credit reports, such as timeliness, completeness, accuracy, truthfulness, and privacy.

If you do not have any credit in your name, open a savings or checking account with a local bank. Open one major credit card in your name, and use it for small purchases infrequently or for emergencies only. Choose the credit card wisely. Department stores, gas company cards, and secured cards are the easiest to get. The best card is a debit card that deducts purchase payments directly from your checking account. If you use student financial aid for your college expenses, you also begin your credit history. Your student loans are reported to the credit bureaus once you sign the promissory note, and the money is disbursed to you. The earlier you establish individual credit in your name, the better.

Building Your Credit, Which Is Better: Individual or Joint Credit Accounts with Your Spouse?

Many couples assume that when they marry they should merge their credit lives (and credit histories). But, in fact, every credit report and score is tied to a single Social Security number. That means that you and your spouse's credit reports remain separate and do not reflect the fact you are married.

Both of your credit reports will, however, do the following:

- List all individual accounts held by each of you
- List all joint accounts that you and your spouse open
- List accounts with one of you named as a cosigner
- Include if a spouse has been added to an existing account as either a joint account holder or as an authorized user of the account

ⓘ **Tip:** Being aware of your spouse's credit history can help to maintain a healthy financial position after marriage and reduce financial strain.

NOTE: Each joint owner has immediate and complete access to all funds in a joint account. Each joint owner can close a joint account. However, a joint account holder cannot be removed from an account without his or her written permission.

Joint: You and Your Spouse as Approved Borrowers

1. When you apply for credit jointly, the lender will consider both of your credit histories when making its assessment and decision. You may be at a disadvantage if your credit history is excellent but your spouse's is not. You could be declined credit or have to pay higher interest rates and fees. This outcome frequently happens with mortgage lending.

2. When you and your spouse open a joint account, you both can use the credit, and you both are individually responsible for the total debt or obligation. For example, if you and your spouse sign for a mortgage loan, you are jointly liable for the amount of the loan. If your spouse passes away, you are held accountable for any remaining amount.
3. If you have good credit history, you can add your spouse to your account to make it joint, and she or he may benefit from your good history on that account that will be factored into his or her score. On the other hand, do not add your name to your spouse's account if there is negative history on that account.
4. If payments are missed or late on joint accounts that are in your name and your spouse's, they can affect *both* of your credit scores negatively. Keep in mind that one recent 30-day late bill payment, if reported by the lender, can negatively impact your credit score by as much as a 110-point drop in score for up to seven years.

You or Your Spouse as an Authorized User

1. As an authorized user of a credit account under your name, your spouse has access to your credit but is not liable for the debt.
2. If you designate your spouse as a user of the account, it will not affect your credit score, and it may or may not affect her or his score.
3. It is easier to remove your spouse as an authorized user of the account than from a joint account as joint owner.

You or Your Spouse as a Cosigner

1. A cosigner is someone who agrees to assume debt and be fully responsible for it if the primary borrower does not pay. If you are a cosigner for your spouse, you must be prepared to manage the account and make payments, if necessary.
2. As a married couple, it is important that you each have separate checking accounts and credit cards. You should sustain your active credit record. If you go for a long time without any individual credit activity, you will find it difficult to take out loans by yourself. You also must pay your bills on time. Late payments are the fastest and easiest way to destroy your credit rating.

Individual: You Are the Approved Borrower

1. You may not qualify to apply individually for credit if you do not have sufficient income and assets.
2. If you have established credit in your name, you will be entirely and solely liable to repay the debt on your own.

3. Once you have credit, your credit history begins and the longer you have a positive credit history, the better your credit score and access to unused credit.
4. States with community property laws may consider credit applications or debts incurred during the marriage as joint debt. Community property laws don't combine your credit histories, but they influence your decision about how to repay debts in a divorce. Sometimes in some states, the individual debts of one spouse may appear on the credit report of the other.

Who Is Responsible for Debt Incurred During the Marriage?

States vary in how they may treat joint and separate debts. It is crucial that you ask a divorce attorney about your state's rules for joint and separate debts and how they will be allocated in a divorce. The following are some general rules.

Community property laws vary from state to state. In most community property states, both spouses are responsible for most debts incurred during the marriage, even if only one spouse borrowed and signed the paperwork. Creditors of one spouse can go after the assets and income of the married couple to collect what they are owed. There is an equal distribution guideline for community property and debt. Add it all up and divide by two. Some good news is that if only one spouse files for bankruptcy in a community property state, all of the eligible debts of both spouses will be discharged.

In community property states, it makes a difference when the debt was incurred. If the debt of one spouse was incurred before the marriage, it is separate property. A creditor can go after only that spouse's half of the community property to repay the debt. Couples in community property states have another recourse as well. They can sign an agreement with a particular store or lender or credit provider that the creditor will look solely to one spouse's separate property for repayment of debt, permanently removing one spouse entirely from any liability.

⚠ **Caution:** Community property states differ on when the marriage is "over" and separate property begins. The time between your separation and the final divorce can be considerable if your divorce drags on, during which your spouse could incur substantial credit card debt for which you could be jointly responsible.

In *common law (equitable distribution) property states*, you should check with a divorce attorney to confirm how debts incurred during the marriage will be characterized. In some states, debts incurred by one spouse are usually that spouse's debts alone. Debts might become owed by both spouses if the debt was for family living expenses, a family necessity (a new car), to maintain a jointly owned asset (a leaking roof), or a mutually agreed to cost for the family (vacation). In other states, as between the spouses, debts incurred during the marriage are automatically marital debts unless a party can prove there were for a nonmarital purpose (a paramour, gambling, etc.).

Creditors of the debtor spouse cannot legally reach the other spouse's *separate* money, property, or wages to repay the debtor's *separate* debt. However, in some states, creditors can go after *jointly owned* property to satisfy the separate debts of one spouse (even if the debt was not family related). Usually, a lender can take only half of the money in a joint account in most states.

In some states, if a couple holds property titled in "tenancy by entirety," a creditor can go only after the property to pay only joint debts, not separate debts of either spouse. If only one spouse files for bankruptcy in a common law state, only that spouse's joint and separate debts would be discharged; the other spouse's separate debts would not be discharged.

What Happens to Debt in Divorce?

It all depends. Dividing debt is extremely critical because all outstanding debts are factored into any determination of your net worth at the time of divorce. It would be ideal, although not easily accomplished, if you could pay off all debts before filing for divorce. If not, courts are charged with allocating your marital debts.

All of the above rules for community property and equitable distribution states apply for distributing the debt unless you and your spouse agree otherwise or the family court orders assignment of debts between you and your spouse. It is possible that you and your spouse mutually agree to assume the other's obligations or to share them. If not, courts will decide and indicate who pays which bills/debts while dividing property and money.

What Happens If Your Ex-Spouse Doesn't Pay?

The first thing to know is that most debts are governed by federal contract law and your divorce decree is governed by your state's laws. Federal law supersedes state law, so lenders are not bound by the terms of your divorce decree if a debt was assigned to you or your spouse. Further, a family court judge does not have the power to alter a lender's rights under the contract.

Consequently, even if the debt was assigned to your spouse in the divorce decree, you will still be held liable for it if your name was on the account, you were a co-signor, or it was a community debt liability. Your only recourse is to make sure you have a correctly worded indemnity clause in your divorce decree that allows you take your ex-spouse back to court if they cause you to have to pay to avert the loan going into default. You have to bring a court action (as part of the divorce case, or, as a separate legal action) to have your former spouse comply with the terms of your divorce decree.

How Can Your Credit Reputation Be Damaged?

Your credit reputation and the increasing use of credit scoring have a broad impact on different financial aspects of your life. Women in the midst of divorce tend to be the most vulnerable if they have not been a wage earner or held individual credit cards, mortgages, bank loans, and other credit lines in their name.

There are several direct and indirect effects of divorce that can hurt your credit score. Here are some ways divorce can bring down your credit score:

1. Your ex-spouse doesn't pay your joint bills.
2. You are unable to pay your bills following the divorce.
3. Your ex-spouse is vindictive and has access to your credit accounts as an authorized user and abuses them.
4. Your ex-spouse has opened credit fraudulently in your name without your knowledge and abused it to harm you.
5. Your spouse is adding charges to joint accounts still open after your divorce.
6. If you live in a community property state, you can be held responsible for debt incurred by your former spouse even if you were unaware of the debt and did not sign an agreement with the creditor.

What Are Credit Damages?

It is relatively common to hear about spouses going through a divorce who cancel credit cards, go into collections on their debts, face foreclosure, file for bankruptcy, or face the loss of employment. With any of these events, your credit reputation is damaged and could be impaired for a very long time. The cost of your debt is increasing, and access to debt is becoming limited. Impaired credit may demand drastic changes to alleviate financial stress (selling assets or paring down expenses) and may require immediate short-term cash flow to pay down outstanding debt. *Most of the time, the damage to your credit reputation and credit privileges is not evaluated during divorce.* This neglect is a particular financial cost that needs to be more routinely recognized and negotiated as an added expense or liability during divorce.

> ⓘ **Tip:** The key to a successful argument for credit reputation damage is to provide evidence of the harmful event. You might need to show a thorough "before" and "after" picture of the injured party's credit situation.

How Can You Protect Your Credit?

If you are the one who depends on joint accounts, then be sure to open your own credit as soon as possible during the divorce to begin using it. Be certain you have some access to credit independently.

If you are concerned about your joint accounts or joint credit lines, it is best to aim to close any in which your ex-spouse is an authorized user before your divorce is final. Only you or your spouse can close a joint account. By law, a creditor cannot close a joint account because of a change in marital status.

If a joint account is closed, a creditor does not have to offer to open an individual account in your name. The creditor can require you to reapply for credit on an individual basis and then, based on your new application, extend or deny you credit. In divorce, you might be required to refinance your mortgage or home equity loan to remove your ex-spouse from it, which might not be possible until you first show at least 6 to 12 months of consistent income (including spousal support).

You have to protect yourself in any situation that may arise when you are divorced. To do so, you must:

- Include a properly worded indemnity clause in your divorce decree
- Pay off as much debt as possible before filing for divorce or make sure the lender gets paid
- Be diligent and know all debt in your name, your spouse's name, or both names
- Make sure any joint debts allocated to your ex-spouse are refinanced as soon as possible.
- Ensure that you have a way to keep track of all loans after your divorce. Get online access to accounts and make sure lenders have a way to send mail to you or update you regularly.

After Divorce, Will You Have to Refinance Debts and Can You Qualify?

Home Mortgages

Usually, mortgages are the largest debts that divorced couples have to split up or allocate to one spouse after divorce. Lenders may not care if you are divorced as long as the mortgage is secured and protected by collateral. Getting your name off of a joint mortgage as a responsible party is not easy. You will still be held accountable for it in the event of default, and the lender will still report that loan on your credit until you can remove your name.

You have a few options for how to handle getting your name or the name of your ex-spouse off of a mortgage. The first choice simply is to sell the property that has the mortgage. Then, you put the joint debt behind you, and you only have to agree how you will share equity or the net sales proceeds. You will need to figure out the amount of equity you own in the property. Home equity is the fair market value of the house less all debts outstanding secured by the house. Your share of home equity is determined by your state's divorce laws and your ability to negotiate.

If the house is "underwater" (that is, it is worth less than the mortgage balance outstanding), then you and your ex-spouse either have to pay off the difference on the mortgage owed upon the sale of the house or you opt for a short sale. A short sale is a sale of real estate in which the net proceeds from selling the property are less than the debts secured by liens against the property. In this case, the mortgage lender agrees to accept less than the amount owed on the debt and allows the sale of ownership to occur. You and your ex-spouse have no equity value in the house, and there is nothing but more debt to share for the payoff.

The second option is to refinance the mortgage in your name alone if you are going to keep the house. If you hold debt, you should own the asset, so be sure to have your ex-spouse quitclaim the deed to you as well. Now, however, you may have to buy out your spouse for his or her share of equity. You can do this with a "trade off" of other assets or by refinancing your mortgage and taking out enough cash to pay off your ex-spouse. The real issue is whether or not you can qualify for a new loan in your name alone after your divorce.

ⓘ **Tip:** Shop around for loan quotes before your divorce is final. Find out what your new monthly payment will be and include it in your budget for quantifying support needs.

Home Equity Line of Credit (HELOC)

Often couples also have a HELOC in addition to a mortgage, which is a major consideration in a divorce. HELOCs can be easily accessed by you or your ex-spouse, and these loans often provide credit cards or checks. The major credit card companies have no systems requiring joint signatures when a credit card is used, and bank checks only require one signature. Any spouse suspecting that the other is engaging in dishonest financial behavior should cancel the credit lines and put the creditor on notice, in writing, that further debts are not your responsibility.

A lender for open-ended credit lines like HELOCs may not make you reapply, change the terms of your account, or close your account because you reached a certain age, retired, changed your name, or changed your marital status. The exception is if you initially qualified for the amount based on your ex-spouse's income and if your income alone is insufficient to support the amount of credit currently available on the account. While your reapplication is pending, the lender must allow you full access to the account. The bank may specify a reasonable period to reapply.

If you and your ex-spouse continue to own the house together for a period of time after the divorce, consider having your divorce agreement note that neither party can access the HELOC and take additional equity out of the house, at least not without the consent of the other person.

Car Leases

Sometimes a lessor will allow you to refinance in your name alone to remove your ex-spouse's name. You enter into a new contract. If your car is leased, you do not own it, and in divorce, its value is zero. You include the lease payment in your budget which usually represents a significant cash outflow.

For the vast majority of leases, the contract purchase price you will pay at the end of a lease term is designed to be close to the value of the car at that time. If you need to value a leased car to renew a lease, turn it in, or trade for another car, most people lose value each time they trade vehicles.

> ⓘ **Tip:** Assume you will lose money when you change your car lease early. Get estimates so you know your outlay and what it truly costs you. Otherwise, determine if it is easier for you to continue to pay for the car even if the lease is in your ex-spouse's name.

After Divorce, What If You Cannot Refinance Your Mortgage or Do Not Want to Sell Your House?

Loan Assumption

A 1982 federal law established a process called loan assumption. Loan assumption is cheaper and may also be quicker than the alternatives. It may help you get your name off a home loan after divorce without having to refinance or sell the house.

Assuming a loan means taking over the seller's (your former spouse's) mortgage and continuing to make payments on it. In reality, however, most loans cannot be assumed because banks do not allow it. *Loan assumption is available only on FHA and VA loans, which are the minority.*

First, your ex-spouse notifies the lender that you are taking over the mortgage due to divorce. Your former spouse must tell the lender that he or she wants a loan assumption, in which you take full responsibility for the loan and remove them from the promissory note. Loan assumptions leave the existing loan intact: You assume the interest rate, loan features, balance, and remaining years of the term of the loan.

Your ex-spouse should request from the lender a release of liability that eliminates their obligation if you fail to pay. This release protects his or her credit from missed payments, late payments, default, foreclosure, and any subsequent liability. However, the lender may not issue this release unless they evaluate your credit and ability to repay the loan on your own. Your former spouse then should be required to remove their name from the house title via a quitclaim deed, making you the sole owner.

What You Need to Know about Making Personal Guarantees

A personal guarantee is often provided for small business loans. It is an unsecured written promise from a business owner or business executive guaranteeing payment on a loan. Since it is unsecured, it is not tied to any particular asset such as a house or property. By making a guarantee, however, the business owner/executive is pledging both themselves and their assets by acting as the loan's cosigner. If the company dissolves, they will be responsible for repayment. Creditors will go after the cosigner if the business fails to repay the loan.

In a community property state, if the lender has not obtained the signature of the spouse, marital assets may be shielded entirely from the reach of the personal guaranty. In a community property state, property acquired by either spouse during the marriage is treated as property equally owned by the marital unit—the "community." Many community property states require a lending company to obtain not only both spouses' signatures, but also name both spouses as defendants to any lawsuit to assert an interest in the community property. This requirement has significant implications should the parties divorce. Other states make the distinction to divide property and debts between spouses in a divorce equitably.

Your Equal Credit Opportunity Rights Are Protected By Law

The Federal Trade Commission (FTC), the nation's consumer protection agency, enforces the Equal Credit Opportunity Act (ECOA), which prohibits credit discrimination on the basis of race, color, religion, national origin, sex, marital status, age, or because you get public assistance. According to the FTC, you can be asked all of this information by creditors, but they are not allowed to use it to decide whether to give you credit or when setting the terms of your credit. Your creditworthiness is based on many different factors, and not everyone who applies for credit gets it or gets the same terms.

The ECOA provides protections and enforces compliance with the law when you deal with any organizations or people who regularly extend credit.

What a Creditor May Not Do When You Apply for Credit as a Divorced Individual

- Discourage you from applying because of your marital status
- Impose different terms or conditions, like higher interest rates or fees, on a loan based on your marital status
- Ask you if you are divorced (he or she may use the terms "married," "unmarried," or "separated").
- Ask about your marital status if you are applying for a separate, unsecured account.
- Ask for information about your former spouse, except if you are relying on alimony or child support
- Ask if you get alimony, child support, or separate maintenance payments, unless they tell you first that you do not have to provide this information if you are not relying on these payments to get credit (he or she may ask you if you have to pay alimony, child support, or separate maintenance payments).

What a Creditor May Not Do When Evaluating Your Income as a Divorced Individual

- Discount income because of your sex or marital status
- Discount or refuse to consider income because it comes from part-time employment, Social Security, pensions, or annuities

- Refuse to consider alimony, child support, or separate maintenance payments (he or she may ask you for proof that you receive this income consistently)

What You Have the Right to Do

- Keep your individual accounts after you change your name or marital status unless the creditor has evidence you are not willing or able to pay
- Know whether your account application was accepted or rejected within 30 days of filing a complete application
- Know why your application was rejected (i.e., the particular reason for rejection) within 60 days
- Find out why your account was closed or why the terms of the account were made less favorable unless the account was inactive or you failed to make payments as agreed

What If You Are in Trouble Handling Debts by Yourself?

If you are in debt over your head and need help, consult with an accredited credit counseling service. Being in trouble with debt includes living paycheck to paycheck or if you are worried about debt collectors or cannot seem to develop a workable budget.

Most reputable credit counselors are not-for-profit, but you should be careful to find a legitimate company with certified and trained credit counselors who will help you in consumer credit, money and debt management, and budgeting. They will discuss your entire financial situation and help you develop a personalized plan to deal with your money problems. You can check out the counseling agency with your state's attorney general's office and local consumer protection agency.

If your financial problems are due to too much debt or your inability to repay debts, they may recommend you enroll in a debt management plan (DMP). A DMP alone is not for everyone. It is when you deposit money each month with the credit counseling agency, and they pay your debts according to a payment schedule they develop between you and your creditors. There are many restrictions on you if you have a DMP, and its primary purpose is to prohibit you from falling into more debt. The FTC governs debt relief and require many upfront disclosures before you sign up for a DMP.

> ⓘ **Tip:** Do not overlook other debt relief options. You can negotiate for free with your creditors to reduce the interest rate, fees, and charges to develop a payment plan. Keep good records, be persistent, and be polite. Your goal is to work out a modified payment plan. Divorce is not an excuse. The other option is bankruptcy. There are serious consequences to declaring bankruptcy, and it should only be your choice of last resort.

Practical Tips about Divorce and Credit

1. In the event you are unsuccessful in removing your name from an account or debt belonging to your ex-spouse, you have the option to add a statement

to the accounts in question, explaining that you are not responsible for making payments on the debt under the terms of your divorce decree.

2. If you discover that your ex-spouse can get a copy of your credit history, you have legal recourse. Using your personal information to access your credit history falsely constitutes fraud and identity theft. You might want to take out a monitoring service if you are unsure.
3. As stated earlier, a divorce decree does *not* legally remove your responsibility for a debt and does not override contracts with your creditors. The divorce agreement is only between you and your ex-spouse. To be removed from any joint debt, such as a mortgage, your ex-spouse will need to pay off the original mortgage and refinance a new one in her or his name. Technically, as long as you a joint holder of debt or a cosigner on an account, you are equally responsible for the debt, and it can continue to appear on your credit report.
4. Understand that you may miss some accounts because not every lender reports to the credit bureaus.
5. You should request a copy of any joint account's statement each month, even if your ex-spouse is obligated for making the payments on that account. Some lenders will agree readily, while others may make you access them online. Also, obtain a free credit report from a different credit reporting agency every four months to track that all payments are being made on time. You're entitled to a free credit report from each of the three major credit reporting agencies every 12 months under federal law.
6. Protect your identity.

15 Divorce and Children with Special Needs

Statistics show that 20 percent of the U.S. population is affected by disabilities. There are few challenges harder than going through a divorce and having a child with special needs. You not only face uncertainty concerning transition, but you are also shouldering the burden of protecting your child's well-being and all their future planning. If you are the custodial parent, chances are you are assuming the responsibility of caring for all of the daily living needs that test your self-reliance and capacity to parent alone. Most children have stress when their parents divorce; however, when there is a child with special needs involved, numerous issues surrounding that child and the family are significantly more complicated to negotiate.

This chapter will help you understand how a child with special needs can have an impact on all aspects of negotiations, including child support, spousal support, property division, and custodial decisions including guardianship. You may have to fashion atypical strategies to avoid adversely affecting the eligibility of potential government benefits because of child or spousal support, to preserve assets with the use of special needs trusts, and to address conflicts related to quantifying future care needs and post-majority age child support.

Divorcing parents with a child with special needs confront unique issues. For example, a child with special needs often has more expenses than a child without special needs. The uncertainty about the nature, cost, and predictability of future care expenses makes a list of child-related add-on expenses relating to any disability challenging to cover in a divorce agreement.

Especially important, the child's eligibility for governmental agency benefits may be threatened or reduced by providing child support, maintenance, or assets in the name of the child. Parents also need to be aware of how to navigate the educational system and take advantage of estate planning strategies to maximize necessary support and health insurance coverage for their child.

Divorce acutely complicates all aspects of family dynamics. Most families are simply unprepared to grapple with the complicated and entangled decisions they must often make to protect both the future and the financial security of their child with special needs.

With more immediate, urgent concerns about daily living holding your attention, you as a caregiver oftentimes have to postpone plans to secure your own future—in spite of your financial anxiety. Not knowing where to begin with financial planning for your child with special needs presents an added hurdle for you to assume during divorce.

Family law legislation does not yet sufficiently recognize the unique considerations of these families in the areas of custody and support. Child support guidelines may be inadequate for resolving life-long issues for families with a child with special needs.

Courts are already overwhelmed when it comes to dealing with divorces and are ill-equipped to deal with the skyrocketing number of families with children with special needs. There is a general disinclination to project post-majority needs of the child and the caregiver's financial needs, and there is often a failure to establish a conflict resolution plan between the parents.

Until divorce laws thoroughly and consistently deal with children and young adults with special needs, divorce attorneys have an unparalleled opportunity and responsibility to educate families and provide viable resolutions by agreement. It is in your best interests to familiarize your divorce attorney with your family dynamics. Make sure your divorce attorney knows what your child's needs are and walk them through a "day in the life" of you and your child. You will enhance your attorney's knowledge and ability to advocate for your family in divorce.

Defining Special Needs

Be aware that legislation and case law are evolving in this area as more family divorce attorneys deal with burgeoning divorce cases that include children with special needs "Special needs are often determined following categories that the public education system considers eligible for special education services, including autism, physical limitation and health impairment, emotional disturbance, learning disability, and developmental delay, among many others."

Special needs cover (1) life-threatening illnesses, (2) chronic and physical disabilities, and (3) mental and behavioral disabilities. Many children with special needs cannot perform many of the six activities of daily living skills, which are defined as eating, bathing, dressing, toileting, transferring (i.e., walking), and continence. Accurately assessing a child's capacities related to activities of daily living is ongoing, and it is critical to determining what type of care the child needs and accessing appropriate services.

The "Best Interests" of the Child with Special Needs

The "best interests of the child" is the doctrine used by most courts to determine a wide range of issues relating to the well-being of children. The goal is to identify and understand how to determine the best interests of the child when that child has special needs. These interests will impinge on the following decisions:

- With whom will the child live? Standard visitation schedules and parenting plans are often unacceptable and unsuitable for the proper care and environment of a child with special needs.
- How much contact ("access" or "visitation") will the parents, legal guardians, or other parties be allowed (or required) to have? Routines versus change

affect every child, but change may have a heightened negative impact on a child with special needs.

- What are extraordinary child-related expenses to evaluate and address?
- For how long will these expenses be shared between parents?
- To whom and by whom will child support be paid and in what amount? When is spousal support appropriate and for how long? How can you preserve the eligibility of a child with special needs to maximize government benefits? Why is age 18 the "magic age" in the life of a child with special needs?

Parenting Plans

A good starting point is to explore both spouses' similar or dissimilar visions of what their child's disabilities and abilities are. If they do not agree, a parenting plan should spell out essential information and instructions. The noncustodial parent who has less frequent contact with the child may not be in the habit of managing behaviors, giving medicines, monitoring consistency of foods, adapting physical surroundings, or understanding specific preferences of their nonverbal child.

Details become paramount in communication between ex-spouses concerning not only their children with special needs, but also their other children. Siblings are undoubtedly affected by the amount of time, energy, and attention required by a child with special needs, and while not intentional, parents often spend much more one-on-one time with their child with special needs. It is important for both parents to recognize that they need to spend one-on-one time with their other children so they also can feel "special" and loved.

Access and Visitation Schedule

A typical visitation schedule used in most divorces may not be appropriate for your family. Very often the parenting plan must be both flexible and structured. Children with special needs often require consistency, structured lives, and familiar routines. However, illnesses or behaviors may interrupt daily routines and planned schedules. You may have to stay within proximity to familiar medical professionals. Early on in the divorce process, you may have to decide if your child with special needs is better off on their own turf where the noncustodial parent visits or if they are capable of traveling. If you have to prepare for travel, determine if your child will go with a caregiver, with your other children, or with you to visit the noncustodial parent. You may have special equipment to send back and forth because insurance usually covers one apparatus of its kind at a time.

Child Support and Add-Ons

Caring for a child with special needs is expensive. There is an increased requirement for specialty medical supports and services. These items may include, but are not limited to:

- Prescriptions
- Therapy services

- Private special education
- Tutors
- Medical equipment
- Physical equipment/furniture
- Nonprescription medicine treatments
- Alternative therapies and treatments (acupuncture, massage, sensory integration, etc.)
- Vitamins and nutritional needs
- Paid respite care for the custodial parent
- Home health aides and nurses
- Modifications to the home
- Modified transportation
- Extra babysitting care for siblings
- Travel for medical care
- Out-of-pocket care/network and expenses not covered by any insurance or agency

The cost of specialized support and services are not typically included or identified in most standard court Financial Affidavit forms. Furthermore, child support calculations do not account for any of these expenses, so deviations from the guidelines are usually warranted. Few state statutes or case law may allow for continuing the support obligation of both you and your ex-spouse for the lifetime of your (adult) child. Advance planning to secure all available public benefits for the child is paramount.

Public Benefits Planning

Spousal support and child support payments need to be structured carefully in consideration with your child's benefit eligibility. It is essential that your divorce attorney works with a special needs attorney and experienced financial adviser to eliminate the risk of forfeiting your child's entitlements.

Securing government and agency benefits for a child with special needs can enable that person to have the resources necessary for long-term care. It is important to know when and what kind of government benefits are available to a child with special needs. It is advisable to consult with a divorce attorney specializing in this area because government programs can be confusing and change often.

There are four government benefit programs available to special needs families: Supplemental Security Income (SSI), Medicaid, Medicare, and Social Security Disability Insurance (SSDI). A child with special needs can receive SSI, SSDI, Medicaid, and Medicare all at the same time.

SSDI and Medicare are *not means-tested programs*. There is no investigation into parents' finances to determine if they qualify for the program based on their income or their resources. Medicare is a form of sponsored health insurance available for the elderly and the disabled. SSDI is available to individuals and minors or children with special needs of a person who has died, retired or become disabled.

A child with special needs who is under age 22 and who is not working can obtain SSDI benefits based on his or her parents' prior earnings.

Both SSI and Medicaid are *means-tested programs*. Eligibility for those programs is based on financial need, and strict requirements must be met before benefits are authorized. With SSI, a disabled person is eligible for food stamps and Medicaid, which pays for a child's medical expenses, mental health services, necessary drug therapy, and home and institutional services that help the child and family.

The distinction between means-tested and nonmeans-tested programs is important to understand.

In the context of support negotiations during a divorce, it is critical to address how support should be configured. Support can be paid with in-kind financial assistance in place of cash maintenance and cash child support or as a combination of in-kind support, payments made to a special needs trust, and cash payments to preserve SSI and Medicaid benefits for the child.

What You Need to Know about Support and When

Age 18 is the "magic age" for a child with special needs. How divorcing parents pay child support and spousal support, share extraordinary expenses, allocate assets, and coordinate efforts to attain benefits for their child, *all must be configured for before and after age 18.*

Deeming of income and resources to the parents ends at age 18, and many disabled youths who were income ineligible for SSI as minors can become income eligible as adults. Divorce agreements must allow for flexibility for the child's changing needs as well as to their aging out of various public benefit and educational programs.

Support for Children with Special Needs under Age 18

- Special educational supports and services may be mandated and provided at no cost to the family under federal and state laws, such as The Individuals with Disabilities Education Act (IDEA). Transition planning usually begins at age 14 for aging out of the educational system at age 21. There are no laws that continue comparable supports and services at no cost after age 21.
- Income and assets held in the custodial parent's name are relevant to determining whether a child is eligible to receive means-tested government programs such as SSI and Medicaid, which may be linked. These resources are "deemed" as available for the child, and as little as $2,000 can disqualify eligibility for SSI benefits.
- Child support paid in cash to a custodial parent is countable income, and two-thirds of a child support payment will cause a dollar-for-dollar reduction in the SSI benefit.
- Most parents' assets and income will disqualify their child under the age of 18 for SSI or Medicaid benefits. In that case, it may be prudent to wait on having support payments assigned to a *pay-back special needs trust* until the child is 18.

Treatment of Child Support in the SSI Program under Current Law

When determining a child's monthly SSI benefit, program rules under the SSA exclude from countable income one-third of the child support payment received from the absent parent. The remaining child support payment is subject to the $20 general income exclusion. The balance reduces the child's monthly SSI benefit dollar for dollar. The example in the following table shows how child support payments are counted for a child who has no other income.

Current Computation for Child Support Payments (in dollars)

Monthly federal benefit rate for 2004	564.00
Average child support payment for June 2003	**199.00**
Minus 1/3 of the child support payment	– 66.33
Minus the $20 general income exclusion	– 20.00
Total countable income	= 112.67
SSI benefit (564.00 – 112.67)	**451.33**
Total income available to child (199.00 + 451.33)	**650.33**

* This example is taken from the SSA website. It assumes that the child has no other income.

NOTE: This calculation is for the federal SSI payment only. Some states provide supplemental payments to children, enabling them to receive higher benefits.

Support for Children with Special Needs over Age 18

- Assets held in the parents' name no longer count against the adult disabled child.
- Assets cannot exceed $2,000 for an adult disabled child to qualify for SSI.
- Child support paid in cash will result in a dollar-for-dollar loss of SSI (up to 100 percent) minus $20. Once child support payments begin, SSI will be reduced, if not eliminated, and Medicaid could also be at risk without a "self-settled" pay-back special needs trust.
- Cash spousal support paid to the custodial parent will no longer be counted as income for SSI purposes for the adult disabled child.
- All entitlements to the many supports and services received during the educational years terminate with aging out of the educational system at anywhere from 18 to 21 years of age.

Practical Tips

1. Make direct payments for bills for private school tuition, entertainment, cable TV and Internet, recreational activities, vacations, and long-term care insurance (these payments cannot be use for food or shelter, which is considered in-kind support).
2. Pay into an SNT or OBRA 93 trust. The non-custodial parent can be ordered by the divorce decree to make a monthly payment for the child's "special

needs" to the trustee of the pay-back special needs trust prepared for this purpose. The custodial parent may serve as the trustee.

If you want to direct child support payments to a special needs trust, it must meet the requirements of Section 42 of U.S Code § 1396p(d)(4)(A) of the SSA. There are several essential features to this trust. The first is that Social Security presumes that the child support payments belong to the child. The second is that any balance remaining in the trust upon the child's death will be paid back to the government. As a practical matter, since the trustee would likely spend all of the child support payments for the child's benefit on a regular basis, there is little chance that much would be left in the special needs trust when the child passes away.

3. Divide and allocate child support between siblings so none is attributed to the child with special needs between 18 to 21 years; avoid unallocated orders.
4. Contribute to a plan for achieving self-support to avoid asset limits under SSI.

Special Education

Through age 18 to 21, federal educational initiatives ensure that children with special needs have access to a free appropriate public education, just like any other child. Some experts go further and state that IDEA emphasizes special education and related services designed to meet their unique needs and prepare them for further education, employment, and independent living. Under IDEA, you as a parent have a voice in the educational decisions the school makes about your child. At every point in the process, the law gives you specific rights and protections.

Your child may receive special education through an individualized education program (IEP) in different settings. Your local school and town (via state funding) will help you determine the appropriate environment. Your child may have access to a school for segregated special education or full inclusion with nondisabled persons in a least restrictive environment to the maximum extent possible, as well as extended school-year services to ensure children with disabilities do not regress over the summer.

In implementing an IEP, you should be aware that a school does not require the signature of both parents even if you have joint custody. It is best to acknowledge this fact in advance during divorce so you can decide the practicality of whether one or both parents should be required to sign an IEP. More significantly, if the school system does not pay for all costs, the divorce agreement should resolve cost-sharing issues. Additional educational expenses include independent assessments, tutors, third-party consultation, required advocacy, necessary legal fees, and other support services for your child as he or she transitions out of the educational system.

Transition Planning

Under IDEA, schools must engage in transition planning starting at age 14 for when the child ages out at age 21. Transition planning enables the school team and parents to focus on how an adult disabled child will access community and vocational activities, as well as adult living arrangements.

In structuring a divorce agreement, unique issues arise when your child transitions into adulthood. These concerns cover a broad spectrum, such as guardianship, eligibility for quasi-government or private agency benefits, employment, recreation and social skills, independent living, and custodial care. Whereas basic child support typically ends at the age majority at 18 or 21, divorcing parents of a child with special needs who has severe impairments face the reality of life-long caregiving and, perhaps, life-long co-parenting.

Incorporating transition planning is critical during divorce negotiations because it often underscores the disparity between the parents' expectations about what their future obligations will be for their young adult child with special needs. It may prompt action to engage and bring in an attorney in this field to have a useful dialogue about eligibility for and securing public benefits.

Spousal Support (Alimony)

You need to consider if managing the care of your child with special needs is your full-time job. According to ClearviewDivorce.com,

> The primary caregiver parent not only provides daily care to their special needs child, but they also manage doctor appointments, therapy sessions, and treatment regimens. They also research and secure funding for the special needs child's expenses, maintain the funding year after year and track the family's medical insurance reimbursements. Since many of these activities can interfere with the primary caregiver parent's employment, they often may find it difficult to maintain a full-time job. Due to these challenges, the primary caregiver parent's income earning potential is often compromised. This should be a factor when determining whether spousal maintenance is required.[7]

Spousal support may be crucial in light of decreased earning capacity, the seeming impossibility for rehabilitation, or the burden of exceptional caregiving responsibilities. When a parent's economic activity is reduced because of the needs of a child, the parent may never catch up financially. Several states recognize this reality and take it into consideration when determining spousal support awards.

7 ClearviewDivorce.com, "Special Circumstances: Why Divorce with a Special Needs Child is More Challenging," June 24, 2011.

Estate Planning

You should set the stage for long-term estate planning in your divorce agreement. Use appropriate vehicles, including special needs trusts, in coordination with public benefits and in contemplation of gifting planning and long-term care insurance.

529 Plans (College Savings Accounts)

These plans are designed for someone planning to attend college. If you set up such an account when your child was younger and it becomes apparent that this child may not use the funds for college education, you have ways to repurpose the account. One strategy is to name an alternative beneficiary on the account (sibling or relative).

Whatever you do, do not name the child as the owner of the account, and do not withdraw the funds and give money directly to the child with special needs. This action could cause a loss of government benefits for the child. It also may trigger a 10-percent penalty in addition to ordinary federal and state taxes on the withdrawn funds.

ABLE Accounts

For the first time in public policy, the ABLE Act (established as of 2014) recognizes the extra and significant costs of living with a disability and allows for tax-advantaged savings accounts for individuals with disabilities and their families. The beneficiary of the account is the account owner, and income earned by the accounts will not be taxed.

ABLE savings accounts will not affect eligibility for SSI, Medicaid, and other public benefits. You can have only one ABLE account per eligible individual. ABLE accounts allow for broader needs than just education. A "qualified disability expense" means any expense related to the designated beneficiary as a result of living a life with disabilities. These may include education, housing, transportation, employment training and support, assistive technology, personal support services, healthcare expenses, financial management and administrative services, and other expenses that help improve health, independence, and quality of life.

Contributions to the account made by any person (the account beneficiary, family, and friends) will be paid using post-taxed dollars and will not be tax deductible on federal income tax returns. Some states, however, may allow for state income tax deductions for contributions made to an ABLE account. The total annual contributions by all participating individuals, including family and friends, for a single tax year, is $14,000. The amount may be adjusted periodically to account for inflation or to correlate to the annual gift tax exclusion amount.

The total limit over time for contributions made to an ABLE account will be subject to the individual state and their limit for education-related 529 savings accounts. Many states have set this limit at more than $300,000 per plan.

However, for individuals with disabilities who are recipients of SSI, the ABLE Act sets some further limitations. The first $100,000 in an ABLE account is exempted from the SSI $2,000 individual resource limit. If and when an ABLE account exceeds $100,000, the beneficiary's SSI cash benefit is suspended until the account falls back below $100,000. It is important to note that while the recipient's eligibility for the SSI cash benefit is suspended, this has no effect on their ability to receive or be eligible to receive medical assistance through Medicaid.

Additionally, upon the death of the beneficiary, the state in which the beneficiary lived may file a claim to all or a portion of the funds in the account equal to the amount in which the state spent on the beneficiary through their state Medicaid program. This is commonly known as the "Medicaid pay-back" provision, and the claim could recoup Medicaid-related expenses from the time the account was open.

Special Needs Trusts

Parents can use a qualified special needs trust to receive funds (assets and cash payments) that would ordinarily be distributed outright to the custodial parent or the adult disabled child. In most cases, these contributions will not preclude the child from receiving government assistance, although special needs trusts are relatively restrictive in their use and operation.

Special needs trusts are designed to protect the assets of a physically or mentally disabled person while still allowing that individual to receive government benefits and have funds to pay for extra care beyond what the government provides. A special needs trust enables a physically or mentally disabled person to have an unlimited amount of assets set aside for their needs without being disqualified from government benefits.

The benefits of a special needs trust include the following:

- ❑ A child with special needs remains eligible for government benefits.
- ❑ Parents' wishes regarding asset management are implemented as intended.
- ❑ Family conflict and turmoil are minimized.
- ❑ The funds are protected from creditors and litigation.
- ❑ A trust creates a succession plan for any assets after the death of a child with special needs.

Maximize your estate planning and your financial health to protect the current and future needs and interests of your child with special needs. Your retirement plans, life insurance, or any other financial accounts where you designate your child as a beneficiary, as well as any lifetime gifts or bequests by anyone in your family, should be directed to a special needs trust or a supplemental benefits trust. These kinds of trusts complement government programs. Effectively channel support in your divorce settlement to provide for more quality-of-life expenditures for your child with special needs.

Divorce presents extraordinary long-term implications for families with children with special needs. Appropriate strategies for paying maintenance and child support, navigating the educational system, setting up special needs trusts, and maximizing estate planning to preserve eligibility for public benefits should be considered by the divorce attorney, together with the assistance of other professionals. Collaborating with experts in this complicated arena will help produce more comprehensive and helpful outcome.

16 College: The Effects of Divorce on College Financing and Financial Aid

College financing and financial aid is a complex subject for families and becomes more so in a divorce situation. The cost of divorce can quickly and easily wipe out liquid assets that would otherwise have been saved for college. Parents have shifting priorities during a divorce, and it becomes clear how tough it is to scramble to pay for their children's college choices while resolving other, more immediate, financial imperatives.

College costs have exploded in recent years and are particularly challenging due to the harsh economic times. Many misinformed parents believe that their child support will automatically end once a child attains majority age and graduates from high school. While that may be the case, many are surprised to find out they may still have a duty to contribute to post-majority support for college costs. It is important to check with your divorce attorney about rules in your state.

Many divorcing parents can reach agreements about how much they will each contribute to college expenses. If parents can't agree, some states allow a court to enter orders for payment of certain post-secondary education expenses. The judge decides how much each parent must contribute after considering many factors, including access to student and parent loans, and he or she can order a noncustodial parent to pay for or contribute to college costs. Parents' obligations under this law are typically limited to the equivalent of a four-year undergraduate degree, and the child must be under the age of 23 (check with your divorce attorney about specific rules in your state).

Other states prevent a judge from ordering a parent to pay for college unless the parents had a previous agreement. Sweeping changes to divorce law are in process in several states that eliminate the confusion and room for disagreement that has led to litigation about college obligations. These revisions are intended to provide clarity, guidance, and definition.

There are differences between a dependent student and an independent student when applying for federal student aid. In this chapter, I discuss the FAFSA application process for dependent students. Federal student aid programs are based on the concept that it is primarily the student's and his or her family's responsibility to pay for his or her education, and because a dependent student is assumed to have the support of both parents, programs will assess the total picture of the family's financial strength.

In states where the court has the statutory or equitable authority to order a parent to contribute to college, often the noncustodial parent bears more responsibility for college costs. The level of the contributions required of noncustodial parents to support college funding varies widely from state to state. Some states specifically prohibit college costs unless there are extraordinary circumstances or the financial ability to pay since child support ends at majority. Courts do weigh several factors to determine if one or both parents should contribute to college costs and, if so, how much. These factors include but are not limited to:

- Each parent's financial status, including the noncustodial parent's assets and debts;
- If each parent received a post-secondary education;
- Whether the parents would expect their child to attend college if their marriage remained intact;
- The child's academic achievements and goals;
- The child's applications for financial aid in the form of scholarships, grants, and loans; and
- The child's ability to earn income while in school.

Language You Should Include in Your Divorce Decree

If you don't want to leave things to chance, you should probably consider a voluntary college support agreement. Courts will likely honor most child support agreements between parents that have provisions for paying for higher education. Agreements should clearly explain and define as best as possible the following elements to be practical and enforceable:

- ❑ What type of post-secondary education will be paid for by the parents—public university, private college, technical school, or trade school
- ❑ What types of expenses will be covered—tuition, room, board, food, travel, books, and other living expenses
- ❑ From which resources these expenses will be paid—Are there any 529 college plans? Will marital assets be allocated to pay college costs? Do the parents agree to contribute additional savings toward future college costs as part of their divorce agreement?
- ❑ Whether the child will be responsible for any expenses
- ❑ With whom the child will live while attending school and whether child support will continue and to what degree if the child resides with a parent
- ❑ Any conditions the child must meet for payments to continue
- ❑ What will happen if the child takes off time before or during college
- ❑ Who will complete the financial aid applications and how both parents will cooperate in this process

The Financial Aid Process When You Are Divorced

Defining Parenthood Criteria

There are various criteria applied to financial aid applications depending on *different kinds of parenthood* (Finaid.org):

1. The parent with whom the child lived the most during the past 12 months (the 12-month period ending on the date that FAFSA application is signed
2. If the student did not live with one parent more than the other, the parent who provided more financial support to the child during the past 12 months
3. The parent who provided the most financial support to the child during the most recent calendar year
4. The parent who provided more than half the child's support (and will continue to do so)
5. The parent who has legal custody
6. The parent who claimed the child as a dependent on their tax return
7. The parent with the greater income

For determining the *custodial parent*, Criteria 1, 2, and 3 are used for determining the custodial parent, with the first criterion being primary. If the parents split all costs equally (without even a penny difference) for the child, Criterion 7 is often used for the final determination. The term *custodial parent* for FAFSA has nothing to do with which parent has legal custody of the child.

Criterion 4 is the most important for determining the household size (the number of family members). Apparently, the FAFSA form instructions allow for a student to be counted as belonging to two different households.

The student's custodial parent gets to list the child as a member of the household, and if the noncustodial parent provides more than half of the student's support, the noncustodial parent gets to include the student as a member of his or her household. (This double counting is not allowed by the IRS on income tax returns.)

Not all information required by FAFSA is used in the financial aid formulas but can be applied to substantiate claims made by a parent. For example, a financial aid administrator may ask a parent for a copy of their tax return to see whether they claimed the child as a dependent. The IRS definition of a dependent includes a 50-percent support test. If the parent cannot claim the child as a dependent (Criterion 6), then they did not provide more than half the child's support (Criterion 4).

Six Things You Need to Know about Divorce and Financial Aid

1. **It matters a great deal with which parent the child lives.** The custodial parent is responsible for filling out the FAFSA. The custodial parent for federal aid purposes is the parent who has taken care of the child for most of the year. The federal government does *not* consider the income or assets of the noncustodial parent in determining a student's financial need.

ⓘ **Tip:** To be eligible for the most aid, make the lower earning parent the custodial parent.

To illustrate how this can be a boon for some families, let's assume that mom is an investment banker who earns $500,000 a year and the dad is a school teacher making $50,000. If the child lived with the dad seven months of the year, he would declare his dad's lower income, and his mom's higher earnings would not affect the aid application. However, the dad would have to include in the FAFSA any child support and spousal support paid by the mom (the noncustodial parent).

Sometimes you need a tie breaker if the student lives with each parent for an equal period of time. In this situation, the parent who spent the most money on his or her care would complete the FAFSA. The time rule is always challenging to validate, so colleges will often ask for a copy of the divorce decree to verify assertions concerning living arrangements and child support. Falsely identifying a parent as custodial to enhance eligibility for financial aid is fraud and a crime.

2. **Make sure you correctly ascertain the child's residency.** Do not use the calendar year. For financial aid purposes, use the 12-month period that ends on the date you sign the FAFSA form. For example, if the FAFSA is submitted on March 15, 2016, then the 12-month period would start on March 15, 2015.
3. **It matters who claims the child as a dependent on their income tax return to benefit from tax credits and deducting direct tuition payments.** The noncustodial parent can only take advantage of the education tax benefits from paying tuition directly if he or she claims the child as a dependent.

   If the noncustodial parent does not claim the child as a dependent on his or her income tax returns but the custodial parent does, the custodial parent can claim an education tax credit based on the tuition paid by the noncustodial parent.
4. **Remarriages matter.** When the custodial parent remarries, the new spouse's income and assets must be reported on the FAFSA. A child's eligibility for financial aid can be jeopardized if the custodial parent remarries. There are no exceptions.

   If the new spouse signs a prenuptial agreement that absolves them from any college-related financial obligations, it will be ignored by the federal aid need analysis process. The federal government will consider the new step-parent a source of income regardless of any prenuptial agreement and even if she or he is unwilling to pay for college.
5. **The CSS/Financial Aid PROFILE form has different rules than** FAFSA and is used mostly by private schools in the United States. Private schools treat divorced parents differently than the FAFSA and routinely require financial information *from both*. The noncustodial parent is viewed as a potential source of support. Schools use this information differently, and it will vary by institution, but it influences the granting of the school's own aid, not federal and state aid.

If schools will require your ex-spouse's income information and your ex-spouse fails to provide it, it can jeopardize your child's financial aid application with the school. If you have been divorced for a long time and cannot locate or know where your ex-spouse lives, the school may waive this requirement.

You better identify ahead of time which colleges require aid forms because the reporting difference can mean your child could qualify for substantial aid at one college and absolutely no aid at another college.

6. **Fill out the FAFSA form soon.** You can fill it out at the beginning of the calendar year in which the student starts college. You base it on year-end data for the previous calendar year. Do not procrastinate until April when you get your income taxes done. There are deadlines for state financial assistance and even help from your child's school, which are generally before April. If you need to estimate numbers in your FAFSA, you can log back in to your online account at a later time to update this information.

It's All about the Financial Aid Calculation

Definition of Expected Family Contribution

The expected family contribution (EFC) is a term used in the college financial aid process in the United States to determine an applicant's eligibility for need-based federal student loan aid and, in many cases, state and institutional (college) aid. The EFC is the number the federal government expects you to contribute toward the cost of college, and it helps determine the amount of federal student aid you will receive. It is a measure of your family's financial strength and is calculated according to a formula established by law.

What Does an EFC Mean?

A school's financial aid office starts by deciding upon your cost of attendance (COA) at that school. Next, they consider your EFC. The amount of your financial need is calculated by this formula: COA – EFC = Your financial need.

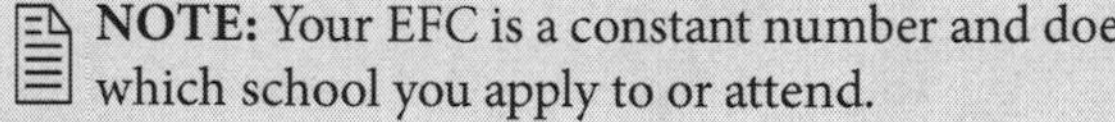

NOTE: Your EFC is a constant number and does not change depending on which school you apply to or attend.

Dissecting FAFSA

How Does FAFSA Define a Parent's Income?

The FAFSA determines your income by taking the AGI figure for the previous calendar year as reported on Line 37 of IRS Form 1040, Line 21 of Form 1040A, or Line 4 of Form 1040EZ. The EFC is recalculated each year based on your income of the previous year.

This figure includes income from work (except work-study income of the student); proceeds from asset sales, dividends, and capital gains; alimony; and withdrawals from IRA/qualified plan distributions. You must also add to your AGI figure any of this additional income:

- Tax-free dividends and interest
- Voluntary retirement contributions
- Nontaxed IRA distributions and pensions received (excluding rollovers)
- Child support received (or you can deduct child support paid)
- Workers compensation, untaxed disability insurance proceeds, and payouts

Common Income Not Counted for FAFSA

There is an income protection allowance that is applied to the custodial parent's AGI. Some income earned by parents and their student is protected to allow for minimal living expenses and payment of taxes. The income protection allowance changes each year.

The following are sources of income that are *not* counted:

- Loan proceeds
- Financial aid grants and scholarships used for college expenses
- Withdrawals from 529 plans
- Portions of money paid for student loan interest, tuition, and fees
- Families who had a total income less than $24,000, filed the 1040A or 1040EZ tax form, and received federal benefits over the previous two years

The Child's Income

The child is expected to contribute 50 percent of income above the Student Income Protection Allowance. This allowance changes each year.

How Are Student and Parent Assets Counted Differently?

All assets owned by the family and the child must be disclosed in their aid applications. Compared to the parent's assets, financial assets belonging to the student have a far greater impact on a family's eligibility for financial aid.

- ❑ Up to 20 percent of the assets owned by a dependent student can be assumed by colleges to pay for college.
- ❑ The parent's assets count for less. Colleges expect parents to use up to 5.64 percent of their "unprotected" assets toward college.
- ❑ A portion of the parent's assets are protected. "Protected" assets are not counted at all. The exact amount protected depends on the number of children and the age of the older parent.

What Is Counted as an Asset?

Money and property owned by the parent or student are counted as assets. This includes the following:

- Custodial accounts count as child's assets.
- 529 savings accounts count as a parent's assets.
- Siblings' assets count as family assets.

Which Assets Are Protected?

- Retirement accounts
- Assets held by others (such as gifts)

What about Transferring Assets?

If parents plan ahead, they should transfer eligible assets held in the child's name at least two years or more before the child starts college. Custodial accounts and trusts cannot be transferred. Others can be moved into a 529 savings plan. Beware that there can be substantial consequences with taxes, and possibly financial aid, if you transfer ownership of assets, investments, and income. In most situations, keeping ordinary investment accounts in the parent's name is the smartest move.

Key Points about the FAFSA Form and the Process

- The lower your EFC, the higher your need for financial aid.
- All schools will first look at your FAFSA when determining your need for federal aid.
- Additional calculations may be applied.
- Your final total award will depend on how much money the particular school has to distribute.

Practical Tips to Maximize Aid in the Tax Year Prior to Applying

1. Student should spend more than 50 percent of the year with the parent with lower income
2. Minimize savings in the child's name (you can always gift money to the child later to repay loans)
3. Minimize income (as appropriate)
4. Maximize qualified retirement plans or IRAs versus nonretirement assets before the base income year (the year ending just before you file your FAFSA application).
5. Use nonretirement assets to pay down consumer debt (but be aware that if your expenses are reduced, this may reduce your need for spousal support).
6. Spend down any assets held in a child's name.
7. Have the noncustodial parent own the 529 account.

8. The custodial parent should not remarry, as the FAFSA form requires a step-parent's financial information. Prenuptial agreements are ignored.
9. If grandparents want to help, ask them to help pay back loans later.

Strategies Beyond Financial Aid

It is important to determine who may be eligible and allowed to take credits and deductions on income tax returns. The noncustodial parent can only take advantage of the education tax credit benefits when she or he claims the child as a dependent. If the noncustodial parent does not claim an education credit, the custodial parent can claim it on the tuition paid by the noncustodial parent.

Credits and Deductions

Credits and deductions include the following:

- The American opportunity tax credit (the maximum amount is $2,500 per student, extended through 2017); or
- The lifetime learning credit (maximum amount is $2,500 per student); and,
- Student loan interest deductions.

The good news is that students whose parents are divorced will in many cases be in line for a more generous financial aid package. It literally pays to be well informed because costs are harder to predict and divorced parents may be overly optimistic about financial aid offers. Have a serious conversation with your ex-spouse (the noncustodial parent) about how to pay for college expenses. Be specific and spell out the terms of how you both intend to handle college expenses in your divorce agreement.

In many states by statute, a parent can be ordered by the court to contribute to a child's education even in the absence of special circumstances or a voluntary agreement of the parties. A court cannot decide what the parents should contribute to their children's college education expenses, will not require either party to invade minimal assets, and may not make any provision that either party borrow money to finance their child's education. However, there is a possibility that a court may order divorced parents to pay or contribute to a child's continuing education beyond their ability or willingness to pay. Thus, it is wise for divorcing parents to negotiate to include specific terms in your agreement.

17 Taxes and Divorce

There are three parties to a divorce: you, your spouse, and Uncle Sam. But when you are going through a divorce, taxes are often the last thing on your mind. A divorce creates tax changes for both spouses, and understanding the tax consequences of your proposed plan is essential before you finalize your proposal for settlement. This chapter will help you identify and address the most important tax-related issues during your negotiations. Given the variety and complexity of tax issues, you are strongly encouraged to consult with a tax expert familiar with divorce.

The court is not obliged to consider the tax effects of your divorce agreement—unless you offer evidence that a proposed provision will adversely affect you tax-wise. Before you finalize your divorce, you should carefully reevaluate the tax impact of your decisions made during divorce concerning the timing your divorce, the characterization of support, and property division.

The timing of your divorce affects these aspects of your taxes:

1. Filing status
2. Exemptions
3. Deductions
4. Credits
5. Income: spousal support versus child support
6. Capital gains from selling your share of marital property post-divorce

ⓘ **Tip:** The IRS has several publications that can help you:

- Publication 17: Your Federal Income Tax for Individuals
- Publication 501: Exemptions, Standard Deduction, and Filing Information
- Publication 503: Child and Dependent Care Credit
- Publication 504: Divorced or Separated Individuals
- Publication 505: Tax Withholding and Estimated Tax
- Publication 508: Educational Expenses
- Publication 521: Moving Expenses
- Publication 523: Tax Information for Selling Your Home
- Publication 551: Basis of Assets
- Publication 552: Recordkeeping for Individuals and a List of Publications
- Publication 555: Community Property (for community property states)

The Timing of Divorce

One of the most important decisions you make is what your legal status will be at year end for tax filing purposes. If you are contemplating divorce and it is close to the year end, you should consider whether it would make sense to wait to be divorced in the new year if your taxes will be lower for the current year filing married jointly.

You should ask your tax preparer to run side-by-side calculations for both you and for your spouse to compare total taxes owed to Uncle Sam based on whether you file jointly or otherwise at year end. This comparison may allow for you to elect a filing status that result in a net tax savings for each of you.

What Tax Filing Status Is Available to You?

Your marital status for tax filing is set as of the last day of the year. If you are divorced prior to December 31, you must file as a single taxpayer or as head of household, if you qualify. You cannot file married, even if you were married up until December 30.

There are four tax filing statuses:

- Married filing jointly
- Married filing separately
- Single
- Head of household

If you are still married as of December 31, here's how it works:

- If you and your spouse lived in the same household and were not legally separated, you must file married jointly or married separately.
- You may be able to file as head of household (see below) if you have been separated or lived apart for six months. Filing as head of household allows you to claim the standard deduction even if your spouse itemizes deductions and allows you to claim additional credits. You may be taxed at lower rates.

If you are divorced or separated as of December 31, head of household status is the most favorable because it results in the least amount of taxes. As a single taxpayer, you may file as head of household if you meet all of these tests:

- You are unmarried or considered unmarried on December 31;
- You file a separate return;
- You paid greater than half the cost of keeping the home for the year;
- You did not live in the same home as your ex-spouse, at any time, during the last six months of the year; and
- A child or other qualifying dependent *for which you or the other parent* is entitled to claim the tax exemption, has lived with you in the home for more than half of the year.

The Impact of Your Tax Filing Status

On average (there are always exceptions), the tax rates get higher in descending order of the filing status listed below:

- Married filing jointly
- Single filing head of household
- Single
- Married filing separately

Just Because You Can, Should You? Your Tax Filing Status

Tax filing status is sometimes used as a bargaining chip because, in most instances, it is to both parties' advantage to file married jointly. Only married taxpayers filing jointly can claim the child and dependent care credit, education credit, and the earned income credit (for low-income taxpayers). Certain other deductions, such as the dependency exemption for a spouse, interest paid on student loans, and the deduction for a spousal IRA contribution, can be taken only on a joint tax return.

In some cases, you might have clear reasons why you *should not* or *cannot file jointly*. Some married couples choose to file separate returns because each wants to be responsible for tax results from their income only and avoid joint liability. On the other hand, if you file separate returns, you almost always will pay more combined federal taxes than you would with a joint tax return and special rules apply.

Advantages for Filing Married Separately

Filing Separately with Similar Incomes

A couple may pay the IRS less by filing separately when both spouses work and earn about the same amount. When they compare the amount of tax due under both joint and separate filing statuses, they may discover that combining their earnings puts them into a higher tax bracket.

Using Miscellaneous Deductions by Filing Separately

Miscellaneous deductions can lower taxable income, but to enter them on Schedule A, they must add up to more than 2 percent of your AGI.

Filing Separately to Save with Unforeseen Expenses

AGI also determines if a couple can use unreimbursed healthcare costs and casualty losses on Schedule A and, as a result, save on taxes. Unless out-of-pocket medical expenses exceed 10 percent of your AGI, they don't qualify as a deduction. Casualty losses must also total more than 10 percent of AGI. If one spouse has a loss or substantial medical outlay that meets or exceeds 10 percent of their individual AGI, then filing married filing separately can trim a couple's overall tax burden.

Filing Separately to Guard the Future

When you don't want to be liable for your partner's tax bill, choosing the status of married filing separately offers financial protection. Among other benefits, the IRS won't apply your refund to your spouse's balance due.

Other Reasons

Some spouses have no alternative but to file separately, such as if your spouse refuses to sign a joint tax return. Or if you and your spouse cannot agree on how to handle your taxes, it is probably wise to file separate returns rather than file late or spend money figuring out the specifics of a joint return.

If you change your mind after filing separately, you can amend both separate tax returns (yours and your spouse's) and file jointly instead. You cannot, however, amend a joint tax return after the due date and subsequently file separately. If you do decide to amend separate returns to file jointly, you have three years to do so.

Itemized Deductions on Separate Returns (IRS Publication 504)

IF you paid . . .	AND you . . .	THEN you can deduct on your separate federal return . . .
Medical expenses	Paid with funds deposited in a joint checking account in which you and your spouse have an equal interest,	Half of the total medical expenses, subject to certain limits, unless you can show that you alone paid the expenses.
State income tax	File a separate state income tax return,	The state income tax you alone paid during the year.
	File a joint state income tax return and you and your spouse are jointly and individually liable for the full amount of the state income tax,	The state income tax you alone paid during the year.
	File a joint state income tax return and you are liable for only your own share of state income tax,	The smaller of: • the state income tax you alone paid during the year, or • the total state income tax you and your spouse paid during the year multiplied by the following fraction: the numerator is your gross income, and the denominator is your combined gross income.

(continued)

Property tax	Paid the tax on property held as tenants by the entirety,	The property tax you alone paid.
Mortgage interest	Paid the interest on a qualified home[1] held as tenants by the entirety,	The mortgage interest you alone paid.
Casualty loss	Have a casualty loss on a home you own as tenants by the entirety,	Half of the loss, subject to the deduction limits. Neither spouse may report the total casualty loss.

[1] For more information on a qualified home and deductible mortgage interest, see Pub. 936, Home Mortgage Interest Deduction.*

* Caution: If you live in a community property state, these rules do not apply. See the section titled Community Property.

Dividing Itemized Deductions

You may be able to claim itemized deductions on a separate return for certain expenses whether you paid the expenses separately with your own funds or jointly with your spouse (see the previous table).

Disadvantages of Filing Married Jointly

When you file a joint income tax return, the law makes both you and your spouse responsible for the entire tax liability. This is called joint and several liability. If you filed jointly and your spouse has historically misrepresented income or deductions or failed to cooperate with you in filing taxes, you are responsible for all taxes owed, as well as any interest and penalties for any tax liability the IRS determines to be due from current or past returns. This is also true even if a divorce decree states that a former spouse will be responsible for any amounts due on previously filed joint returns.

When you file jointly, you expose yourself to 100-percent liability for total taxes owed, even if you do not know what information is included on the return. If your spouse wants to file a joint return, you don't necessarily have to agree, but if you don't file an objection for tax relief with the IRS based on fraud, identity theft, or lack of consent or file your own separate return first, then the joint return is valid even without your signature.

If your ex is going to file a joint return and you intend to file under the status of married filing separately, file your return as soon as possible. If you expect this issue to be a problem, discuss it immediately with your spouse and divorce attorney. Do not expect tax relief by asserting that you are an "innocent spouse." The rule allows you to escape relief from *additional* tax liability only in very limited circumstances.

According to the IRS, you cannot ignore the information contained in the tax return you sign. If you have doubts, always ask your tax preparer to evaluate your risk for filing jointly. If you do sign a joint return, make sure your divorce agreement includes a tax indemnification clause that says that the spouse liable for any amounts due on previously filed joint returns based on income reported or deductions taken will pay and will hold the other spouse harmless. The right to indemnification from your former spouse is an imperfect protection because the IRS collection efforts may cause you hardship.

The indemnification clause isn't binding for the IRS. The IRS can go after the assets of both of you, or either one of you, even after the marital property has been divided in a divorce. Your recourse is to pursue your rights of indemnification against your former spouse in court, and/or you can ask the IRS for another kind of tax relief called "separate liability relief," which only applies to the portion of tax affected by improper reporting.

Your divorce agreement should address how you will deal with any tax refund, liability, penalty, and charges due on past joint tax returns; how refund payments shall be made to the other spouse; and how much of the refund should be shared.

Courts generally cannot compel a resisting party to sign a joint tax return. Only in some states and under very specific, limited, and unusual circumstances does a court has the authority to order an unwilling spouse to sign a joint federal tax return or pay any of the increased tax, interest, and penalty caused by the refusal to sign. Often, if the court finds a recalcitrant party to be willfully refusing to sign a tax return because they want to intentionally damage the other party, the court may use its equitable authority to use other assets to rebalance the total financial outcome.

Once you are divorced and a joint tax liability arises, the IRS has authority to settle or compromise federal tax liability up to 10 years from the date of assessment to collect. At any point, your ex-spouse could file for a collection appeal or cut a deal with the IRS without your knowledge. Unfortunately, this grim situation could leave you on the hook with the IRS if you are not a party to the settlement. Worse yet, if you remarry and were not covered by your ex-spouse's IRS settlement, your new spouse also could be subject to unforeseen tax liabilities if you file jointly and your separate property has been transferred to joint names. If you are aware of a tax liability, you cannot ignore it and must resolve it.

What Is a Tax Exemption?

A tax exemption comes in many forms, all of which either reduce or eliminate an obligation to pay tax. In divorce, an exemption usually refers to an additional exemption for claiming a child as a dependent. Only one parent can claim the child as a dependency exemption in a given year.

Unless otherwise agreed to in the divorce agreement, usually the parent who has primary physical custody of the child (i.e., has the child more than 50 percent of the time) is entitled to claim the dependency exemption for a child, provided the child is under 19 years old (or under 24 if a full-time student) and does not provide more than half of their own financial support during the tax year.

Usually, the primary custodial parent files as head of household, claims the dependency exemption, and receives corresponding tax credits, such as the child and dependent care tax credits and the earned income credit. In most cases, the tax credits (which reduce taxable income dollar for dollar) are more valuable than the exemption itself. Regardless who claims the child, both parents can claim the child as a dependent to the extent the parent made contributions to a child's medical expenses and reimbursements.

The parent with the highest AGI will usually benefit most from taking the exemption. However, if the custodial parent's income is too high to take advantage of claiming the child dependency exemption (either because it is phased out or is subject to AMT), the parents can trade the exemption or release it so that the lower income parent can claim the full tax benefit.

Releasing a Child Dependency Exemption to the Other Parent

IRS Form 8332

To release the dependency exemption to the noncustodial parent if you want to change any filing status or to balance the tax benefits of having dependency exemption, you may do so by using IRS Form 8332. Both parents have to file this form with their income tax returns.

Should both parents claim the same child as their dependent in the same year, they each will be required to document their claim of majority support, and the IRS will make its determination of eligibility. This action may result in an audit and even a penalty.

NOTE: Tax filing status and dependency exemptions are different. By agreement, either parent may claim a dependency exemption.

What Is a Tax Deduction?

Tax deductions reduce your taxable income by the amount of the expense you paid during the year. The IRS allows many kinds of deductions for expenses. They are reported on Schedule A of Form 1040 if you itemize. If you do not itemize, or you choose to file the short-form tax return, you may take a "standard deduction" (the amount changes annually per the IRS).

Specified Deductions on Schedule A

- Taxes you paid
    - State and local sales tax
    - Disability insurance tax (some states)
    - Occupational taxes
    - Real estate taxes (state, local, or foreign)
    - Portion of condo and coop maintenance that includes real estate tax
    - Personal property taxes, such as auto and boat registration, license fees, etc. (only if charged on the basis of value and a yearly basis; varies by state)

- Interest you paid
  - Mortgage interest
  - Student loan interest
  - Late payment charges on mortgage payments
  - Prepayment penalties
  - Points on refinancing
  - Mortgage insurance premiums
- Other expenses
  - Job search expenses
  - Medical and dental expenses
  - Tax preparation and tax advice fees
  - Other professional fees (accounting, investment advisor, financial planner, etc.)
  - Legal fees (fees relating to collecting spousal support, keeping your job, tax advice, etc.)
  - Home renovation accommodations (for disability)
  - Business use of home and car
  - Safety deposit box
  - Tuition and fees
  - Charitable donations
  - Casualty and theft losses

Home Mortgage Deduction

The amount of home mortgage interest and property taxes paid can be substantial deductions. The question is which taxpayer can claim the mortgage interest and property tax deductions. The IRS requires that in addition to actually making these payments, the home must be your primary residence and your name must be on both the title and the mortgage. A divorce agreement should identify the party responsible for paying the mortgage interest on a jointly owned home, as well as the right of one party or the other to live in the house.

Jointly Owned Home

If you and your former spouse continue to jointly own the house after divorce and you are ordered to pay all of the mortgage payments, real estate taxes, and home insurance, then you can deduct—and your former spouse must include—one-half of all payments as spousal support. As an itemized deduction, you can claim the balance of the payments of one-half of the mortgage interest and taxes (but none of the insurance). If both you and your former spouse are paying the mortgage interest, then the deduction can be shared with your ex-spouse. However, you cannot claim as a deduction more than what you have actually paid.

If *you are still living* in the house after the divorce and you are paying all of the mortgage interest, the IRS will continue to allow you a mortgage interest deduction but you cannot claim spousal support. The IRS states that payments cannot be spousal support if spouses are members of the same household when the payment is made as ordered under a divorce decree.

Change of Ownership

If you change ownership of the house after divorce, what you can claim as a tax deduction or as spousal support depends on (1) who owns the house and (2) who pays the mortgage, taxes, and insurance. If you take *sole ownership of the home*, but your ex-spouse lives in it and your divorce judgment provides for you to pay for all house expenses, you can deduct the full amount of mortgage interest, but you can't claim any of the mortgage interest payment as spousal support.

If *your ex-spouse owns the home* and lives in it and you take responsibility for the house payments, then you can deduct all that expense as spousal support. Your ex-spouse must report the spousal support as income and can claim all of the mortgage interest deduction as the owner.

Expenses for a Jointly Owned Home (IRS Publication 504)

Use this table to find how much of your payment is alimony and how much you can claim as an itemized deduction.

IF you must pay all of the . . .	AND your home is . . .	THEN you can deduct, and your spouse (or former spouse) must include as alimony, . . .	AND you can claim as an itemized deduction . . .
Mortgage payments (principal and interest)	Jointly owned	Half of the total payments	Half of the interest as an interest expense (if the home is a qualified home).[1]
Real estate taxes and home insurance	Held as tenants in common	Half of the total payments	Half of the real estate taxes[2] and none of the home insurance.
	Held as tenants by the entirety or in joint tenancy	None of the payments	All of the real estate taxes and none of the home insurance.

[1] Your spouse (or former spouse) can deduct the other half of the interest if the home is a qualified home.

[2] Your spouse (or former spouse) can deduct the other half of the real estate taxes.

What Is a Tax Credit?

A tax credit is a dollar-for-dollar offset against your income taxes. It is a reduction of the amount of taxes you pay. In most cases, a tax credit equals the amount of expenses you have paid during the year. Tax credits save you more money than deductions. Deductions only reduce the amount of income subject to taxes, whereas credits reduce taxes directly. Tax credits can have a huge impact on your taxes when you are divorced.

There are many different types of credits. Some of the most valuable credits for divorcing parents help them reduce the actual cost of raising and caring for children.

These credits are the child and dependent care credit, the child tax credit, and the earned income tax credit (EITC).

According to the IRS, only one parent can claim all the child-related tax benefits for a child. The tax benefits include the dependency exemption, the child tax credit, the dependent care credit, the exclusion for dependent care benefits, head of household filing status, and the EITC.

For divorced or separated parents or parents who have lived apart for the last six months of the calendar year, a special rule provides that the noncustodial parent may claim the dependency exemption for a child if the custodial parent releases the exemption. The noncustodial parent may also claim the child tax credit if the other requirements for the child tax credit are met.

The dependent care credit may only be claimed by the custodial parent. Likewise, only the custodial parent may claim the EITC since the child must meet the residency test; that is, the child must live with the parent for more than six months of the year except for temporary absences. Custody is determined by the number of nights the child slept in the home of the parent or the parent who had responsibility for the child for the evening.

The Child and Dependent Care Credit

This credit helps you cover childcare costs so that you are able to work or look for work. Expenses for before-school and after-school care of a child may also be claimed as childcare costs.

The credit can be as much as 35 percent of your care expenses (at lower income levels) but is reduced to 20 percent at higher income levels, with a maximum of $3,000 for one child and up to $6,000 if you have more than one child. The total $6,000 limit does not need to be divided evenly between the children.

Child Tax Credit

The child tax credit gives taxpayer parents—with incomes below certain amounts—a $1,000 credit for each qualifying child under age 17. If your AGI is over $75,000, as a single taxpayer, the credit is lowered and possibly not available at all. The custodial parent usually takes this credit. However, the noncustodial parent may take it if the custodial parent releases the dependency exemption to the noncustodial parent.

EITC

The EITC gives a tax break for workers with low wages. Whether any taxpayer can take the credit depends entirely on the amount of the taxpayer's earned income and AGI.

Important aspects of the EITC, provided you are separated or divorced:

- Only the custodial parent may take the EITC. The child must have lived with the parent in the United States for more than one half of the year. A non-custodial parent can't take the credit even if the custodial parent releases the dependency exemption.
- Determine if you have earned income. Spousal support and child support paid to you is *not* "earned income" (even though the spousal support you receive is taxable income and taxable to you). If you have no earned income, you do not qualify for the tax credit.
- Determine if you qualify based on workers rules if you don't have a child or do not claim a child. You may be able to take the EITC based on your own income even if your ex-spouse claims the EITC as the custodial parent.
- Even if you're the custodial parent with a qualifying child and satisfy the other EITC requirements, you may not claim the EITC if you are claimed as a dependent by someone else (e.g., if you and your child live with your parents after the divorce).

The EITC is complicated. The IRS frequently finds that the taxpayer claiming the credit is not entitled to it. Before claiming or overlooking the credit, review the IRS EITC materials carefully and talk to a tax professional.

Summary of Tax Facts in Divorce

Spousal Support

Spousal support is usually taxable to the recipient and tax deductible to the payor. Spousal support is considered earned income for purposes of making contributions to IRAs. As the payor of spousal support, you can deduct against income the amount you are legally ordered to pay in the written divorce agreement or by court order. The agreement or order must provide that spousal support payments terminate in the event the recipient dies. More details, strategies, and practical tips, including tax traps, concerning spousal support are included in Chapter 13.

Child Support

Child support is not taxable or tax deductible. It is an ongoing, periodic payment made by a parent for the financial benefit of a child following the end of a marriage or other relationship. More details, strategies, and practical tips, including tax traps, concerning child support are included in Chapter 12.

Retirement Assets

All qualified tax-deferred pension and retirement benefits can be divided between divorcing spouses without penalty or loss of any tax advantages of the plan. The funds are taxed when withdrawn. These asset transfers are accomplished via a QDRO or a direct transfer from one spouse's IRA to the other spouse's IRA.

The following documents are required to make this a tax-free transfer:

- A decree of divorce (judgment of dissolution);
- A decree of separate maintenance; or
- A written instrument incident to such decree, or a document.

More details and practical tips, including tax traps, are included in Chapter 9.

Property Transfer and Capital Gains

Dividing marital property, incident to divorce, does not result in any taxes. The original basis (cost or purchase price) of the property stays with the asset and goes to the spouse who is the new owner. Subsequently, when the recipient spouse goes to sell the property, they may incur a capital gain or loss. More details, strategies, and practical tips, including tax traps, concerning spousal support are included in Chapters 8 and 11.

Impact of Taxes in Divorce

Far too many couples negotiate their divorce without consideration of the tax impact of their decisions. The tax implications concerning the timing of divorce, type of support, the manner in which property is to be divided, and avoidable tax consequences require education and attention.

There is no "redo" on many decisions, and Uncle Sam will not take a back seat to your divorce agreement. A useful place to start is with the IRS publications and its websites, which provide mountains of useful, current information to help you better understand the consequences of the decisions you will need to make during your divorce.

18 Getting to "Yes": Negotiating a Settlement

Negotiating What Is Acceptable, Affordable, and Durable

The vast majority of divorce cases reach a successful conclusion without a trial. The statistics are in your favor—fewer than 2 percent of all cases do not settle and are decided by a judge after trial. The other 98 percent are able to reach agreements with the help of their attorneys and/or mediators. Most cases settle—whether they are simple, complex, friendly, or contested—because both parties realize the following:

1. Contentious divorces are almost always expensive.
2. As long as your divorce continues you will be emotionally, physically, and mentally impaired.
3. Once you put your financial future in the hands of a judge who does not know you or your family, you surrender all control.

To make the most of your opportunity to negotiate a settlement, you must have a pretty clear idea of what you want before the negotiating begins. If you have done your homework and have worked with the professionals on your team, you can advocate on your own behalf and frame your position in negotiations.

The process usually goes like this. Both you and your spouse, independent of each other, decide what you want; one makes the first proposal; the other responds; and either accepts or rejects the proposal in whole or in part. If the second party rejects the proposal, they can offer a counterproposal indicating what they want. Proposals and counterproposals often go back and forth before a compromise is reached when both parties give in on some of the terms they originally wanted.

In theory, everything is negotiable. However, in reality, you may decide that specific items are nonnegotiable from the start. The objective is to find a reasonable and legally acceptable balance between what is personally acceptable and what is affordable.

If you and your spouse can agree on most issues, it's worth reaching out on outstanding issues in order to save money and to spare yourself the uncertainty of what would happen in court. It is almost unheard of to get everything you want in a settlement; it is not a realistic goal.

⚠ **Caution:** When you consider negotiating, reflect on the potential risks or disadvantages you may face trying to collect what you are owed from your spouse. Prepare for unforeseen contingencies and rank the likelihood of actually receiving your benefits now and in the future.

Rarely are two spouses equal when it comes to their negotiating abilities; recognize if it is you or your spouse who has the advantage. Don't let yourself be rushed or coerced into an agreement before you are ready or before you have all of your questions and concerns addressed. On the other hand, delay tactics may backfire and destroy any potential meaningful negotiations. There is a fine line to observe and respect concerning settlement negotiations. The yin and yang of back-and-forth proposals provide the opportunity to vent your emotions, fears, priorities, and values to reach a resolution. A general rule of thumb in negotiating is never to start with your bottom line.

ⓘ **TIP:** Be careful not to abuse this opportunity and be diligent in making all decisions from a position of knowledge. Information is power. Go to the bargaining table prepared for compromise and a deal to be closed.

What Are Some Effective Strategies for Settlement Negotiations?

Most couples talk to each other informally without counsel during the divorce process about who should get what and why—these conversations directly influence the negotiations. To deal with situations where you are alone with your spouse, it helps to plan ahead for diffusing difficulties that arise during this one to one talk. If you are not confident that you can unemotionally assess strategies and tactics, or you fear spousal talks will be a free-for-all or simply rehash old wounds, take the following points into consideration.

Timing Is Everything

One spouse is usually far ahead of the other when planning to divorce. The spouse who has been contemplating divorce (secretly), and therefore has had much longer to plan his or her goals, may insist on getting you to agree to an issue before you are ready. Both of you will feel impatient, frustrated, and anxious.

You need to defuse this situation by moving the spotlight away from the item in question, by taking it off the table temporarily, and asking what would happen if this one issue didn't exist? Acknowledge that you need more time to think it over and agree to reconsider later and see how it all fits into the bigger picture. You could suggest you sideline the issue and involve a neutral mediator to help resolve the sticking point. Be patient.

Numbers Are Fatal Early in the Game

Once a party sees a number (dollar value or percentage), they will fixate on it. The methodology used to get to a number, the assumptions on which it is based, and even the result or goal attained pale beside the suggestion of a specific monetary value. Numbers prematurely put on the table can be dangerous; often the other spouse will not listen to anything else.

When your spouse asks you for a ballpark figure that will resolve the case—or to get a better idea of where you are coming from, you don't have to respond directly. You may not know your "target number," and if you reveal your number, you tip your hand; your spouse will have the opportunity to nitpick each and every expense that you claim in order "to prove" your number is inflated.

To avoid shooting yourself in the foot, you can suggest that you do not know your "number" yet and that after the financial phases of the divorce process you will be in a better position to respond.

How to React When You Get an Ultimatum

When your spouse says, "Take it or leave it—it's the best offer you will ever get," how do you respond? Is this simply posturing?

- Does your spouse offer ultimatums casually, frequently, seriously, and/or threateningly?
- Is your spouse used to being in control?
- Does your spouse feel unheard, fearful, frustrated, desperate, or guilty?
- Is your spouse fully engaged in the negotiation process?

Ultimatums arise from any number of emotions and situations. You must diffuse them while saving face for your spouse to salvage the negotiations. You could offer to reply with a counter proposal now that you have something to analyze and review. You could ask more questions about the specifics—clearly and without blame—of the "proposed deal" and the nature of its urgency, and/or you can suggest that you need more time to consider it.

You could also suggest that while you may agree with aspects of the proposal, you need the opportunity to come up with your own ideas. Ask your spouse to put themselves in your shoes and ask how they would react to the situation. No one should make split second decisions under duress or threat. The significant financial decisions you make during the divorce process will have lifetime consequences.

Separating You from Your Attorney or Negotiating Apart from the Formal Process

Attorneys can serve as a much-needed buffer between spouses to minimize a highly emotionally charged interaction. Let them do so. However, if you and your spouse feel that your divorce attorneys are aggravating the hostility, poor communications, or inhibiting productive progress, the parties may make headway on their own (or should change one or both of their attorneys).

Assume you and your spouse both want to settle, but you just cannot get to "yes." What is the problem? Are you dealing with a difficult attorney? Is it the opposing attorney or your spouse who is sabotaging settlement?

Tell-Tale Signs of Sabotage

- Counsel
    - Opposing counsel demands are so outrageous that you might as well take your best shot at trial because you won't do any worse than what the other side is offering.
    - Opposing counsel refuses to take your attorney's phone calls and/or refuses to respond to written offers.
    - Opposing counsel files routinely frivolous motions and needlessly drags you into court.
    - Opposing counsel fails to communicate your proposals to your spouse; your spouse has no idea about your efforts to try to settle.
    - Opposing counsel is unskilled in the techniques of good negotiation, unfamiliar or inexperienced with divorce law, inattentive or overworked with caseload, and/or arrogant and seems to churn the file (inflating billable hours).
- Your Spouse
    - Your spouse would rather stay in a failed marriage even if the situation is objectively untenable. Your spouse believes that your marriage is perfectly "good enough."
    - Your spouse enjoys the battle enough to drag out the divorce interminably.
    - You spouse has more often than once fired their divorce attorney and hires new counsel without good reason or cause. Switching attorneys as a delay tactic is routinely recognized by the court and considered improper.

Responding to Sabotage

In some of these situations, it may be entirely appropriate for you and your spouse to talk to each other directly and then jointly suggest to your divorce attorneys that you will try mediation (without the attorneys) if you are close to a settlement. You can threaten to fire your reasonable attorney to hire the meanest in town (if you are prepared to do so). In the end, you simply may have to prepare for trial as a last resort.

Communications with Your Spouse

Don't negotiate over the phone or by email. Communication when the other party is out of sight is easily misunderstood. A spouse who is unprepared for an email exchange or a phone call is unlikely to focus immediately on negotiations. Often a response will be more damaging than productive.

If your spouse insists on communicating with you, document everything. If you have a toxic spouse, you should collect hard evidence of threats to share with your attorney. Documentation also gives you a clear record of everything that has occurred up to that point in time in case there is a dispute. Stay organized during your divorce. The more organized you are and have complete logs of finances and communication, the easier it will be to refute any gross exaggerations or lies that your spouse tells.

Seven Deadly Sins of Divorce Negotiation

- Wrath: Emotions that jeopardize a deal
- Greed: Irrational expectations
- Lust: Power of control and imbalance
- Envy: Baseless assumptions and comparisons to the divorce experience of others
- Pride: Unreasonable positioning and escalating demands
- Sloth: Inertia, procrastination, and keeping the status quo
- Gluttony: Overindulgence and inflated sense of entitlement

The basic rule for negotiations is to understand what options exist for both of you and to bring closure to a legal separation agreement. You may not get everything you want, but you can get everything you negotiate.

Once You Agree, How Do You Conclude Your Divorce?

First, be sure that all issues have been resolved. Have you agreed on:

- When to end your marriage?
- Child custody and visitation?
- Support issues (including child and spousal)?
- Division of property and allocation of debts?
- Health and life insurance?

In a negotiated divorce, if you and your ex-spouse are close to making a deal but some issues remain unresolved, you and your divorce attorney request a *settlement conference*. A settlement conference offers your attorneys an opportunity to hammer out the final specific details of your divorce agreement. A settlement conference provides an opportunity to address each issue and confirm an agreement on each point. Let your attorney suggest whether you and your spouse attend the conference. If your divorce is contentious or if either of you have a hard time keeping your emotions under control, don't attend. Be available by phone to give your attorney feedback on any last-minute negotiated compromises.

If you and your spouse simply cannot agree on something, no matter how hard your attorneys try to craft a mutually acceptable compromise, they may recommend mediation or even arbitration. If you don't want to give these options a try and you don't want to keep negotiating, your only other option—assuming that you and your spouse still want to get divorced—is to have your case tried in court.

State by State

In some states, judges are allowed to modify the negotiated agreement. In others, judges can only accept or reject an agreement. If the judge rejects your agreement, you go back to the drawing board to work out a new, more acceptable one. A judge may deny your agreement because he or she doesn't think it's fair to one or both of you, because it's unenforceable or violates your state's laws, or because it isn't in the best interests of your minor children, among other reasons.

The Settlement Agreement (or Separation Agreement)

A clear, comprehensive, separation agreement brings about a satisfactory dissolution of your marriage. This final document legally memorializes all of the issues you agreed to. Once you and your spouse have agreed upon all of the key elements of the settlement, your divorce attorneys (or mediator) draft an agreement that reflects the spirit and intent of what you both want to achieve.

The agreement is signed by each party and by the attorneys. The agreement is presented to a judge for review and approval. The divorce is final when the court clerk enters the judgment into the court record. The document will be date stamped, and copies will be provided to your attorneys. The effective date of divorce is the date entered by the court clerk unless your state has an appeal period (that can be waived).

If the decree contains a judge's orders, be sure to read the orders. If you request clarification, ask your attorney. If there is a mistake that dramatically affects the outcome, make sure your attorney addresses it and possibly files a request with the court to make a change.

However, if your ex-spouse objects to the change(s), altering a divorce decree can be more difficult. In such cases, your attorney will have to file a motion with the judge for a new hearing to determine whether to make any changes. You have up to 30 days after the final divorce decree order to request a new hearing in most states. It is very important to read the documentation when the divorce papers are signed.

Obey the Divorce Order

Forgetting to follow through on implementing the terms of your divorce agreement can be one of the easiest things in the world to do and one of the costliest. No matter how you feel after you reach settlement, you must obey orders. If you signed an agreement, you are saying you are and it is time to follow through on the actions required by your divorce order.

Make a checklist of tasks you need to execute to comply with your orders and do them in order of their timeliness and priority. Stay on track and remember the last thing you want to do is lose what you've worked so hard to secure.

These may include:

- Paying support (child and spousal)
- Transferring ownership of assets to your former spouse (such as a car or house)
- Transferring interest(s) in retirement assets or a pension plan to your former spouse (confirm hiring another attorney to perform a QDRO)
- Making bill or debt payments
- Obtaining your own insurance(s)
- Changing beneficiary designations on life insurance if permitted, retirement accounts, bank accounts, etc.

In many cases, there are deadlines to perform these actions. Delays may result in further penalties, including your ex-spouse taking you back to court for lack of compliance.

Checklist of Post-Divorce Actions

- ❑ COBRA enrollment or other health insurance
- ❑ EFT for bill payments, support payments, and children's add-on expenses
- ❑ Re-issuing or separating joint policies in life and long-term care insurance
- ❑ Cashing out or dividing into separate annuities
- ❑ Completing QDRO papers
- ❑ Revising personal documents to reflect your new single status

Where to Find Divorce Records Online or Get a Copy

The cost and rules for obtaining a court-certified copy of your divorce agreement vary by state.

Some divorce records are kept at the state level; some are kept at the county level. To find out where the divorce records you want are located, you can contact your state's vital records department or the court clerk of the court where your divorce case was held or look online.

NOTE: To find out where to write or access vital online records, you can also go to http://www.cdc.gov/nchs/w2w/index.htm and click on the link for your state.

Divorce records are an abundant source of information available to the general public. Most divorce records can be obtained for a small fee. They are not confidential and reveal in-depth information regarding the divorce settlement, custody arrangements, whether or not alimony was ordered, and the grounds for which the divorce was filed, as well as if any restraining orders were filed.

Only in some cases will records be completely sealed for extenuating circumstances, such as:

- The need to protect children from identification in divorce records;
- The need to protect victims of domestic violence;
- The need to keep sensitive information such as Social Security numbers and bank account numbers private;
- The need to protect proprietary business information; and
- The need to prevent the instigation of false allegations in the future.

Courts do not take it upon themselves to file divorce records under seal. You and your spouse have to make the request to the court, and you stand a better chance if you both are in agreement. Courts do not consider embarrassing information alone as causing harm or a reason for keeping court records from the public. A request to seal divorce records has a better chance to succeed if it is narrowly tailored to redact or seal particular (rather than all) information. Attend the hearing with the judge and present evidence and arguments in favor of the motion to seal divorce court records. The judge will issue their decision following the hearing.

19 The Light at the End of the Tunnel: Your Financial Situation after Divorce

Once you finalize your divorce and all of the terms of your judgment have been executed correctly, you can finally focus more of your energy on yourself. You begin now the process of redefining and restructuring your new life after divorce. As with most challenges, achieving financial security is essential, and it is more important than ever to plan for your long-term well-being.

Divorce is one of life's transitions, but few see financial planning as part of their response to a divorce. Ignoring your situation can have far-reaching consequences simply because you may need to adapt to changes you didn't anticipate or adjustments that are different from what you expected. The good news is that you have a fresh start. You have options within your control for dealing with the future. Now is the time to explore the possibilities.

At some point, we have all fantasized about having full control and complete access to money we never had before. Your net worth will have changed because of the assets and debts you received or exchanged, as well as the cash flow you receive. One unique aspect of divorce is that you may come into sudden money with a divorce settlement. This outcome can impact you in any number of positive and negative ways. You may feel like you are experiencing a windfall, but it is not a cure-all. If not handled appropriately, you may end up going broke within a few years, just like 70 percent of the general population who come into sudden money.

Immediately after divorce is *not* the time to take risks, make impulsive choices, lock yourself into long-term contracts, or fall prey to inertia (no "woe is me"). It is premature to make life-changing financial decisions during a time of transition. Do not underestimate the emotional exhaustion and physical toll divorce may have on you.

Whatever your situation is, it is best to *take your time* to study how you are going to make decisions about:

- Your money
- Your children
- Your social life
- Your career

Setting Goals

Change is simply a process comprised of one step at a time. You are going to redesign your goals to make new plans. Financial planning strategies can be very helpful for the short and long term.

It typically takes about three months following divorce for things to settle down. You should view this time as a "test" period for working through your new economics. You should be tracking everything until you believe you have a good handle on how to match your inflows with outflows, which establishes your bottom line.

After this trial three-month period, you should be ready to sit down and work on a new spending plan with new financial goals. Sample goals include:

1. Don't spend more than you earn: A simple rule of thumb is that your inflows should match your outflows.
2. Invest in you first and foremost: Pay yourself first, ratchet up your savings, and do it with discipline.
3. Save as much as you can for your retirement: Max out your retirement savings annually. If possible, aim to max out your employer's contributions as well.
4. Get out of debt: Elect for "plastic surgery" and cut up all nonessential credit cards. Pay off expensive debt first. Make payments on time and as much as possible, and pay *more* than the minimum amount each month.
5. Invest smarter: Do your homework and understand the basics of investing. Put your money to work for you! Get professional help.

What Is a Budget?

A budget is a plan for your future inflows and outflows that you can use as a guideline for spending and saving. The key is to spend less than you make. Budgeting makes it easier for you to make conscious decisions about how you *prefer* to spend your money. It helps you get out of debt, save for emergencies, make significant purchases, and plan for your retirement. Spending wisely is a consistent, learned behavior that results in a long-term successful solution.

The biggest unconscious spending habits are credit card abuse, excessive dining out, and personal entertainment. To avoid these bad habits, start by organizing expenses into three categories:

- Fixed (mortgage, rent, taxes, insurances, auto leases, loan payments, etc.)
- Variable (groceries, utilities, auto gas, auto registration/license, dues, prescriptions, out-of-pocket medical/dental, etc.)
- Discretionary (personal grooming, entertainment, clothing, restaurants, vacation, etc.)

There are multiple approaches to budgeting and how much you should spend in proportion to your income on different kinds of expenses. You do not need to be overwhelmed and afraid of spreadsheets and sophisticated software with detailed spending categories. The good news is that you may prefer first to get a global snapshot of your finances. How much does each expense category represent of the total pie?

This approach is called the percentage budgeting concept. It is relatively straightforward. Instead of allocating a fixed dollar amount for each expense category, you establish a target percentage. This process allows for you to see the trade-offs in your spending decisions and can show you where you may need to consider cutting back or where you may be able to afford to spend a little more.

The following chart presents some budget percentage guidelines to consider.

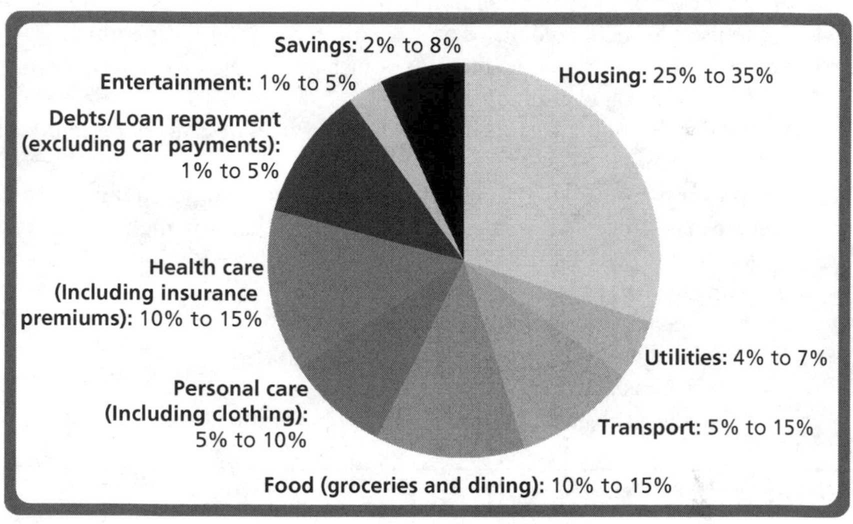

Another budgeting approach is the 50/20/30 rule:

- 50 percent of your income goes to necessities (living expenses and essentials, such as your mortgage or rent, utilities, transportation, etc.);
- 20 percent of your income goes to financial goals (long-term savings, investments, and debt-reduction payments); and
- 30 percent of your income goes to lifestyle choices (flexible spending for everything you buy that you want but don't necessarily need).

Usually, these percentages are the maximum you should spend. All suggested target ranges allow for some flexibility and personal fine tuning. Your action steps are clear but also be gentle with yourself.

There is a learning curve to the mastery of personalizing your preferences and regaining control over your spending. A budget is a "living" thing. You must reevaluate it from time to time. Remind yourself what you are doing for yourself. If you are struggling or falling behind in this effort, you may need to seek professional assistance to put a little more discipline into your life.

Practical Tips for Budgeting

1. Maintain a spending book. At the end of each month, sort your spending into categories and free up some cash for an emergency fund, savings, or retirement.
   a. Keep all receipts because it is tempting to lose sight of what you spent.
2. If you can, set up a reliable system for paying bills such as automatic bill paying or reminders to get your payments in on time.
3. Take out enough cash for only the week. Paying in cash versus with a debit or credit card draws your attention to how fast it goes!
4. Try to use one main credit card or checking account for all spending.
5. Balance your checkbook or monitor your bank account. A couple of mistakes can cost you overdraft fees or charges.
6. Renegotiate rates for everything and stop services you do not need. Call your service providers.
7. Always shop around to get the best mortgage rate and get multiple offers. Prepare in advance with a little research to know what you might qualify for: FHA, conventional, refinance, or the Home Affordable Refinance Plan.
   a. Mortgage tips to save you money:
      i. Improve your credit score
      ii. Manage your debt to income
      iii. Have cash reserves
      iv. Make a substantial down payment (minimum 20 percent)

Eliminating Debts with a Payment Plan

One out of every three households carries credit card debt from month to month. Some manage modest amounts of debt fairly well, while others struggle to make minimum payments and are fending off bankruptcy.

Simple Steps to Eliminate and Stay Out of Debt

1. Calculate your exact budget and start downsizing your expenses.
2. For some people, the quickest way to restrain the use of debt is to pay only in cash.
3. Stop spending with credit cards or use only a debit card.
4. Consolidate debts into a manageable payment plan or eliminate some debts before others:
   a. The ladder approach: You pay down debts with highest interest rates or reduce some debts before others.

b. The snowball approach: You pay down the largest balances outstanding instead of starting with the ones with the highest interest rates.

5. Explain your payment strategy to the creditors and ask for help before the situation is out of control. They may have methods for dealing with one-time hardship.
6. Seek nonprofit credit counseling if you need discipline, guidance, and instruction.
7. Visualize being debt free and keep yourself motivated.

Make Sure You Have an Emergency Fund

An emergency fund is an amount of cash set aside to cover the financial surprises life throws at you. It is for unexpected events that can be costly and stressful. Nearly 80 percent of us will have a major negative economic event in any given 10-year period. You need an emergency fund to survive. Most of the time, you shouldn't touch an emergency fund at all—it just sits there until you need it.

Common Emergencies People Face

1. Job loss
2. Delayed or default on support payments you rely on
3. Medical or dental emergency
4. Unexpected home repairs
5. Car troubles
6. Unplanned travel expenses

Obvious consequences of not having enough cash in the short term are that it costs you to find it. Painful strategies include:

- Increasing debt at a cost
- Withdrawing from retirement funds, perhaps incurring a penalty in addition to taxes
- Delaying bill paying and negatively impacting your credit score
- Declaring bankruptcy

How Big Should an Emergency Fund Be?

The more stable your household is, the less you need in your emergency fund. If you are somewhat unsettled following divorce, a good rule of thumb is to set aside an amount equal to at least three to six months of expenses, but the exact amount depends on a few variables. Estimate your costs for critical expenses, such as housing, food, utilities, healthcare (including insurance), transportation, and debt repayment.

How to Build an Emergency Fund

Remember something is better than nothing. If you can't save enough, do not panic. Start saving with small amounts weekly, and it will build up.

Practical Tips for Saving

1. Set a monthly savings goal. Determine how much you need and then break it down to figure how much you can put in each month. Based on your contributions, you can see how long it will take you to reach your target amount.
2. Make it automatic. Schedule automatic debits from your checking account to your savings. Maybe divert a portion of your paycheck to go directly to your emergency fund.
3. Squeeze all your sources and keep the change:
    a. Stop wasting money from leaks in your budget (expensive credit card fees, leaving lights on, or ordering too much take out)
    b. Earn supplemental income
    c. Stop reinvesting interest and dividends in your investment accounts until you establish your emergency fund
    d. Clean out your change

Emergency Fund Essentials

1. Low/no risk—Cash is king
2. Liquidity—Ready to be used; minimal efforts to obtain cash
3. Accessibility—How fast can you get your hands on it?

Where to Keep Your Emergency Fund?

Your emergency fund should be where you can immediately access your cash and where it is safe from market risk. Options are:

- A regular savings account
- A money market account
- A short-term interest-bearing account or CD
- Cash in a lockbox

Re-Evaluating Your Risk Protection: Insurance

The chances are that following divorce, you have to update your insurance: automobile, homeowners, renters, umbrella, personal liability, and perhaps professional insurances. As you know, you buy insurance to protect your income, your family, and your assets from financial ruin. But just any old insurance won't do. You owe it to yourself and your loved ones to obtain and maintain the correct type and amount of coverage from a financially secure insurance company.

How should you go about evaluating your insurance options and understanding what your needs are post-divorce? You have to become an informed consumer by doing your research. Check out the quality of companies and the types of insurance you feel you need before you contact an agent.

Major Issues to Consider When Evaluating Your Current Insurance Coverage or Considering Purchasing New Policies

1. Contact your previous insurance company(s) to ask about updating or entering into a new policy(s) based on your needs now. Recognize that a captive agent working for one insurance company will not be in a position to provide policy comparisons across different insurers. Always compare prices.
2. What is the financial strength of the company? Insurance is worth nothing if the company isn't around to pay claims when you're in need. And you obviously don't want to waste money paying for insurance that won't cover you when the need arises.
3. What are the claims payment history and customer service ratings? Check out the insurance company's complaint history with your state insurance regulators.
4. You may be required to review your coverage to maintain or purchase life insurance pursuant to your divorce decree, to secure your support obligations, to cover college funding, or to replace lost income to meet living expenses for your children.
   a. How much life insurance should you purchase?
      i. A very simplistic measure is to buy an amount as a percentage of your income.
      ii. Comply with your divorce order that usually requires coverage at the outset to be equal to total support obligations and any additional expenses, such as college.
      iii. Evaluate your family's needs by considering family size, ages of dependent family members, income, expenses, debts, existing assets, and personal goals. There are online capital needs assessment calculators you can access that also include anticipated inflation and rates of return.
      iv. Equally important to selecting the amount of life insurance is determining if you should have temporary (term) or permanent life insurance. Term provides coverage for a limited period, such as 5, 10, or 20 years. The advantage is cost.

         Permanent life insurance provides a lifetime of coverage as long as you continue to pay the premium; it is more expensive than term. Another feature of permanent insurance is that it accumulates a cash value on a tax-deferred basis. Cash value accumulates and is applied against premium payments, and you can borrow against it or withdraw it (usually after the surrender period).

5. Working with one broker is helpful when you need to assess your needs, close coverage gaps, and reduce liability exposure. Your broker should view your entire lifestyle and portfolio of assets for holes in coverage and potential exposure. Placing all your coverage with one carrier is more cost effective because it allows for premium credits and elimination of costly redundant coverage. Your broker should analyze, assess, and determine the best value and insurance carrier for you. Having a broker allows you to contact a single point person to call in the event of loss, who then notifies all insurance companies on your behalf.

Keeping Up with Changes in Your Tax Status

Filing taxes after divorce may be trickier than you think. The biggest taxable events play out after divorce.

Points to Consider When You File Your Taxes for the First Time after Divorce

1. **Who claims the kids?** You get a valuable tax deduction if you can claim a dependency exemption as well as significant tax credits (refer to Chapter 16). You may have to use IRS Form 8332, Release/Revocation of Release of Claim to Exemption for Child by Custodial Parent, and it must be signed each year by the custodial parent for use by the noncustodial parent.
2. **What's your tax filing status?** Your tax filing status is set as of December 31. If you are divorced, you are considered single and unmarried for the whole year. You must qualify to file as head of household per IRS criteria.
3. **Spousal support (alimony) and child support.** Spousal support is taxable to the recipient and tax deductible for the payor. Child support is nontaxable to the recipient and nondeductible by the payor. Review your income changes and withholding deductions for how you will be affected post-divorce. If you are not employed and receive only spousal support, you will need to make quarterly estimated tax payments. If you are receiving spousal support or other taxable income, you may need to make estimated tax payments. If you are employed, your withholding is probably not enough to cover your taxes for the coming year. You may want to consider having extra tax withheld from your paycheck or set up quarterly estimated tax payments to avoid owing additional taxes and penalties at the end of the year. If you are paying alimony, you might update your withholding on Form W4 if your tax filing status changes to either single or head of household.
4. **Division of property**. In divorce, any marital property transferred between former spouses is a nontaxable event. However, if you sell or liquidate any assets after you are divorced, you alone are responsible for any taxes owed. The assets you receive in divorce retain their original cost basis. In some instances, your capacity to shield sale profits from taxes is reduced as a single person. For example, if you sell your house, you can exclude up to $250,000 profit on the sale, not the $500,000 for married couples.

5. **Splitting income in the year of your divorce.** As a taxpayer, you are required to include in gross income all income from every source. Taxation of the income from jointly held property is determined by state law for deciding who is entitled to the income from the property. If you and your ex-spouse had an equal right to the income from the property, the usual rule is that one-half of the income from the property is properly taxable to each spouse.
6. **Dividends and interest from joint assets.** In general, both parties on a joint account must report one-half of the annual income from dividends and interest from joint assets. If in divorce, the entire account is transferred to your former spouse, including the accumulated income, you may still be issued a Form 1099 if your name was listed first on the account. You have to include this income on Schedule B of your 1040, but you can make it known that the amount was paid to your former spouse. You enter the same amount as a negative number for "Paid to the nominee and your spouse's social security number." You must inform your ex-spouse that income is attributed to them as the nominee. When the account is divided and transferred post-divorce, the income will be reported in your name alone.
7. **Splitting deductions in the year of your divorce.** You and your former spouse may each claim any itemized deductions you actually pay. If expenses were paid from a joint account, each of you could claim equally the deductions. However, the IRS provides special rules in the situation of divorce, and you must further comply with the provisions of your divorce decree or legal separation agreement.
   a. **Mortgage interest**: Home mortgage interest is typically one of the most significant itemized deductions. The deduction for home mortgage interest and real estate taxes for the post-divorce period of the year will be determined by the terms of the judgment or settlement agreement and the form of ownership following the divorce. If the home continues to be held in some form of joint ownership, either as tenants in common or joint tenancy, you and your spouse are both entitled to take deductions for half of the mortgage interest and real estate taxes. However, if the entire interest in the marital residence is transferred to one party as part of the settlement, only that person can take the mortgage interest deduction.
   b. **Medical expenses**: You can claim as itemized deductions all medical and dental expenses not covered by insurance as long as they exceed 7.5 percent of your AGI. You can deduct all medical expenses, including insurance premiums, that you paid for yourself, for your former spouse, and for dependents. To include medical expenses paid for your spouse, you must have been married at the time the medical services were received or when the expenses were paid. If medical expenses were paid from a joint checking account, each former spouse could claim half the expenses. You could not claim expenses if they were paid from an HSA or flexible spending account.

   c. **Other itemized deductions**: For other itemized deductions, such as charitable contributions, you could claim the expenses you paid separately and half the expenses that were paid from a joint account while you were married.

8. **Splitting estimated joint tax payments**. If you and your spouse made joint estimated tax payments for the year of divorce, either of you could claim all of your payments or you could divide them in any way on which you both agree. If you cannot agree, seek professional help before you claim any taxes paid.
9. **Dividing overpayments applied to the year of divorce.** If taxes were prepaid or applied toward your joint tax liability in the year you divorce, you must allocate the overpayment between yourself and your ex-spouse. Either of you can claim all of your payments, or you can divide them in any way on which you both agree. However, if you cannot agree on the allocation, seek professional help with the calculation.
10. **Paying joint tax liabilities.** If you filed joint tax returns during the marriage for which taxes are still owed, you and your former spouse are severally and jointly liable for all taxes owed. The IRS will go after both of you to collect. Even if joint tax liabilities were ordered by the court to be assigned to one spouse, this does not resolve your standing with the taxing authorities. A court order allows you to sue your former spouse but does not prevent the IRS from collecting from you.

Taking Care of Your Estate

Having just gone through your divorce, you probably are not inclined to visit another attorney. However, you want to make sure you have updated financial arrangements that kick in upon your death. States have different provisions regarding inheritance and former spouses. They vary greatly from state to state, and they may or may not apply to all of your assets. The only way to be sure your assets will go to those you want to have them is to update your estate planning—and the sooner the better.

Revoke your old will and any power of attorney. Destroy old copies of outdated documents. Everything should reflect your new legal status and current name, as well as current lifestyle. If you don't, your property and personal effects may be distributed and taxed in ways you do not expect or desire.

Seven Simple Steps to Take as Soon as Possible after Divorce

1. Update your will
2. Name an executor for your estate
3. Name a guardian for your children
4. Update all beneficiary designations on:
   a. Financial accounts (bank and brokerage accounts)
   b. Life insurance policies

   c. Annuities
   d. Retirement accounts like IRAs and 401K plans
5. Amend living trusts (most can be changed)
6. Update your healthcare directive
7. Update your financial power of attorney
8. Update your living will

How Do You Define Success?

Feeling victorious seems far-fetched for most people going through a divorce. Sheer survival is more realistic than triumph. How do you let go of the negativity and see the light at the end of the tunnel?

Practical Tips for Moving Forward

1. Identify what you want and have a clear vision that will guide you in decision-making.
2. Take control of your financial situation: save more and invest wisely.
3. Silence the naysayers and focus on people who positively influence you and support you.
4. Honor your values and re-identify with what makes you tick. How are you unique and gain insight into yourself? Know what you do best. Prepare yourself to do it.
5. Set your intentions for positive co-parenting and be respectful.
6. Rise above. Nothing breeds success like success. The desire to live a successful life is half the battle. The rest is planning, passion, focused attention, and diligent execution. Before you know it, you will see positive results!

I hope that this book has provided you with knowledge, practical tools, strategies, and tips for navigating the divorce process. The fundamental components of every divorce for anyone are few: support, division of property, and parenting of children. The variables, challenges, and consequences, however, are many. With this book, you should gain a keener insight into both basic concepts as well as more nuanced issues of divorce. *Money and Divorce* will help guide you in determining exactly what you need to do and know to succeed in your divorce and life.

Glossary

A

ABANDONMENT – a reason for divorce

ACTION – the legal term for lawsuit

ACTIVE APPRECIATION – an increase in value at least in part because of efforts or contributions by one or both spouses

ACCRUE – to increase by addition or growth; often financial, such as interest on money

ADDENDUM – an additional document or phrase attached to the original document

ADJUSTED GROSS INCOME – total gross income minus specific deductions, which is located at the bottom of the first page of your income tax return (Line 37); however, the way you calculate income for child support and spousal support may be different from the way you would calculate income for tax purposes

ADMISSIBLE, ADMISSIBILITY – evidence that is presented formally before a trier of fact (a judge) to consider when deciding a case

AFFIDAVIT – a written statement of facts made under oath and signed before a notary public

AGREEMENT – a transcribed or written resolution of the disputed issues when the parties have resolved issues in the case

ALIMONY, SPOUSAL SUPPORT, MAINTENANCE – payment of support from one party to another (usually taxable to payee and deductible for payor)

ALIMONY PENDENTE LITE – a temporary order of the court that provides support for one spouse and/or children while the divorce is in progress

ALLOWABLE DEDUCTIONS – any item or expenditure deducted from income to reduce the amount of income subject to income tax

ALTERNATIVE DISPUTE RESOLUTION – processes that help parties resolve disputes without a trial: mediation (a neutral third-party negotiates between the parties and the decision is nonbinding), arbitration (the decision is binding by a neutral third party), and collaborative

ALTERNATE PAYEE – for purposes of dividing qualified retirement plans by a qualified domestic relations order, an alternate payee is any spouse, former spouse, child, or other dependent of a plan participant who is recognized as having the right to receive all or part of the benefits payable under the participant's plan

AMORTIZATION – the paying off of debt with a fixed repayment schedule over a period of time in regular installments, such as a mortgage or car loan

ANCILLARY RELIEF – in an action for divorce, this is additional or other help asked for beyond a judgment of divorce, such as maintenance, division of property, responsibility for bills, child support, etc.

ANNULMENT – the legal ending of an invalid marriage

ANNUITY – an annuity is a retirement vehicle sold by insurance companies that provides a steady series of equal payments made at equal intervals for a specific time period, often for the recipient's life

ANSWER TO COMPLAINT (PETITION) AND COUNTERCLAIM – the response to the complaint or petition to divorce that admits or denies the petition's allegations and also may make claims against the other party

ANTENUPTIAL AGREEMENT (ALSO CALLED PRENUPTIAL) – a written contract between two people who are about to marry, setting out the terms of possession of assets, treatment of income, control of the property, and potential division if the marriage is later dissolved

APPEAL – the process by which a higher court reviews the proceedings resulting in an order or judgment of a lower court and determines whether there is a reversible error

APPEAR, FILE AN APPEARANCE – formal method of telling the court you submit to the court's jurisdiction

APPRAISAL – an expert estimate of the value of something

APPRECIATED VALUE – an increase in value of an asset

APPORTION – to divide and allocate

ARREARAGE – the amount of money that is past due for child or spousal support

ASSETS – property owned by a person that has an economic value or a useful or desirable quality

ASSIGNMENT OF WAGES – the transfer of the right to collect wages from the wage earner to the creditor

ATTACHMENT, MOTION FOR ATTACHMENT – seizure of a debtor's property by order of the court

ATTORNEY FOR CHILD – an attorney appointed by the court to represent a child in contested custody matters; the attorney represents what the child wants and advocates for the child in court (this is not the same as a *guardian ad litem*).

AUTOMATIC RESTRAINING ORDERS – mutual orders issued by a court and signed by a judge that become effective immediately upon filing for divorce, legal separation, nullity, or paternity action; they apply to both parties and freeze money and property

AUTOMATIC STAY ORDERS – a legal provision that temporarily prevents creditors from pursuing debtors for amounts owed; it goes into effect immediately when a debtor files for bankruptcy

B

BANKRUPTCY – a legal declaration that one is unable to pay one's debts and needs to have debts forgiven or reorganized

BENEFICIARY – a person that receives benefits, profits, or advantages; different types include irrevocable, revocable, contingent, primary, secondary, etc.

BEST INTEREST OF THE CHILD – a court will use different factors to assess your child's best interests; this process is used in custody disputes

BIFURCATION, BIFURCATED TRIAL – some states will allow a divorce to be split into two parts: (1) to resolve marital status and (2) to conclude other matters, such as property division, child custody, child support, and spousal support

BLACK SCHOLES MODEL – a methodology for valuing options that takes into account whether an option is in the money or out of the money, the volatility of the underlying asset, the time to expiration of the option, whether the option is a put or a call, and the current rate of return on a risk-free asset such as a Treasury bill

BURDEN OF PROOF – a party's duty to prove the truth of his or her claims in the lawsuit

BUSINESS VALUATION – the estimation of a business' worth by a professional expert using any number of different techniques for the purpose of dividing the marital estate

BUY AND SELL AGREEMENT – a legally binding agreement between co-owners of a business that governs the situation if a co-owner dies or leaves the business

BUYOUT, LUMP SUM ALIMONY – the payment of spousal support or its equivalent in one payment, rather than through periodic payments made over a designated period of time

C

CAPITAL GAINS – the excess by which proceeds from the sale of a capital asset exceeds the cost

CAPITALIZATION – the company's stock price per share multiplied by the total number of shares outstanding; a business valuation methodology

CASH FLOW – cash that comes into or goes out of a person's or company's account

CASH VALUE – the cash amount offered to the policy owner by the issuing life insurance carrier upon cancellation of the contract; also called the surrender value of an insurance contract

CERTIFIED DIVORCE FINANCIAL PLANNER, CERTIFIED DIVORCE FINANCIAL ANALYST – a financial professional trained and skilled at analyzing data and providing expertise on the financial issues of divorce

CHANGE IN CIRCUMSTANCE – term used as cause to modify an existing court order, either increasing or decreasing amounts of child or spousal support

CHANGE OF VENUE – the transfer of a case from a court in one location to a court in another for reasons of fairness or for the convenience of the party's witnesses

CHATTEL – an item of personal property

CHILD CONTINGENCY RULE – the IRS rule that prevents spousal support deductions for what is essentially child support or a property settlement

CHILD CUSTODY – having rights to your child; these rights can be legal, physical, or joint

CHILD SUPPORT – money that a noncustodial parent pays to the custodial parent for their child's support (nontaxable for the payee and nondeductible for the payor)

CHILD SUPPORT GUIDELINES – guidelines established by statute or rule in each jurisdiction that set forth the manner in which child support must be calculated; generally based on the income of the parents and the needs of the children

CLEAR TITLE – a title without any kind of lien or levy from creditors or other parties and poses no question as to legal ownership

COBRA – the Consolidated Omnibus Budget Reconciliation Act of 1985 is a law that gives workers and their families who lose their health benefits the right to choose to continue group health benefits provided by their group health plan for limited periods of time under certain circumstances

COHABITATION – a living arrangement in which an unmarried couple lives together in a long-term relationship that resembles a marriage

COLA, COST OF LIVING ADJUSTMENTS – begun in 1975, Social Security general benefits increases have been based annually on increases in cost of living as measured by the Consumer Price Index

COLLABORATIVE LAW, COLLABORATIVE DIVORCE – see ALTERNATIVE DISPUTE RESOLUTION

COLLATERAL – assets used as security for a loan

COMMENCEMENT OF ACTION – formal procedure for initiating legal action

COMMINGLE – when a spouse's separate property is mixed with the other spouse's marital property; the mixing of assets, both separate and marital

COMMON LAW PROPERTY DISTRIBUTION – property is distributed according to the manner in which title is held, in contrast to equitable distribution; this is more frequently used in the probate context than the divorce context

COMMUNITY PROPERTY – generally, the money earned and property and debts acquired during a marriage as a result of both parties' work and effort

COMPARABLES – term for comparing two or more things that are similar and can be compared to each other; generally used for informal real estate appraisals

COMPOUND INTEREST – interest paid on interest from previous periods in addition to principal

CONSENT ORDER – a legally binding order of the court that is voluntarily and jointly agreed to by a divorcing couple to finalize all financial obligations arising from their marriage

CONTESTED DIVORCE – any case in which the court must decide one or more disputed items

CONTINGENT INTERESTS – an interest that is uncertain, either as to the person who will enjoy its possession or as to the event upon which it will arise; it is future interest that can only come on the happening of a specified event

CONTEMPT OF COURT – the willful and intentional failure to comply with a court order, judgment, or decree by a party to the action, which is punishable in a variety of ways

CONTINUATION – the postponement of a legal proceeding

CO-PARENTING PLAN – a plan devised jointly between the parents, or submitted by one parent and accepted by the court, that defines how the parties will share rights, time, and responsibilities regarding their child/children

COST BASIS – the original value of an asset, usually the purchase price, which is used to determine the capital gain

COURT DOCKET, INDEX NUMBER – court dockets contain all materials filed by the court or by any party in a court proceeding; courts assign each newly filed action with a docket number

COURT ORDER – a written document issued by a court that becomes effective only when signed by a judge

COVERTURE, COVERTURE FRACTION – term used to separate the portion of benefits that was earned during the marriage from the portion of benefits that were earned outside the period of marriage; often used for valuing pensions

CREDITOR – a person or company to whom money is owed

CUSTODY – the control and care of a person or property; types of custody are legal, physical, sole, joint, and shared

CUSTODIAL PARENT – the parent who has either sole physical custody of the child or the parent with whom the child resides the majority of the time

D

DAMAGES – a lump sum of money the law imposes for a breach of some duty or violation of some right

DATE OF SEPARATION, DATE OF CUTOFF, DATE OF DIVORCE, DATE OF MARRIAGE – the essential date(s) that a state uses for determining property interests, income accumulation, etc.; if the date is unclear or contested, states may look at different tests to determine essential dates

DEATH BENEFIT – the dollar amount that is payable upon the death of the person whose life is being insured

DEBT – a debt is an obligation to repay an amount owed

DEBTOR – person or company who owes money

DECREE, DECISION, JUDGMENT, DISSOLUTION, FINAL JUDGMENT – the court's written order or decision signed by the judge finalizing the divorce, often issued in conjunction with the court's judgment

DEED – a written instrument that has been signed and delivered, by which an individual conveys title to real property to another individual

DEFAULT JUDGMENT – failure to answer a petition or complaint for divorce and an award by the court of everything requested by the filing spouse

DEFENDANT – the person against whom legal papers are filed; also called the respondent

DEFERRED ANNUITY – an annuity that commences not less than one year after the final purchase premium

DEFERRED COMPENSATION – a voluntary or involuntary arrangement in which a portion of an employee's income is paid out at a date in the future (after the income is actually earned); examples include pensions, employee stock options, restricted stock, etc.

DEFINED BENEFIT PLAN – a retirement plan, known as a pension, in which the retiree receives a set amount of benefits each month for the rest of their life or a lump sum amount upon retirement; the pension amount depends on employee's age at retirement, final salary, and number of years on the job

DEFINED CONTRIBUTION PLAN – a retirement plan, known as profit sharing, in which an employee and/or employer contribute a set dollar amount each month on a pre-tax basis to an account in employee's name; contributions are invested before the retiree makes withdrawals, and retirement income is not guaranteed

DEPENDENCY EXEMPTION – a tax deduction in the amount of a personal exemption that is based on a qualifying child or relative

DEPOSITION – part of the discovery process of a legal proceeding, in which the attorney for the other party asks you questions, you answer with your attorney present, and a transcript of the proceedings is prepared

DEPRECIATION – the decrease in value of a tangible asset because of age, wear, or market conditions; corporations can choose between several types of depreciation, which affects the value of assets and corporate earnings; depreciation is an income tax deduction and does not affect cash flow

DIRECT TRANSFER – a transfer of assets from one type of tax-deferred retirement plan or account to another

DIVIDEND – a share of a company's net profits distributed to a class of its stockholders

DISCOUNTING – a financial calculation or process for determining the present value of a payment or a stream of payments that is to be received in the future

DISCOVERY, DISCLOSURE – the information-exchanging process of a legal proceeding, including serving interrogatories, requests for production of documents and taking depositions

DISSIPATION OF ASSETS OR INCOME – the wasteful use of an asset or income for an illegal or inequitable purpose, such as the spouse's use of marital property for personal benefit when a divorce is imminent; intended to deprive the other spouse of the use and benefit of the asset

DISSOLUTION – another word for divorce

DISTRIBUTIVE AWARD – any payment in real or personal property, payable in a lump sum or over time, in fixed amounts, made from separate property or income, and not from marital property and are not payments of spousal support

DIVERSIFICATION – minimizing risk by investing in a wide variety of securities held in a portfolio

DIVISIBLE PROPERTY – divisible property includes post-separation increases and decreases in the value of marital property, property received after the date of separation that was acquired as a result of the marital efforts of either spouse before the date of separation, passive income generated by marital property and received after the date of separation, and post-separation increases in marital debt

DIVORCE – the legal termination of a marriage
DOMICILE – place of residence
DOUBLE DIPPING – the concept of double counting of a marital asset, once in the property division and again in the support award
DURATION – the time during which something continues; in finance, this is a measure of the sensitivity of price to a change in interest rates
DRO (DOMESTIC RELATIONS ORDER) – a judgment or court order concerning the distribution of assets and benefits after a divorce

E

EARNING CAPACITY – the amount of money someone should be able to earn, given the person's talent, skills, training, and experience
EMANCIPATION – the point at which a child may be treated as an adult and in some states when the duty to support may terminate; the release of a child from the responsibility and control of a parent
ENCUMBERED – restricted or burdened; a property owned by one party but on which a second party reserves the right to make a valid claim (e.g., a bank's holding of a home mortgage encumbers the property)
ENJOIN – to legally prohibit or restrain by a court injunction (order)
EQUITABLE DISTRIBUTION, EQUITABLE ASSIGNMENT, EQUITABLE DIVISION (OF PROPERTY) – a system of distributing property in connection with a divorce proceeding on the basis of a variety of factors without regard to who holds the title
EQUITY – ownership; in real estate, this is the difference between what the property could be sold for less any debts claimed against it
ERISA – the Employee Retirement Income Act of 1974 is a federal law establishing minimum standards for pension plans and health plans in private industry
ESOP – a qualified defined contribution plan, also known an employee stock ownership plan, designed to invest primarily in the stock of the sponsoring employer
ESTATE – a person's property
EVIDENCE – documents, testimony, or other demonstrative material offered to the court to prove or disprove allegations
EX PARTE: HEARING, MOTION, ORDER – an application for court relief without some other party being present
EXPECTANCY – the possibility of future enjoyment of something one counts on receiving, usually referring to real property of the estate of a deceased person; a future interest in property that is expected but not vested
EXPERT WITNESS – a person who is a specialist in a subject, often technical, who may present his or her expert opinion that is strictly within this subject area
EXTRAORDINARY EXPENSES – federal guidelines for child support define what are basic, necessary, and reasonable expenses; states may also consider specific situations of each family to determine what constitute special and extraordinary expenses

F

FACE VALUE (ALSO NOMINAL, PAR VALUE) – the nominal value or dollar value of a security stated by the issuer or the price at which a company's security was initially offered for sale; for stocks, it is the original cost of the stock shown on the certificate, and for bonds, it is the amount known as "par value"

FAIR AND REASONABLE – a financial term used to describe the price point for a good or service that is fair to both parties involved in the transaction

FAIR MARKET VALUE – a selling price for an item to which a buyer and seller can agree

FEE AGREEMENT, RETAINER AGREEMENT – a retainer agreement is a work-for-hire contract

FICO SCORE – a person's credit score calculated with software from the Fair Isaac Corporation (FICO)

FIDUCIARY – a person to whom property or power is entrusted for the benefit of another

FINANCIAL AFFIDAVIT, STATEMENT OF NET WORTH, CASE INFORMATION STATEMENT, INCOME AND EXPENSE DECLARATION – a legal document sworn to under oath that gives a complete list of a person's income from all sources, expenses including nonprorated and prorated expenses, assets, and liabilities; it is filed in all cases involving child support, post-separation support, and/or spousal support

FINDING OF FACT – refers to the decision or opinion of the judge or jury regarding issues of fact in a lawsuit

FINANCIAL NEUTRAL – a financial professional or specialist trained in the collaborative process who works with the attorneys and couple

FORECLOSURE – a situation in which a mortgage lender takes possession of the property because the borrower has not made payments on interest or principal for a certain period of time

FORENSIC, FINANCIAL FORENSIC, FORENSIC ACCOUNTING – the application of accounting concepts and techniques to legal problems, such as fraud, dissipation, and wrongdoing; sometimes called investigative accounting

FORFEITURE OF ASSETS – the involuntary relinquishment or seizure of an asset without compensation as a consequence of a breach or nonperformance of some legal obligation or the commission of a crime

FUTURE VALUE – the value of an asset at a specific date in the future based on an assumed rate of return of growth over time

FRAUD – a material and intentional misrepresentation, by omission or commission, to induce someone to surrender something of value; fraud means acting in bad faith and that substantial harm was caused

FRAUDULENT CONVEYANCE – the intentional transfer of property to another person for the purpose of making the asset inaccessible to creditors; in divorce, this includes the retitling of property to reduce the size of a spouse's available property at the expense of the other spouse or an outside creditor

G

GARNISHMENT, WAGE GARNISHMENT, WAGE ATTACHMENT – the process of deducting money from an employee's monetary compensation as a result of a court order

GOOD FAITH – honesty of intention; absence of intent to defraud

GOODWILL – the accounting concept measures goodwill using excess earnings and excess value; legally in divorce, goodwill is an intangible asset, may be commercial or professional, and may or may not be considered a marital asset in your state

GROUNDS FOR DIVORCE – regulations specifying circumstances under which a person will be granted a divorce; a legally sufficient reason for divorce

GROSS INCOME – each state's child support guidelines define gross income (and may differ from tax reporting); financially, gross income is income from all sources before taxes and deductions

GUARDIAN AD LITEM – an attorney or mental health professional appointed by the court to represent a child's best interest in a divorce case; the *guardian ad litem* will form an opinion to make a recommendation to the court and is not the same as an attorney for the child

H

HARDSHIP – a condition which causes financial strain on the ability of a parent to support his or her children, such as loss of job, medical condition, etc.

HEAD OF HOUSEHOLD – tax filing status for single or unmarried taxpayers who keep up a home for a qualifying person

HEARING ON MERITS – any proceeding before the court for purpose of resolving disputed issues through presentation of testimony, offers of proof, and argument

HEIR – a person entitled to receive property (and, in some jurisdictions, the corresponding title) from a deceased person

HOLD HARMLESS, HOLD HARMLESS AGREEMENT – a situation in which one spouse assumes liability for a debt or other obligation and promises to protect the other spouse from any loss or expenses in connection with it

HOMEMAKER CONTRIBUTIONS – the noneconomic contributions of a homemaker may be considered in both the award of spousal support and the distribution of property

I

IMPUTED INCOME – the income level assigned to an individual that is greater than their actual earnings

INDEMNIFY, INDEMNIFICATION – the promise to reimburse another person in case of anticipated loss; same as hold harmless

IN KIND – paid in goods or services instead of money

INHERITANCE – the passing on of property, titles, debts, rights, and obligations upon the death of an individual

INNOCENT SPOUSE RULE – claiming innocent spouse relief of the responsibility of paying tax, interest, and penalties if a former spouse improperly reported or omitted an item on a prior joint tax return

INSURABLE INTEREST – a person has an insurable interest in something when loss or damage to it would cause that person to suffer a financial loss

INSURANCE – a contract between a client and a provider whereby the client makes monthly payments (called premiums) in exchange for the promise that the provider will pay for certain expenses

INTESTATE – dying without a valid will

INVESTMENT RISK – the probability or chance that an investment's actual return will differ from the expected return; intangible assets; measure of uncertainty

INTEREST – a financial term to refer to money paid at a particular rate of return for the use of money lent or invested (such as in stock)

INTERSPOUSAL GIFTS – definition depends on whether it is a gift to a spouse or a gift to the marriage; gifts to the marriage are generally marital property, while gifts from one spouse to the other are generally separate property

INTERROGATORY – a series of written questions served on the opposing party to discover certain facts regarding the disputed issues in a matrimonial proceeding; answers must be given under oath and served within a prescribed time

IN THE MONEY, OUT OF THE MONEY – *in the money* describes an option where the strike price is less than current price and one can turn a profit on sale; *out of the money* describes an option that is worthless today because its strike price is higher than current market price

IRA – a custodial account or trust in which individuals may set aside earned income in a tax-deferred retirement plan

IRRECONCILABLE DIFFERENCES – no-fault grounds for divorce

IRRETRIEVABLE BREAKDOWN – no-fault grounds for divorce

IRREVOCABLE BENEFICIARY STATUS – a beneficiary in a life insurance policy or separate account or trust who cannot be removed or changed without his or her consent

J

JOINT CUSTODY – the shared right and responsibility of both parents awarded by a court for the possession, care, and rearing of their child/children

JOINT PETITION – some states allow couples to file jointly for divorce as a simplified uncontested or no-fault divorce

JOINT PROPERTY – property held in the name of more than one person

JOINT AND SEVERAL LIABILITY – two or more persons are fully responsible equally for the full amount of the liability; a claimant can sue any party for the full amount

JOINT TENANCY – a form of legal ownership when two or more people each own an equal share (or interest) in a property and has the equal, undivided right to keep or dispose of the property; creates rights of survivorship

JUDGMENT – see DECREE

JURISDICTION – the authority of a court to rule on issues relating to the parties, the children, or their property

L

LAPSE – termination of an insurance policy due to nonpayment of premiums

LEASE – a legal contract for renting land, buildings, etc., to another at a specified price and for a specified term

LEGAL CUSTODY – a parent with legal custody can make long term decisions about raising a child and key aspects of a child's welfare, including a child's schooling, religious upbringing, and medical care

LETTERS OF CREDIT, LINES OF CREDIT – a credit arrangement in which a financial institution agrees to lend money to a customer up to a specified limit

LIABILITY – to be responsible for something; money owed

LIEN – an encumbrance on one's property to secure a debt the property owner owes to another person

LIFE EXPECTANCY – the average period that a person may expect to live; a mortality or annuity table is used as a reference

LIFE INSURANCE – insurance that pays out a sum of money either on death of the insured person or after a set period of time; two types are whole life and term

LIFESTYLE STANDARD, LIFESTYLE ANALYSIS – the level of wealth, comfort, material goods, and necessities available to the parties during the marriage, subject to a number of exceptions; methodologies include the preparation of the Financial Affidavit, a narrative description of the station in life the parties achieved, and a comprehensive lifestyle analysis by a forensic accountant

LIQUID ASSET – a security that can easily be sold for cash

LIQUIDATION VALUE – the amount of money with which you could sell an asset and settle a liability on a rush basis; probably lower than fair market value

LIS PENDENS – a pending legal action or a formal notice of this

LIVING TRUST – an agreement where the trustee holds the legal possession of a fund or asset that belongs to another person, the beneficiary; must be created while the person is alive

LIVING WILL – a medical directive to physicians to give explicit instructions about medical treatment to be administered when a patient is terminally ill or incapacitated

LUMP SUM ALIMONY, LUMP SUM SETTLEMENT – a single payment of spousal support that serves as a complete payment

M

MAINTENANCE SPOUSAL SUPPORT – see ALIMONY

MANDATORY FACTORS – the factors a court must consider before making a final decision relating to property division and spousal support

MARITAL PORTION – a share of a pension accrued during the marriage or stock options that vest before, during, or after the marriage

MARITAL PROPERTY, MARITAL ASSETS, MARITAL ESTATE – accumulated income and property acquired by spouses during the marriage, regardless of which person is named as owner; subject to certain exclusions in some states

MARKETABILITY DISCOUNT – an accounting method used to calculate the value of small business ownership or of closely held or restricted stock that has limited marketability

MARRIED FILING JOINTLY – tax filing status for couples who are married as of December 31 in the tax year

MEDIATION – see ALTERNATIVE DISPUTE RESOLUTION

MEDICAL SAVINGS ACCOUNT – an account into which tax-deferred amounts from income can be deposited to pay for medical expenses; generally associated with self-employed individuals

MEDICAL DIRECTIVE – see LIVING WILL

MINOR – a child is considered a minor for purposes of legal decision-making authority, child custody, and parenting time as long as they are under age of majority, typically 18; see EMANCIPATION

MINORITY DISCOUNT – a reduction is an economic concept reflecting the notion that a partial ownership interest may be worth less than its proportional share of the total business; a discount for lack of control applicable to a minority

MODIFICATION, MOTION TO MODIFY – a party's formal written request to a court to change a prior order regarding custody, child support, spousal support, or any other order that the court may change by law

MORTGAGE – a legal agreement in which a person borrows money to buy a property and the loan is secured by the property

MOTION – a written application to the court for some particular relief, such as temporary spousal support, injunction, or attorney's or expert's fees

N

NEGOTIATED AGREEMENT, NEGOTIATED SETTLEMENT – a settlement that disputing parties reach between themselves, especially with the help of their attorneys

NESTING – refers to a transitional arrangement where parents continue to share the family home and take turns being "on duty" with their children

NET – profit or loss on a transaction

NET INCOME – income after all expenses and taxes have been deducted

NET WORTH STATEMENT – see FINANCIAL AFFIDAVIT

NO-FAULT DIVORCE – when divorce is granted without a party having to prove the other party's marital misconduct; all 50 states are now no fault

NOMINAL VALUE – see PAR, FACE VALUE

NONCUSTODIAL PARENT – the parent who does not have physical and/or legal custody of his or her child by court order

NONMARITAL PROPERTY – any real or personal property that was owned by either spouse before the marriage and not subject to division by a court upon the dissolution of the marriage

NONQUALIFIED PLAN – a type of tax-deferred, employer-sponsored retirement plan that falls outside of ERISA guidelines; designed to meet specialized retirement needs of key executive employees

O

OPINION – a written statement by a court, judge, or legal expert as to the legality of an action, condition, or intent

OPTION – gives a buyer the right, but not the obligation, to buy or sell an asset at a set price on or before a given date; classified as "in the money" or "out of the money" for valuation purposes

P

PARTY – a plaintiff or defendant in a legal proceeding

PAR VALUE (ALSO NOMINAL) – see FACE VALUE

PASSIVE ASSET, PASSIVE APPRECIATION – an increase in value of an asset as a result of changes in the market and not because of efforts or contributions made by either spouse

PAYEE – a person to whom money is to be or has been paid

PAYOR – a person who is responsible for paying something to someone

PENDENTE LITE – a Latin term meaning "awaiting the litigation" or "pending the litigation" that applies to court orders that are in effect while a matter (such as a divorce) is pending

PENSIONS – a retirement benefit paid by an employer of a fixed amount paid at regular intervals to a person

PERJURY – the crime of telling a lie in court

PERSONAL GUARANTOR – a person who guarantees to pay for someone else's debt if he or she should default on a loan obligation

PERSONAL PROPERTY (DIVORCE) – all property that is not real property; personal property is something that you can pick up or move around

PHYSICAL CUSTODY – the parent that the child lives with or spends the majority of time with; see CUSTODY

PLAINTIFF – a person who brings a case against another in the court of law

PLEADINGS – the formal presentation of claims and defenses by parties in a lawsuit

POSTNUPTIAL AGREEMENT – a written agreement executed by a couple after they are married

PRELIMINARY RELIEF, PRELIMINARY IN JUNCTION – a temporary order made by a court at the request of one party that prevents the other party from pursuing a particular course of conduct until the conclusion of a trial on the merits

PREMARITAL PROPERTY, NONMARITAL PROPERTY – assets and liabilities acquired or incurred by either spouse prior to the marriage

PREMARITAL AGREEMENT, PRENUPTIAL AGREEMENT – see ANTENUPTIAL AGREEMENT

PRESENT VALUE – the current value of a future sum of money or stream of cash flow given a specified rate of return; future cash flows are discounted at the discount rate because of the time value of money; see DISCOUNTING

PRETRIAL DISCOVERY – discoveries that are conducted before trial to reveal facts and develop evidence

PRIVILEGE – in common law jurisdictions, legal professional privilege protects all communications between a professional legal advisor and a client; the privilege is that of the client and not that of the attorney

PRO BONO – without charge to the client

PRO SE – a Latin phase meaning "for oneself" or "on one's behalf" (i.e., legal representation without an attorney or self-representation)

PROPERTY AGREEMENT – a contract that divides the assets and liabilities of the spouses seeking divorce and is incorporated into a divorce decree

PROPERTY SETTLEMENT NOTE – a structured settlement that is a series of smaller payments paid over time, as opposed to a lump sum payment, almost always for spouses involved in a divorce

POST-JUDGMENT ORDER – anything that occurs after a judgment has been issued by a court

PUBLIC RECORDS – any information, files, accounts or documents which a governmental body is required to maintain which are accessible to scrutiny by the public

Q

QUALIFIED DOMESTIC RELATIONS ORDER – a judicial order entered as part of a property division or legal separation that splits a retirement plan or pension by recognizing marital ownership interests in the plan; see DOMESTIC RELATIONS ORDER

QUALIFIED RETIREMENT PLAN – a type of retirement plan established by an employer for the benefit of employees that gives them tax breaks for contributions

QUITCLAIM DEED – a legal instrument which is used to transfer interest or ownership in real property

R

RANGE OF VALUE – the difference between the lowest and highest values; for example, real estate brokers often estimate a range of values for a property

RATE OF RETURN – the gain or loss on an investment over a specified period of time expressed as a percentage of the investment's cost

REAL ESTATE – property comprised of land and buildings as well as natural resources of the land

REAL PROPERTY (DIVORCE) – land and anything attached to the land, such as a building, home, or trees

REBUTTAL – to introduce evidence to defeat, dispute, contradict, or remove the effect of the other side's arguments in a presumption, particular case, or controversy

RECAPTURE OF ALIMONY RULE – applies only to the payor when spousal support decreases substantially or ends during the first three calendar years or when the tax benefit was improperly taken at an earlier time and must be paid back

REFINANCE – when an old loan or debt is paid off and replaced with a new loan offering different terms

REIMBURSEMENT ALIMONY – spousal support that reimburses an ex-spouse for economic sacrifices (expenses) that she or he made during the marriage and that enhanced the future earning capacity of the other spouse

REHABILITATIVE ALIMONY – spousal support for a short period of time to encourage a dependent spouse to become completely self-supporting after a divorce

RELEASE – a legal release relinquishes a claim or right under the law to another person against whom the claim or right is enforceable

REPLACEMENT COST – refers to the value or amount that an entity would have to pay to replace an asset at the present time, according to its current worth; a method for determining the value of an insured item

RESIDENCY – certain residency requirements that must be met to file for divorce in a state; residency only requires a person to be present in a state (domicile is more complicated)

RESPONDENT – the person who is served with divorce papers; see DEFENDANT

RESPONSE – a written answer to a divorce petition by the defendant (aka respondent)

RETAINER AGREEMENT – see FEE AGREEMENT

RETROACTIVE RELIEF – the court corrects what should have been done earlier; retroactive relief applies to the date of divorce, child support, spousal support, and college expenses

RETURN DATE – the date on which the stipulated waiting period for a divorce begins; also, the date by which the defendant should file an appearance

REVERSAL – the successful appeal of a divorce judgment by an appellate court

REVERSE MORTGAGE – a financial agreement in which a homeowner relinquishes equity in their home in exchange for regular payments to supplement retirement income

RIGHTS OF SURVIVORSHIP – the power of successors of a deceased individual to acquire the property of that individual upon his or her death

RISK TOLERANCE – the degree of variability in investment returns that an investor is willing to withstand

S

SANCTION – a threatened penalty for disobeying a law or rule

SECRETION OF ASSETS – the hiding of assets

SEPARATE DEBTS – usually separate debts belonging to one spouse; debts incurred before the marriage are separate debts

SEPARATE PROPERTY (DIVORCE) – everything each spouse owns separately as defined by each state; this property is not available for equitable distribution

SEPARATE SUPPORT – a way for one spouse to continue to support the other before, during, and after a legal separation (similar to spousal support in divorce)

SEPARATION AGREEMENT – an agreement between two married people who have agreed to live apart for an unspecified amount of time that addresses spousal support, child support, custody arrangements, payment of bills, and management of assets/liabilities

SETTLEMENT, SETTLEMENT AGREEMENT – a formal, voluntary, written agreement on all of the issues surrounding divorce; it must be formally signed and acknowledged

SET OFF – a debt or obligation owed by one spouse to the other; also a method of asset distribution by which one spouse receives a sum or money or assets in exchange of his or her release from an interest in marital assets

SEVERABILITY – a clause in a contract that allows for the terms of a contract to be independent of one another so that if parts are found to be illegal or otherwise unenforceable, the remainder of the contract should still apply

SEVERANCE PAY – money that is paid by the employer to an employee who is dismissed because of lack of work, other reasons beyond the employee's control, or through mutual agreement

SHARED CUSTODY – a situation where a child spends about an equal amount of time in the care and home of each of the two separated parents and the parents share the legal rights in regard to the child

SINGLE – a separate person; also a tax-filing status if you are unmarried as of December 31 of the tax year that determines whether you can claim certain tax deductions or credits

SOLE CUSTODY – one parent has both physical and legal custody of a child; the other parent cannot make any major decisions about the child

SOURCE OF FUNDS – an approach for determining whether money used to pay for property came from separate or marital estates in proportion to the contributions

SPECIAL MASTER – a person appointed by the court to carry out some sort of action on its behalf; they may be a unique blend of dispute-resolver facilitators and can reduce litigation

SPLIT CUSTODY – a child custody decision that results in the splitting up of the children

SPOUSE – a husband or wife

SPOUSAL SUPPORT – see ALIMONY

SPOUSAL SOCIAL SECURITY BENEFITS – if you qualify and are eligible, you may be able to collect spouse's retirement benefits instead of on your own record

STANDARD OF LIVING – see LIFESTYLE STANDARD

STATUS CONFERENCE – a meeting of the judge and attorneys in a pending legal matter to determine how the case is progressing

STAY, STAY OF PROCEEDINGS – an action to delay or postpone a proceeding to a later time

STIPULATION, STIPULATED AGREEMENT – where both spouses voluntarily agree on the facts and agree that the court can rely on those facts in deciding a case

STRIKE, MOTION TO STRIKE – the removal from the record and docket of material found to be irrelevant, scandalous, or without proper notice

STOCKS AND SECURITIES – an ownership share(s) in a corporation; also equity and common stock

STOCK OPTION – a benefit given by a company to an employee to buy stock in the company at a discount or at a fixed price within a certain period of time

SUBPOENA – a document that requires production of documents or a request to appear in court or other legal proceeding

SUCCESS FEE – a conditional fee arrangement paid to attorney for a favorable result over and above the amount which would be normally payable

SUMMARY JUDGMENT – a judgment is entered by a court for one party and against another party without a full trial, the court finds no factual issues that remain to be tried, and the judge can then make a final decision to resolve the lawsuit; can be based on the merits of the entire case or on discrete issues in that case

SUMMATION – the final or closing argument in a court case

SUMMONS – an official order to appear in a court of law

SUPPORT – there are two kinds of support: child support and spousal support; payments from one spouse to another

SURRENDER VALUE – see CASH VALUE

SURVIVORSHIP BENEFIT PLAN – a monthly benefit paid to a designated beneficiary of a retired deceased person; usually an annuity of a monthly payment for the lifetime of the beneficiary

T

TAX CREDIT – an amount of money a taxpayer is able to subtract from taxes owed to the government; value depends on the nature of the credit

TAX DEDUCTION – a reduction in income that is able to be taxed, commonly the result of expenses; deductions reduce taxable income

TAX SHELTER – a legal method of minimizing or decreasing an investor's taxable income and tax liability

TEMPORARY ORDER – a court order to keep the status quo from the time a divorce is filed until a final divorce settlement is negotiated; may apply to child support, spousal support, custody, etc.

TENANCY BY ENTIRETY – a type of shared property ownership between a husband and wife, with each spouse holding an equal and undivided interest in the property

TENANTS IN COMMON – co-owners who each own a separate and undivided interest in the same real property and have equal rights and use of the property

TESTATE – having made a legally valid will before death

TITLE – the legal basis of ownership of property that is recognizable and enforceable in court

TORT, DOMESTIC TORT, MARITAL TORT – a private or civil wrong or injury arising from the conduct, deliberate carelessness or intent, or negligence of another; some states allow for a marital or domestic tort for misconduct that occurred during the marriage

TRACING – asset tracing is simply the process of the documentation and supporting of a claim that an asset is or is not part of the marital estate

TRANSFER – when you divide property in divorce, you move assets and debts from one spouse to the other; incident to divorce, no gain or loss is recognized on a transfer of property between divorcing spouses

TRANSMUTATION OF ASSET – the change of the character of property, either from separate to marital or from marital to separate, by conversion, gift, or other legal transfer

TRIAL – a formal examination of evidence before a judge who makes decisions based on facts and case law

TRIAL MEMORANDUM – a presentation to the court setting forth your case, goals, and justifications; a pretrial memorandum often explains the position or argument of the party

TRUSTS, TRUSTEE – an arrangement or entity created to hold assets for the benefit of certain persons, with a trustee managing or taking care of the property

U

UNCONTESTED DIVORCE – an agreement where the spouses reach a decision as to all of the terms of their divorce without going to trial, including but not limited to the division of marital property and debts, child support, and spousal support; or, where one spouse fails to appear in a divorce action

UNEMANCIPATED CHILDREN – children who are under the financial care of their parents; see MINOR

UNVESTED INTEREST (ALSO NONVESTED) – refers usually to stock options and the right of an employee to earn them after a period of time with the company; the term is also used relative to a trust and means there is no guarantee of present or future value

V

VACATE, MOTION TO – a request filed with the court to set aside a prior court order or ruling

VALUE – the monetary, material, or assessed worth of an asset, good, or service

VALUATION PROCESS – a complex process for determining the worth of a business involving numerous factors that address intangible and tangible property

VENUE – jurisdiction with the authority to decide legal issues, usually in same county as the marital home

VESTED INTEREST – the equity a person has in certain assets; a right to the immediate enjoyment of an interest

VISITATION – access to a child granted especially to a parent who does not have custody

VOCATIONAL ASSESSMENT – a court-ordered examination of a person's skills, talents, and competence, designed to investigate the basis of his or her claim of unemployability

W

WAIVER – knowingly, intentionally giving up rights or claims; in divorce, a waiver may also refer to a fee waiver, a waiver of service (i.e., a waiver of citation), or a waiver of final hearing

WARRANTY DEED – a document that may be used to legally transfer property (there are two types: general and special); also a guaranty of title, which means that the seller may be held liable for damages if the buyer discovers the defect

WITH PREJUDICE – a case that is dismissed, is over and done with for all, and can't be brought back to court

WITHOUT PREJUDICE – a case that is not dismissed forever and leaves the plaintiff free to bring another suit based on the same grounds

WORKERS COMPENSATION – a form of insurance providing wage replacement and medical benefits to an employee injured in the course of employment in exchange for the mandatory relinquishment of the employee's right to sue his or her employer

Y

YIELD – the income return on an investment, such as the interest or dividends received from owning a particular security; expressed as an annual percentage rate based on the investment's cost, current market value, or face value

Index

E